Improving Intelligence Analysis in Policing

This book explains how improvements in intelligence analysis can benefit policing. Written by experts with experience in police higher education and professional practice, this accessible text provides students with both practical knowledge and a critical understanding of the subject. The book is divided into three key parts:

- Part One outlines how the concept of intelligence was initially embraced and implemented by the police and provides a critique of intelligence sources. It examines the strategic use of intelligence and its procedural framework. It provides a summary of the role of the intelligence analyst, establishing the characteristics of effective practitioners.
- Part Two describes good practice and explains the practical tools and techniques that effective analysts use in the reduction and investigation of crime.
- Part Three examines more recent developments in intelligence analysis and looks to the future. This includes the move to multi-agency working, the advent of big data and the role of AI and machine learning.

Filled with case studies and practical examples, this book is essential reading for all undergraduates and postgraduates taking courses in Professional Policing, and Criminal Justice more widely. It will also be of interest to existing practitioners in this field.

Stuart Kirby previously served as a Lancashire Police Officer (UK). As a Detective Chief Superintendent (Specialist Crime and Operations Division), he had responsibility for Intelligence, Forensic, Major Crime, Organised Crime and Counter Terrorism. On retirement he started a second career in academia, becoming a Professor of Policing. As current Director of Crimeinsights Ltd. he acts as a policing consultant to national and international public sector agencies.

Scott Keay is a senior lecturer in Policing at Edge Hill University (UK). He worked for the Lancashire Constabulary for almost 20 years, in various analytical roles from criminal intelligence through to community safety and partnership intelligence. He is currently conducting a PhD, exploring how the police define, identify and respond to vulnerability.

Routledge Advances in Police Practice and Knowledge
Series Editors
Dr Tom Cockcroft, Leeds Beckett University, UK, and Dr Martin Wright, Canterbury Centre for Policing Research, UK

Routledge Advances in Police Practice and Knowledge is a new series of books which brings together established academics and authors in the field of police studies to provide themed textbooks that will support students engaging with professional police studies within higher education. The focus of the series is to provide academically rigorous accounts of research and knowledge and to contextualise them in the practical and applied context of policework. In doing so, the books that make up the series will provide an invaluable resource to students studying policing through a variety of academic and vocational routes.

The Editors, Dr Tom Cockcroft and Dr Martin Wright dedicate this series to the memory of Professor PAJ (Tank) Waddington who believed policing to be an honourable profession, and whose career's work embodied the values that inform the direction of the series.

Policing Structures
Colin Rogers

Improving Intelligence Analysis in Policing
Stuart Kirby and Scott Keay

Improving Intelligence Analysis in Policing

Stuart Kirby and Scott Keay

Routledge
Taylor & Francis Group

LONDON AND NEW YORK

First published 2021
by Routledge
2 Park Square, Milton Park, Abingdon, Oxon OX14 4RN

and by Routledge
52 Vanderbilt Avenue, New York, NY 10017

Routledge is an imprint of the Taylor & Francis Group, an informa business

British Library Cataloguing-in-Publication Data
A catalogue record for this book is available from the British Library

Library of Congress Cataloging-in-Publication Data
Names: Kirby, Stuart, 1959- author. | Keay, Scott, author.
Title: Improving intelligence analysis in policing / Stuart Kirby and Scott Keay.
Description: Abingdon, Oxon ; New York, NY : Routledge, 2021. |
Series: Routledge advances in police practice and knowledge |
Includes bibliographical references and index.
Identifiers: LCCN 2020054437 | ISBN 9780367481117 (hardback) |
ISBN 9780367481124 (paperback) | ISBN 9781003038047 (ebook)
Subjects: LCSH: Crime analysis. | Crime prevention. | Domestic intelligence. | Police.
Classification: LCC HV7936.C88 K57 2021 | DDC 363.2/3—dc23
LC record available at https://lccn.loc.gov/2020054437

ISBN: 978-0-367-48111-7 (hbk)
ISBN: 978-0-367-48112-4 (pbk)
ISBN: 978-1-003-03804-7 (ebk)

Typeset in Times New Roman
by Taylor & Francis Books

For my girls – Ann, Hannah and Kate

Stuart

For my boys – Isaac and Samuel

Thanks to Ken Pease for his continued guidance and wisdom.

But mostly a huge thanks to my co-author for being a great mentor, PhD supervisor and introducing me to the 'art' of publishing.

Scott

Contents

Illustrations

Figures

Tables

Box

Preface

Egon Bittner (1974:17) once commented that 'the police are the best known but least understood' of institutions. Since then many have attempted to redress this gap, with the topic expanding significantly as an academic subject. However, one of the many challenges in studying police work is the ability to understand the dynamics and nuances of operational activity (which comes with practitioner experience), whilst continuing to maintain academic objectivity and rigour. To navigate this dilemma the concept of 'pracademics' has emerged in many professions, including the police. This means that researchers, who have benefited from police operational experience, also use their academic skills to analyse the subject matter (Braga, 2016).

Both Stuart and Scott can be viewed as pracademics, having worked together in an operational police setting as well as academic research projects. Stuart spent 30 years engaged in a variety of uniform and detective roles, during which time he managed and commanded intelligence led operations. Previous roles included the Head of Intelligence, Divisional Commander and finally as Detective Chief Superintendent in command of the Specialist Crime and Operations Division. Upon leaving the police he moved into academia working in a number of universities eventually attaining the role of Professor of Policing. Scott's route involved 20 years as an established and award-winning senior police analyst. He has experience of developing and leading analyst teams and responding to intelligence commissions from practitioners and partner agencies. He made the transition to academia during 2019, when he became a senior lecturer of policing at Edge Hill University, UK.

During their time together they have both enthused and expressed frustration at the way intelligence is used to direct policing. However, they agree that effective intelligence analysis is only possible when managers and practitioners work in harmony, understanding the parameters and constraints the other works within. This work harnesses their different perspectives to bring a unique and wide-ranging exploration of the subject into one accessible book. In essence, it brings academic knowledge and practitioner experience together, to explain how individual and organisational improvements can be made.

Further, it extends this analysis by looking at whether current approaches will be fit for purpose in the future.

The book is broken down into three parts. The first phase comprises four chapters and provides an overview of past and current practice. Chapter 1 is an introductory chapter showing how the concept of intelligence was initially embraced and implemented by the police, whilst Chapter 2 provides an overview of intelligence sources. Chapters 3 and 4 emphasise the strategic use of intelligence and its procedural framework whilst also exploring analyst working practices. Part two, which incorporate Chapters 5 and 6, highlight the practical tools and techniques that analysts can use in the reduction and investigation of crime. Part three, then examines more recent developments in intelligence analysis and looks to the future. Chapter 7 explains how analysts are increasingly used in a multi-agency environment, with Chapter 8 introducing the concept of big data. Chapter 9 concludes by examining the transformation needed to ensure intelligence analysis can deliver its potential in an increasingly digital, interconnected and data led world.

References

Bittner, E. (1974) Florence Nightingale in pursuit of Willie Sutton: a theory of the police. In H. Jacob (ed.), *Potential for Reform*. Beverley Hills: Sage.

Braga, A. (2016) The value of 'pracademics' in enhancing crime analysis in police departments. *Policing: A Journal of Policy and Practice*, 10 (3): 308–314.

Chapter 1

Defining intelligence analysis and understanding its role in policing – past, present and future

Introduction

Policing is big business and extends far beyond government funded police agencies. This is because public police forces (such as the 45 in the UK or 18,000 in the USA), are supplemented by many other public, private and third sector organisations who attempt to reduce offending within society. These organisations base much of their activity on intelligence analysis, which is dependent on competent staff. Whilst this book is primarily written for those working (or hoping to work) in the law enforcement sector it should also be helpful for anyone involved in the collection, analysis or dissemination of intelligence in wider commercial settings. By deconstructing all the elements that play such a vital role in intelligence analysis it hopes to show how the process can be improved, both now and in the future. In doing so it will serve as an important reference material to both students and practitioners of the frameworks that currently aid (or frustrate) good intelligence analysis. It also seeks to provide fresh insights as to how intelligence analysis can improve through future individual and organisational improvements. This introductory chapter is the first step in this journey and is spread across three sections.

- Section 1: Defines the concept of intelligence and goes on to explain its origins, both across the military and commercial sector.
- Section 2: Explains how intelligence was widened to encompass policing, from the initial emergence of the intelligence cycle to intelligence-led policing (ILP) and the National Intelligence Model (NIM).
- Section 3: Looks to the future. It suggests how society will change and how this will affect intelligence development. From this it will propose further ideas and concepts that are built on in ensuing chapters.

Section 1: Intelligence – its history and value

What is intelligence?

The term intelligence is said to originate from late Middle English, via Old French, from the Latin word *intelligentia*, which means 'to understand'. The *Oxford English Dictionary*, defines the term in two ways:

a   'The ability to acquire, and apply, knowledge and skills'.
b   'The collection of information of military or political value'.

Similar to other general definitions of 'intelligence' it emphasises the military. This is because warfare and counter-terrorism operations were the first to see the benefits of intelligence when directing operations. However, as the concept of intelligence started to expand, a unified definition proved difficult to establish. Legg and Hutter (2006:402) have tracked down over 70 definitions of 'intelligence' arguing if the critical elements were merged it might be articulated as, 'Intelligence measures an agent's ability to achieve goals in a wide range of environments'. Meanwhile, Brown (2007:340), simply defines the concept as, 'Intelligence is information which is significant, or potentially significant, for an enquiry or potential enquiry'.

The process of transforming information into 'actionable' intelligence is a further theme that preoccupies commentators; Warner (2002) believes data or information cannot be viewed as intelligence until it is deemed actionable. Others agree by saying intelligence is the by-product of a sequential process, whereby individual elements of raw information are collected, evaluated, and analysed to form accurate and timely judgements (Morehouse, 2000:7). However, this perspective is contradicted by those who argue intelligence does not always need to be the product of analysis (Petersen, 1997), due to the fact that some information is so valuable it can be immediately actioned (Brown, 2007). The Guidance on the National Intelligence Model (ACPO, 2005) points out that information is the raw material and intelligence relates to information that has been put through a defined evaluation and risk assessment process to support decision as to whether it is actionable. Europol endorse this view in their own definition, which proposes,

> Intelligence is based on raw information which can be about a crime, event, perpetrator, suspected person, etc. Intelligence is the enhancement of this basic information which provides additional knowledge about the activities of criminals. Intelligence provides information that is normally unknown by the investigating authorities and is intended to be used to enhance the efforts of the law enforcement investigators, it is 'information designed for action' (Europol, 2003).

Unsurprisingly, as intelligence is such a pervasive term, its purity is tainted as it is adapted to describe various roles, functions, structures, products and processes (Ratcliffe, 2003). For example, in the law enforcement environment terms such as 'intelligence proformas' and 'Field Intelligence Officers' are used to describe aspects of processes and activity, not associated with formal analysis (Maguire & John, 2004). Other commentators have attempted to deconstruct the term, often separating strategic intelligence from operational or tactical intelligence. Strategic intelligence has been defined as, 'a systematic and continuous process of producing needed intelligence, of strategic value, in an actionable form to facilitate long-term decision-making' (Global Intelligence Alliance, 2004:1). This type of intelligence is often associated with the ability to acquire a bigger picture and is focused decision making to benefit future responses. In contrast tactical or operational intelligence focuses on the information that allows a strategy to be implemented. Specifically, it describes the tasks that need to be performed as well as the means to deliver them. Tactical intelligence therefore focuses more on the present day, generating real-time analysis for more immediate action.

The emergence of intelligence and recognition of its value

Whilst contemporary society sees many aspects of life influenced through intelligence analysis, its origins are associated with the military. Sun Tzu, a Chinese general and military strategist, who lived in ancient China during the period 544–496 BC, is reported as saying, 'the reason the enlightened prince and the wise general conquer the enemy, whenever they move, and their achievements surpass those of ordinary men, is foreknowledge' (SunTzu, 1963:144). In fact, historians have repeatedly shown that smaller armies, even when constrained through poorer technology and tactics, can vanquish their opponents when possessing more accurate intelligence.

Two famous illustrations of this are the Battle of Bull Run on the 21 July 1861, and the six-day war, which commenced on the 5 June 1967. The former was won by the US Confederate army over the Union army. Months before the battle the Confederates had put in place a network of Washington sympathisers who supplied accurate details of opposition numbers and routes. These agents comprised bankers, clerks, couriers, housewives, and even the owner of a social establishment that senior government and military officials frequented (Time-Life Books, 1985). Their information allowed the Confederates to position their forces on the most advantageous ground, which proved decisive in winning the battle. The second example relates to the military achievement of Israel which faced attack from Egypt to its south, Syria and Lebanon from the North, and Jordan from the east. The combined Arab forces had superior resources: 2–1 in combatant staff, 7–1 in artillery, 2–1 in tanks, 3–1 in aircraft, and 4–1 in warships. The conflict came to a head on the 18 May, when Egypt announced it was combat ready and blockaded the Israeli port of Eliat. Israel was in a difficult situation, compounded by the fact that it faced a hostile international community, and lacked support from its main ally (the USA) who wanted to avoid provoking the Soviet Union (which was aligned with Egypt). Without a diplomatic solution the Israeli's decided to attack, and whilst inferior in capacity and capability they had superior intelligence. Their intelligence network (which included intelligence officers embedded in the Egyptian catering corps) generated detailed information, including: the location of each aircraft and details of the pilot; the name and background of each base commander; the schedules of Egyptian radar controllers, pilots and ground crews; Egyptian battle codes and communications networks; and information to establish when senior air officials would be absent from their commands and unable to direct operations (Steven, 1980:229–231). This intelligence allowed the Israelis to simultaneously strike against 18 Egyptian airbases, immediately making 300 of 420 combat aircraft and 100 of their 350 qualified combat pilots inoperable (Steven, 1980). Assisted by significant deficiencies in Egyptian intelligence (Pollack, 1996, the Israelis won the conflict. Since this time military combatants across the world attribute battle success to high quality intelligence.

In complete contrast intelligence also emerged in commercial profit driven industries as it assists companies secure greater market share and maximise profits. This is through introducing new products and competitive pricing, whilst minimising losses through recalling less desirable items. A useful illustration was provided by Dunnhumby, the company behind Tesco PLC's decision to introduce a loyalty card in 1995, making it one of the first to learn from Big Data Analytics (Pati, 2014). The loyalty card enabled them to escape from an arduous trading period and increase their market share by over 10% in the decade that followed. The scheme allowed them to understand customer behaviour by receiving detailed information on nearly two thirds of customer purchases. This benefited Tesco in three ways. First, they improved their targeting of discount coupons and raised their redemption from 3% to 70%. Second, they changed product lines, focussing 'Tesco Value' products at one demographic cohort, whilst their 'Tesco Finest' products were aimed at more affluent customers. Third, consumer gaps were identified and removed. For example, noticing that their customers preferred to buy a competitor's baby products, they launched a baby club that captured 24% of the market. Through predictive analytics Tesco saved millions of pounds in both stock and energy costs. As Tesco's chairman, Lord MacLaurin, was said to observe, 'What scares me about this is that you know more about my customers after three months than I know after 30 years' (Smale, 2014:1).

Section 2: The relationship between policing and intelligence

How intelligence benefits the police and the policing process

This section describes how policing services came to rely on intelligence analysis. However, at the outset it will distinguish between the terms 'police' and 'policing' illustrating that many organisations involved in policing also rely on intelligence to direct their activity.

The term 'police' is primarily associated with government funded police agencies and since their formation there has been a debate as to their purpose and activity. Whilst some see the police as ostensibly 'crimefighters' this view isn't supported by the evidence. An enduring finding across international studies shows only about 20% of incoming police calls relate to crime, with a recent UK study showing it at 17% (College of Policing, 2015). This means the other 80% of police calls contain a wide array of public safety and welfare incidents (Higgins & Hales, 2016). Goldstein (1977), endeavoured to describe the functions of the police, in an attempt to illustrate the breadth of their role. These included:

1   To prevent and control conduct that is widely recognized as threatening to life and property (serious crime).
2   To aid individuals who are in danger of physical harm, such as the victim of a criminal attack. To protect constitutional guarantees, such as the right of free speech and assembly.
3   To facilitate the movement of people and vehicles.
4   To assist those who cannot care for themselves: the intoxicated, the addicted, the mentally ill, the physically disabled, the old, and the young.
5   To resolve conflict, whether it be between individuals, groups of individuals, or individuals and their government.
6   To identify problems that have the potential for becoming more serious problems for the individual citizen, for the police, or for government.
7   To create and maintain a feeling of security in the community.

Since Goldstein generated this list other factors have increased in significance, including terrorism (from Islamic extremism to white supremacism), and organised crime. This means that an intelligence analyst can potentially find themselves working on a wide range of projects, from traffic management to the identification of repeat callers and terrorist suspects. However, it is important to highlight that it is not just police employees who engage in intelligence analysis. Mawby (1999:17) explains the term *policing* goes much wider than the police institution. It relates to the *process* of preventing and detecting crime and maintaining order, which encompasses a vast range of agencies. Indeed, agencies involved in 'policing' have expanded significantly in recent decades, through what Garland (2001) explains as a policy of 'responsibilization'. In this approach whilst the government engages in a regulatory role (steering), its citizens become responsible for resourcing the activity (rowing). Loader (2000), assists this understanding by listing five organisational categories involved in policing:

• *Policing by government.* As discussed, this involves publicly funded agencies which are commonly referred to as the police or law enforcement. Examples are NYPD or the Metropolitan Police, as well as Drug Enforcement Agencies and Anti-Terrorist Units.
• *Policing through government:* This relates to government funded agencies, outside the police, but nevertheless associated with the control of behaviour, for example, street wardens, antisocial behaviour officers, and social services.

- *Policing above government.* This includes transnational law enforcement agencies such as United Nations, Interpol, or Europol.
- *Policing beyond government:* This often relates to policing activities provided by private or commercial agencies, privately funded by citizens or corporations (i.e. private security to supervise buildings or events; or commercial businesses which require an investigative or policing capability, such as insurance companies).
- *Policing below government:* agencies engaged in voluntary and community activities (such as neighbourhood watch and community support groups).

This widespread involvement of other agencies engaged in the policing of society has led to a mixed economy, often termed pluralisation. Many of these 'policing' agencies employ their own analysts to understand data patterns and establish more effective and efficient business practices. Within this expansion it is the private security industry which has shown most growth, stimulated by an increased sense of insecurity, ironically during a period when reported crime started to decrease. Private security services are available at a fraction of the cost of the public police (Johnston, 1992) and have been able to respond more flexibly to globalisation, being able to provide security and protection across jurisdictional boundaries. Similarly, the gentrification of public space and shopping outlets has added to this expansion. An international review of Private Security Companies (PSC) across 70 countries, found a ratio of 1.8 private security personnel to every one publicly funded police officer. In total this could mean approximately 255 million privately funded police officers across the world (Small Arms Survey, 2011). The exact ratio differs across the world, with the public police still the majority in 56% of the surveyed countries, including the UK (0.9:1). At the time of this survey countries where the public police were in the minority included: India (5:1), South Africa (2.6:1), USA (2.3:1), Australia (2.2:1), China (1.9:1), and the Russian Federation (1.3:1). This means there are commercial companies who have a significant footprint in policing with the private security firm G4S reported as employing 530,000 staff in 115 countries over a decade ago (Abrahamsen & Williams, 2009:2). In fact, whilst there are about 200,000 police staff in the UK there are around 250,000 licensed security staff who undertake a wide variety of tasks. In summary many agencies are invested in intelligence analysis relating to 'policing'.

The emergence of intelligence analysis in the police

Intelligence analysis (sometimes referred to as crime analysis) has been defined as follows.

> Analysis is the process of collecting and interpreting a range of data and making inferences and recommendations. Intelligence analysts use defined

analytical techniques to identify and explain patterns of crime and incidents and to infer who might be responsible. Analysis supports strategic decision making and the tactical deployment of resources to prevent crime, and to detect and disrupt criminal activity (Pearce 2008:145).

Whilst military intelligence has been tracked back to ancient China, intelligence analysis in relation to policing is a more recent endeavour. During the 1950s the FBI were known to hold dossiers on specific individuals, whilst in the 1970s, major police stations in the UK had a 'collators' office which would collect information on people of interest. However, in these early times there was concern about the lack of rigour relating to the type of information collected and how it was stored. Across the US and the UK these deficiencies started to be exposed when activists lobbied for reform. In the UK a lapse of police security in 1979, led to an expose by the *New Statesman* publication (Campbell, 1979:189), which pointed out that the police 'regularly record gossip, hearsay and unsubstantiated information; that they permanently file details of any type of police activity against an individual, irrespective of any charge or conviction; and that they open and update files on people who have never been convicted or even suspected of any criminal offence'.

The dominant thinking of that time relied on a model, widely referred to as the intelligence cycle, which is still referred to today. Whilst the originator is unknown, the concept can be found in books as early as 1948 (Wheaton, 2011), and whilst the intelligence cycle has been slightly adapted over time, its fundamental steps remain both constant and resilient (Stark, 2016). They include the following.

- Stage 1: *Direction*. This is the natural starting point of the cycle and simply directs what intelligence needs to be gathered and for what purpose.
- Stage 2: *Collection*. This is the gathering of raw information and can include both open and covert data, from both human and technological sources.
- Stage 3: *Analysis and production*. This is where the raw information is interpreted. Specific consideration should be given to the reliability, validity and relevance of the information and the product should be transformed into a product suitable for the recipient.
- Stage 4: *Dissemination*. The last step is the distribution of the intelligence product to the consumers, often the people who directed its collection.

Whilst there have been a number of minor amendments to this cycle, primarily emphasising the importance of evaluation, the cycle remains important to both the military and law enforcement. However, perhaps the most significant driver of change in the intelligence community was the National Intelligence Model (NIM), which emerged in the UK in 2000 (ACPO, 2005). To appreciate the origins of the NIM, one needs to refer back to 1993 when the UK Audit Commission (a government sponsored agency directed to examine effectiveness and efficiency in public services), started to examine the police. Their report showed the previous decade had seen a small rise in police officers (6%), but a much larger increase in recorded crime (74%), significant increases in calls for service, and a 9% reduction in the detection rate. The report was critical of police policy that randomly deployed resources with little analysis as to place, type or time of the incident. They recommended police practice should change in three ways: a) develop integrated crime strategies that clarify roles and responsibilities (i.e. Detectives, patrol, administration); b) make the best use of resources (i.e. reduce duplication); and c) target the offender rather than reacting to crime incidents (Audit Commission, 1993). The response became known as intelligence-led policing (ILP).

> Intelligence-led policing aims to reduce crime through the informed direction of enforcement agencies. Information is collected from a variety of sources, to produce 'intelligence'. This is then used to direct the activities of enforcement agencies in ways that enable them to disrupt, disable or undermine criminal behaviour (Tilley 2008:146).

Whilst ILP appeared to make an impact, there remained concerns (especially amongst politicians), that proven good practice was not being consistently replicated. In 2000 the British Government sought to change this with the introduction of the National Intelligence Model (NIM). The National Criminal Intelligence Service (NCIS) (2000:11) explained the approach as something that,

> involves identifying and limiting the activities of volume criminals and dangerous offenders, controlling disorder and tackling the many problems that adversely affect community safety and quality of life. The specific outcomes required are improved community safety, reduced crime rates and the control of criminality and disorder.

The introduction of the model was supported by significant resources, which generated extensive guidance in the form of processes, protocols and documentation. It attempted to bring a consistent method of working across the 43 police agencies of England and Wales, using three innovations. These included: distinguishing policing into three levels; standardising intelligence techniques and products; and devising different levels of Tasking and Co-ordinating Groups from which priorities were set (specified in strategic or tactical assessments) and actioned. These are explained more extensively in Chapter 3 and there is no doubt the NIM significantly raised the profile of intelligence-led policing. Jones and Newburn (2007) said this was 'the pre-eminent intelligence model internationally' and it was adopted or adapted in a variety of other countries notably in Australia, New Zealand Canada, Abu Dhabi, and parts of Europe (Brown, 2007:336; Kirby, 2013; Ratcliffe, 2016). In 2003, the US

Government endorsed the National Criminal Intelligence Sharing Plan, followed in 2004 when the Hague Programme of the European Union officially declared 'intelligence-led policing' within its five-year strategy (Council of the EU, 2004:22).

Section 3: Future challenges associated with the improvement of intelligence analysis

Context

Whilst the principles of intelligence analysis remain consistent (explained by the intelligence cycle and the National Intelligence Model), the means to collect intelligence changes as it adapts to social, political, economic, technological and legal advances. The purpose of this section is to highlight some of the challenges associated with this evolution. At the outset it is important to provide some context, specifically by illustrating the speed of change within society and what that means for intelligence analysis.

Conscious and adaptive opponents

One of the reasons why intelligence remains important is that law enforcement faces conscious and adaptive opponents (Sparrow, 2008). In essence offenders are able to combat law enforcement agencies by withdrawing and returning with new approaches (Kirby, 2013). Indeed, Ekblom (2003) explains that law enforcement practitioners and offenders are engaged in a constant *arms race* where each looks for ways to out-think the other. A useful international illustration relates to car theft. Vehicle crime wasn't a significant problem in the early 20th century due to the scarcity of cars. However, this changed during the 1960s as vehicle numbers increased, as did the opportunities to steal them. As thefts reached a significant level the intelligence analysis indicated poor vehicle security was facilitating the problem, which resulted in security accessories being designed and introduced (i.e. steering locks). Unfortunately, these weren't completely successful as many vehicle owners refused, or forgot, to use them which meant thefts continued, albeit at a reduced rate. During the 1980s and 1990s, as the problem increased, more pressure was put on manufacturers to design better security, which led to inbuilt central locking, car alarms, and electronic immobilisers. As these tools were only fitted to new vehicles, the overall impact was initially limited and vehicle crime continued to rise until 1993 when the technology encompassed a critical mass of vehicles (Morgan et al., 2016). Indeed, the most significant change occurred after governments made these interventions compulsory. A study across seven nations found that whilst effective preventative security appeared between 1989 and 1992, it took between 8 and 14 years to protect half of all available vehicles, when a sharp decline in theft took place (approximately 40%). Unfortunately, this trend has recently started to change. The introduction of keyless cars has allowed *conscious offenders* to find ways around the security, using equipment bought online. Since 2014/15 in the UK there has been a significant year on year increase in theft. Further, as the Home Office estimates, the average cost of a stolen vehicle is £10,290 and a commercial vehicle at £35,180, this presents a £1b problem to the UK. This means manufacturers, insurers, police and other stakeholders are once more looking for strategic and coordinated responses to reverse this trend. In essence the pace of change creates opportunities for offenders and law enforcement alike. It is important for intelligence analysts to identify these trends in order that they can be exploited for the benefit of society. On that point it is important to look ahead to establish the future challenges for intelligence analysis.

A new epoch for intelligence analysis?

As will be explained throughout this book, crime and other policing issues often occur as a result of opportunities. At a macro level this pace of change is likely to accelerate in both complexity and speed, creating new policing challenges. Schwab (2015) argues that seismic shifts in society are associated with industrial revolutions. The original industrial revolution started with the introduction of the steam engine and the realisation of its potential. This was followed by the mainstream use of electricity, and more recently by computer and communication technology. Schwab argues the world is in the early stages of a fourth industrial revolution which will harness and connect digital, physical, and biological innovation. He explains that we live in an increasingly interconnected interdependent world, which he predicts will become increasingly integrated and driven by big data. This fourth industrial revolution will change the way we communicate, produce and consume. Further, an increasingly digitised world will lead to wider changes in the physical environment, including the emergence of smart traffic systems and smart cities. Successful cohabitation in such an integrated society will rely on close co-operation between government, private business and civil society. It will also require a new economic model to cope with these changes and maximise human well-being.

Building on this theme Deloitte (2018) argue this epoch has ramifications for the police. Going back in history they argue that version 1 of the police (1829–1900) introduced the (then) radical civilian policing model that shaped policing across the world. Version 2 (1900–1960) evolved by embracing electric power and technological advances in investigation (i.e. fingerprinting). Version 3 (1960 to the present), responded to a more diverse and mobile society, which was increasingly connected through digital technology. However, whilst police forces have undoubtedly modernised, they have remained faithful to traditional policing approaches. Deloitte argue the emerging version 4 requires a much more innovative data management approach, producing seamless connectivity with wider agencies involved in governance and policing. They argue this may require innovative insight to design and deliver workforce modernisation, digital transformation, and new structures and collaborations. This means the police must prepare for six new realities:

1   Serving a fully digital world. In this, each police related incident has a digital footprint.
2   Police working from disproportionately smaller budgets compared to private sector agencies involved in crime, as well as other public sector agencies who require bigger budgets (health, social care, and pensions).
3   The unprecedented speed of change in society will demand an unprecedented speed of response.
4   A requirement to harness cyber-physical systems.
5   Managing an unknowable volume of knowledge to establish 'what works'.
6   Operating with near total transparency.

All of these challenges will have at their heart the collection, interpretation, analysis, dissemination and management of information as the world copes with:

•   A growing and ageing society.
•   A globalised economy.
•   Ongoing urbanisation.
•   Technological acceleration and data abundance.
•   Political extremism.

For intelligence analysis this suggests advances are needed at individual, process and structural levels. In relation to individual factors, personal knowledge and skills will be increasingly important for both analysts and managers. This point has been highlighted since the emergence of intelligence-led policing in the 1990s. Indeed, Cope (2004) examining two UK police forces, concluded there was insufficient understanding of crime analysis and crime intelligence, which had been neglected in operational planning. Harfield and Harfield (2008) concluded that ten years following the implementation of NIM there was insufficient evidence to show the police had fully embraced the intelligence profession. Janet Evans (a practitioner) and Mark Kebbell (an academic), who are based in Australia, argue the dynamics generate a *vicious* intelligence cycle. This commences with intelligence staff, who are poorly selected and generate weak intelligence products. As this results in intelligence requirements not being achieved, police commanders lose faith in the intelligence model. This culminates in reduced investment, which affects the quantity and quality of recruitment, and so the negative process continues. As they point out 'Police agencies frequently lack the skills for effective evaluation and fear that what they have done may not withstand scrutiny' (Evans & Kebbell, 2012:84). Many commentators, including Keay and Kirby (2018) concur with these views pointing out that insufficient investment is focused on intelligence analysts, and much more needs to be done in relation to their knowledge, understanding and skills.

In relation to *process and structural levels* it is well documented that implementation failure can occur at organisational and operational levels. For example, Chainey (2012), argues 'hypothesis testing' should be used extensively by analysts when testing theories. However, this advice can actually be found within the NIM and Chief Officer guidance (ACPO, 2008), distributed to each UK police headquarters. Unfortunately, this may be hidden within the NIM guidance which comprises 213 pages and nine volumes of supporting documents (totalling 816 pages). This issue of implementation failure will be explored throughout this book as it is apparent a considerable amount of knowledge is present but poorly implemented, leading to failures emerging in a myriad of ways. Whilst these frailties can be found internationally, an infamous organisational failure was observed in the UK. Following a murder in Soham UK in 2004 an inquiry, led by Sir Michael Bichard, examined how a person suspected of sex offences could be recruited as a school janitor. Bichard highlighted, 'systemic and corporate' failures in intelligence handling which he said was 'all the more surprising given the emphasis all the witnesses placed on the importance of intelligence and the need to identify patterns of behaviour as early as possible'. He highlighted that IT systems were not sufficiently searchable; matters were not routinely referred by police to social services; intelligence records sometimes not submitted; and records at times being inappropriately deleted. He concluded by saying there was 'a widespread failure to appreciate the value of intelligence' (Bichard, 2004, paras 8–15 cited in Brown, 2007:337–338). His comments led to a code of practice which covered record creation, review, retention, deletion and information sharing.

Conclusion

This chapter has served as an introduction to the origins and growing use of intelligence within policing, as well as indicating future trends. Whilst significant achievements have been made from intelligence analysis, there does seem scope for improvement. This is especially relevant as society is continually evolving and will continue to generate opportunities for offenders who can only be disrupted through better intelligence analysis. The chapters that follow will deconstruct the process of intelligence analysis in finer detail. Whilst the next chapter lists the intelligence sources on offer, Chapters 3 and 4 will provide strategic and tactical discussions on intelligence providing both managerial and analyst perspectives. Chapters 5 and 6 provide practical advice on how analysts can use their knowledge and skills to facilitate the reduction and investigation of crime. Later chapters then examine how intelligence evolved, specifically in a multi-agency environment and through the impact of data science. The concluding chapter will summarise the book, exploring how intelligence analysis may be improved in a future policing environment.

References

Abrahamsen, R. and Williams, M. (2009) Security beyond the state: global security assemblages in international politics. *International Political Sociology*, 3: 1–17.

ACPO. (2005a) *Guidance on the National Intelligence Model*. Wyboston: NCP.

ACPO. (2008) *Practice Advice on Analysis*. London: NPIA.

Audit Commission. (1993) *Helping with Enquiries: Tackling Crime Effectively*, Vols 1 and 2. London: HMSO.

Bichard, M. (2004) *Bichard Enquiry Report: Introduction and Summary*. Available at http://www.bichardenquiry.org.uk [Accessed 3 February 2020].

Brown, S.D. (2007) The meaning of criminal intelligence. *International Journal of Police Science & Management*, 9 (4): 336–340.

Campbell, D. (1979) Keeping tabs on everyone. Available at https://www.duncancamp bell.org/menu/journalism/newstatesman/newstatesman-1979/Keeping%20tabs%20on %20everyone.pdf [Accessed 13 September 2020].

Chainey, S. (2012) Improving the explanatory content of analysis products using hypothesis testing. *Policing: A Journal of Policy and Practice*, 6 (2): 108–121.

College of Policing. (2015) *College of Policing Analysis: Estimating Demand on the Police Service*. Online report. Available at http://www.college.police.uk/documents/ demand_report_21_1_15.pdf [Accessed 1 February 2020].

Cope, N. (2004) Intelligence-led policing or policing-led intelligence: integrating volume crime analysis into policing. *British Journal of Criminology*, 44 (2): 188–203.

Council of the EU. (2004) The Hague Programme: strengthening freedom, security and justice in the European Union (16054/04 Jal 559). Available at http://www.europa.eu/ justice_home/doc_centre/doc/hague_programme_en [Accessed 24 January 2006].

Deloitte. (2018) *Policing 4.0: Deciding the Future of Policing in the UK*. Available at https://www2.deloitte.com/content/dam/Deloitte/ie/Documents/PublicSector/deloit te-uk-future-of-policing.pdf [Accessed 18 May 2020].

Ekblom, P. (2003) Organised crime and the conjunction of criminal opportunity framework. In A. Edwards and P. Gill (eds), *Transnational Organised Crime: Perspectives on Global Security*. London: Routledge.

Europol. (2003) *Intelligence Handling Booklet*. The Hague: Europol.

Evans, J. and Kebbell, M. (2012) Integrating intelligence into policing practice. In T. Prenzler (ed.), *Policing and Security in Practice*. New York: Palgrave MacMillan.

Garland, D. (2001) *The Culture of Control: Crime and Social Order in Contemporary Society*. Oxford: Oxford University Press.

Global Intelligence Alliance. (2004) *Introduction to Strategic Intelligence*. Available at https://www.academia.edu/33107444/INTRODUCTION_TO_STRATEGIC_INTEL LIGENCE [Accessed 24 June 2019].

Goldstein, H. (1977) Policing a free society. University of Wisconsin Legal Studies Research Paper No. 1349. Cambridge (MA): Ballinger Pub. Co. Available at http:// ssrn.com/abstract=2596883 [Accessed 6 May 2020].

Harfield, C. and Harfield, K. (2008) *Intelligence: Investigation, Community and Partnership*. Oxford: Oxford University Press.

Higgins, A. and Hales, G. (2016) Police effectiveness in a changing world: Paper 1. The Police Foundation. Online report. Available at http://www.policefoundation. org.uk/uploads/holding/projects/changing_world_paper_1 [Accessed 3 March 2020].

Johnston, L. (1992) *The Rebirth of Private Policing*. London: Routledge.

Jones, T. and Newburn, T. (2007) *Policy Transfer and Criminal Justice.* Maidenhead: Open University Press.

Keay, S. and Kirby, S. (2018a) The evolution of the police analyst and the influence of evidence based-policing. *Policing: A Journal of Policy and Practice,* 12 (3): 265–276.

Kirby, S. (2013) *Effective Policing?: Implementation in Theory And Practice.* Basingstoke: Palgrave MacMillan.

Legg, S. and Hutter, M.A. (2006) Collection of definitions of intelligence. Available at http://www.vetta.org/documents/A-Collection-of-Definitions-of-Intelligence.pdf [Accessed 24 May 2019].

Loader, I (2000) Plural policing and democratic governance. *Social and Legal Studies,* 9(3): 323–345.

Maguire, M. and John, T. (2004) The National Intelligence Model: early implementation experience in three police force areas (Working Paper Series No. 50). Wales: Cardiff University School of Social Sciences.

Mawby, R.I. (1999) *Policing Across the World: Issues for the 21st Century.* London: Routledge.

Morehouse, R. (2000) The role of criminal intelligence in law enforcement. In M. Petersen, R. Morehouse and R. Wright (eds), *Intelligence 2000: Revising the Basic Elements,* p. 7. Lawrenceville, NJ: International Association of Law Enforcement Intelligence Analysts.

Morgan, N., Shaw, O., Feist, A. and Byron, C. (2016) Reducing criminal opportunity: vehicle security and vehicle crime, Home Office research report 87, London: Home Office.

National Crime Intelligence Service. (2000) *The National Intelligence Model.* London: NCIS.

Pati, R. (2014) Supermarket giant Tesco pioneers big data: turning customer loyalty into royalties. Available at https://dataconomy.com/2014/02/tesco-pioneers-big-data/ [Accessed 22 March 2020].

Pearce, K. (2008) Intelligence Analysis. In T. Newburn and P. Neyroud (eds), *Dictionary of Policing.* Cullompton: Willan Publishing.

Petersen, M. (1997) The role of analysis in intelligence-led policing. In A. Smith (ed.), *Intelligence-led Policing: International Perspectives on Policing in the 21st Century.* Lawrenceville, NJ: International Association of Law Enforcement Intelligence Analysts.

Pollack, K.M. (1996) The influence of Arab culture on Arab military effectiveness. PhD Dissertation Submitted to the Department of Political Science at the Massachusetts Institute of Technology.

Ratcliffe, J. (2003) Intelligence-led policing. *Trends and Issues in Crime and Criminal Justice,* No. 248. Canberra: Australian Institute of Criminology.

Ratcliffe, J. (2016) *Intelligence-led Policing.* Abingdon: Routledge.

Schwab, K. (2015) The fourth industrial revolution: What it means and how to respond. Available at https://www.researchgate.net/deref/https%3A%2F%2Fwww.foreignaffairs.com%2Farticles%2F2015-12-12%2Ffourth-industrial-revolution [Accessed 23 April 2020].

Smale, W. (2014) The couple who helped transform the way we shop. Available at https://www.bbc.co.uk/news/business-30095454 [Accessed 27 January 2020].

Small Arms Survey. (2011) Small arms survey: States of security. Available at http://www.smallarms.survey.org/publications/bytypre/yearbook/small-arms-survey-2011.html [Accessed 28 August 2016].

Sparrow, M.K. (2008) *The Character of Harms*. Cambridge: Cambridge University Press.

Stark. B. (2016) The Intelligence Cycle. Available at http://www.intelligence101.com/an-introduction-to-the-intelligence-cycle/ [Accessed 14 May 2020].

Steven, S. (1980) *The Spymasters of Israel: The Definitive Look at the World's Best Intelligence Service*. New York: Ballantine Books.

Sun Tzu. (1963) *The Art of War*. New York: Oxford University Press.

Tilley, N. (2008) Modern approaches to policing: community, problem-oriented and intelligence-led. In T. Newburn, (2nd edn). *The Handbook of Policing*. Devon: Willan Publishing.

Time-Life Books. (1985) *Lee Takes Command: From Seven Days to Second Bull Run*. SanDiego: Bluestocking Books.

Warner, M. (2002) Wanted: a definition of 'Intelligence'. Available at http://www.cia.gov/csi/studies/vol46no3/article02 [Accessed on 11 October 2005].

Wheaton, K.J. (2011) Who invented the Intelligence Cycle? Available at https://sourcesandmethods.blogspot.com/2011/01/rfi-who-invented-intelligence-cycle.html [Accessed 5 May 2020].

Chapter 2

Understanding the value and danger of intelligence sources

Introduction

The previous chapter has explained how the concept of intelligence was introduced into the police. The purpose of this chapter is to show the multitude of available intelligence sources and explain their strengths and weaknesses, as higher quality sources improve intelligence analysis. In essence the chapter, which is set out in three sections, hopes to provide a useful reference for those involved in the collation, analysis and dissemination of intelligence.

- Section 1: Human intelligence (HUMINT). Will explore the different types of intelligence that emanate from human sources, both in the police and public domain.
- Section 2: Will explore the intelligence opportunities provided through technological and scientific methods, including elements such as CCTV, Forensic, and Behavioural sciences.
- Section 3: Open source intelligence (OSINT). Will explore this increasingly available and relevant source, created through the opportunities presented by the internet.

Section 1: Human intelligence, witnesses, Covert Human Intelligence Sources, and undercover police officers

Whilst humans are central to the intelligence process, they are fallible. This is because the brain, a core element in both analysis and decision making, can generate irregularities. Although physical similarities exist (all brains comprise about 1.4 kg of human tissue and accommodate approximately 100 billion nerve cells or neurones), each organ operates at a personal level. During each second a million new, and often subconscious, connections are generated to regulate human thoughts, experiences, memories and habits (Phillips, 2006). In practice this means that individuals can witness the same information but process it in different ways due to many idiosyncracies, including prior experience. These nuances are constantly illustrated by human intelligence sources and personified through eye witness testimony.

Eyewitnesses

Witnesses are a common source of intelligence, especially following the commission of crime. Police analysts often use witness statements as a core intelligence document; however, research shows this testimony can be fallible and is often a critical factor in false convictions (Connors et al., 1996; Huff et al., 1996). This unintentional inaccuracy can be generated both through the processing of the information, as well as the way the information is extracted from the witness. Understanding these factors can help intelligence practitioners assess the reliability of the information they analyse.

The accuracy of eyewitnesses can be overtly affected by both physical or psychological disabilities, which can affect both senses and memory. However, even without the existence of a specific medical condition, most healthy people find it demanding to remember and recount a fleeting event. The process an eyewitness takes part in can be understood in three-stages: the acquisition of the information, the retention of the information, and its subsequent recall. In terms of acquisition, psychologists have shown that the viewing context is important. For example, studies show individuals find it easier to identify the characteristics of people with whom they share the same ethnicity, whilst the stress associated with viewing a violent incident can reduce the accuracy of the memory (Clifford & Hollin, 1981). Secondly, retention is also a factor as, with the exception of facial recognition, most memories deteriorate over time. This means the sooner a witness can make a statement the more likely it is to be accurate. The final stage is *retrieval*, where a number of factors can also influence accuracy. Particularly important is the way the police officer obtains the information. Witnesses are often eager to assist the police, therefore if the investigator asks leading questions or introduces unreliable information it can unwittingly affect the accuracy of the account, even making it possible for the witness to recount something that never occurred (Porter et al., 1999). Witnesses are also more accurate when recalling the circumstances of the event, rather than describing the physical characteristics of the offender. Finally, the statement-taking process can generate inaccuracy, especially if the investigator is under time or media pressure to discover a specific fact, or the eyewitness feels a particular responsibility to answer the questions in a specific way.

Some practical tips were provided in the famous case of R. V. Turnbull 1977, which provided the mnemonic ADVOKATE (Kebbell & Wagstaff, 1999). This suggested a witness should be asked a number of questions to help understand the accuracy of their memory, including:

- Amount of time under observation.
- Distance between the witness and incident.
- Visibility at the time of the observation.
- Obstruction between the witness and incident (i.e. street furniture, vegetation).
- Known or seen before (witnesses are more able to recognise the features of those they already know).
- Any reason to remember (if the incident happened on a birthday the witness may place specific relevance on it).
- Time lapse between the incident and being asked to recall it.
- Errors or material discrepancies.

As well as these points there has also been considerable research to advise how an investigator should engage with the witness. First it is important for the interviewer to show empathy, rapport and good listening skills as these competences are associated with greater accuracy. This can also be enhanced by the use of social and cognitive cues set out in the Cognitive Interview model (Geiselman, et al., 1984), which proposes four interview techniques. The first cue asks the witness to consider the physical or emotional environment at the time, as reinstating the context in which the memory was formed makes it more likely to be recalled. The second cue involves asking the witness to initially recount all the event details, no matter how minor, as free recall initially generates better accuracy than being asked to respond to specific questions. The third cue is to ask the witness to recall the events in a different order (reverse order, forward or backward from highly memorable points) as this can tease out hidden memories. The final cue is to ask the witness to recall the event from a different perspective, for example to consider what they may have seen if walking on the opposing footpath. Again, it generates access to different memories without the need to ask leading questions.

Covert Human Intelligence Sources

The discussion so far has examined the testimony of a public-spirited volunteer. However, there are those who provide information for more complex reasons and they require more scrutiny. One such example relates to Confidential Informants, referred to in the UK and other parts of the world as Covert Human Intelligence Sources (CHIS). The benefits of using informants is well established, as they can potentially provide low cost, relevant, and accurate information, which prevents the need for expensive and lengthy police activity. As an example, consider a violent robbery which can lead to the serious injury of innocent people. If the police respond after the crime is committed, they require time-consuming and expensive follow up enquiries, forensic analysis at the scene, house to house enquiries and media requests to help discover witnesses. If this process is ultimately successful then the suspects can be identified, although this is often not quick enough to prevent criminal profits, weapons and other forensic evidence being concealed. A lengthy and challenging court case then ensues whereby circumstantial evidence is presented, and witnesses are coaxed into giving their testimony. Consider these human and financial costs against a single (and relatively small) financial payment to an informant who identifies all those involved, where and when the crime will take place, and how the weapons and stolen property will be disposed of. Ideally this allows an intervention to take place before the harm materialises, or at least allows the police to arrest the offenders and capture important evidence immediately after the crime occurs.

Due to these benefits informants have provided critical information throughout history and have even been mentioned in accounts of the White-chapel murders of 1888. These endorsements were enhanced further when the Audit Commission (a UK government organisation tasked with highlighting value for money in the public sector), supported their use in 1993 as a means to target persistent offenders more effectively. However, history has also shown the unintended consequences of using informants to obtain intelligence. A critical point is that informants are often criminals themselves and their motivation for assisting the police can be varied. This includes seeking revenge against the person they are informing on; attempting to disrupt an investigation by providing false information; diverting the police away from their own crimes; obtaining information from the police; or obtaining financial reward. Their use has generated many scandals over the years, which have included: informants encouraging others to commit crime; informants committing crime themselves with the implicit consent of the police; and police officers diverting informant money into their own pockets.

These issues have led the UK (and other countries) to introduce more control in terms of the police–informant relationship. As the UK police watchdog stated, 'Informants are considered necessary and useful, but they should be properly targeted and controlled (including such areas as risk assessment, registration, payment and supervision)' (Her Majesty's Inspectorate of Constabulary (HMIC) 1999:4). As a result, checks and balances, in the form of legislation and procedure have increased and it is generally accepted only experienced officers should manage informants. In the UK these guidelines are explained within S.71 Regulation of Investigatory Powers Act 2000. As with other types of covert intelligence use, the authorisation to use informants should only be provided if it is compatible with Human Rights legislation and principles. This means it should be proportionate (the scale of the deception and intrusion must be appropriate to the crime); it is legal; there is accountability associated with the decision (recorded/authorised); and the approach is necessary (the information cannot reasonably be obtained in any other way). In the management of the process, the 'informant handler' is designated as the person who deals directly with the informant, and they are assigned a specific supervisor, known as an 'informant controller'. Each informant will be referred to by a pseudonym (often an identifying number), and good practice dictates there will only be one person, in any agency, who has access to the identity of all informants (often referred to as the registrar).

Police surveillance officers

One of the disadvantages of using a member of the public to provide intelligence is their unpredictability. Questions also surround their veracity, their ability to respond under pressure, the reasons for involvement, and the dangers inherent in their involvement. It is for these reasons that primary intelligence (i.e. occurrences that are personally seen or heard), from police officers or specialist police staff are particularly valued. Whilst all members of staff are able to submit items of intelligence, certain individuals are specifically assigned specialist intelligence duties, with surveillance being one such example. Here improvements in technology (in movement tracking, the use of drones, and auditory or visual recording) have improved the safety of operatives as well as providing corroboration. Whilst surveillance technology is nothing new (pinhole cameras and covert recording devices have been used for many years), their reliability and size allow them to be used more inconspicuously. This has created an expectation that they will be used to support human testimony wherever possible.

Human surveillance is generally categorised as mobile or static. The closer to the target and more covert it has to be, then (generally speaking) the more challenging it is to conduct. Static surveillance relies on identifying a suitable observation point, unobserved monitoring of the subject and recording relevant intelligence. There are many dangers associated with this process. The first challenge is identifying a suitable observation post, which often lies within (or extremely close to) a hostile environment. Any person assisting with a suitable location has to be protected to reduce the chance of future reprisals. Further, the closer the location to the subject of interest, the more risk the surveillance operative runs of being identified and challenged. One of the most challenging environments is to conduct static surveillance in open and hostile environments. Operatives who conduct this are known as CROP officers (Covert Rural Observation Post), and their expertise allows them to blend into the environment and conduct covert observations. Whilst more often associated with rural surroundings, they can also be deployed in urban situations. The risk of using CROP officers was spelt out in January 1985 when two operatives were deployed to watch a man called Noye, who was suspected of handling stolen gold from the Brinks Mat bullion robbery in 1983. Their surveillance location was discovered by two rottweilers who were running loose within the grounds. Concerned that the noise from the dogs would alert Noye, one of the officers retreated, however before the other could escape he was repeatedly stabbed and killed. Noye was acquitted of charges relating to the death but sentenced to 14 years in relation to the robbery.

Whilst static surveillance has its dangers, the threat generally increases with mobile surveillance, due to it being less predictable, more challenging and expensive to conduct. Identifying and maintaining observation on mobile suspects is inherently more difficult as they can increase their speed, change direction, or swap methods of transportation. As such a mobile surveillance team require significant resources to respond to these challenges and maintain their covert nature by frequently changing personnel. An example of the challenges surrounding mobile surveillance was illustrated in the tragic death of a Brazilian man called Jean Charles de Menezes. Following an attempt to detonate a bomb in London on the 21st July 2005, military and law enforcement officers were deployed to watch flat premises which were associated with a suspect. A soldier informed the group that de Menezes (who was mistakenly identified as the suspect) was leaving the premises. It was reported afterwards that due to a surveillance officer taking a comfort break, it was impossible to transmit a photograph to the control room, which would have shown they had identified the wrong person. Faced with this ambiguity the officers on the ground decided (wrongly) he was the suspect and followed him into Stockwell underground station. Shortly after he was forced to the floor and shot seven times in the head, an accepted tactic to prevent a terrorist detonating a bomb. The inquest delivered an open verdict, and although individual charges were not pressed, the Metropolitan Police Service (MPS) was found to be in contravention of the Health & Safety at Work Act 1974 (failure to provide for the health, safety and welfare of Mr de Menezes). The MPS commander said at the time, 'Our job is to reduce the risk to everybody as best as possible. But I do fear that, in the future, a bomber might not be prevented from setting off a bomb. And equally, I pray it doesn't happen, but it is possible an innocent member of the public might die like this' (*The Independent*, 2008). This tragedy shows the many challenges associated with static and mobile intelligence gathering.

Police undercover officers

Some argue that deploying undercover officers provides the benefits of an informant (CHIS) without the added complication of having to manage an untrained, unpredictable (and often criminal) civilian. However, numerous international scandals surrounding the use of undercover officers have led to the approach being researched in the UK, Canada and the USA, utilising the academic disciplines of Law, Criminology, Sociology and Psychology. It has been explained across three elements:

a   Surveillance (passively observing and reporting back);
b   Prevention (where the operative attempts to stop an offence taking place i.e. is part of a protest and attempts to diffuse aggression);

c   Facilitation (where the operative encourages commission). This is where the operative is close to the offending group and plays an active part. It is said to be the most controversial aspect of undercover work as it often faces allegations of agent provocateur and entrapment. However, from a police perspective it is the most cost effective, as it can lead to suspects being caught in the commission of the offence using the least resources.

The decision making associated with undercover policing appears to be a moral maze with significant levels of discretion existing at all levels of the operation (i.e. its authorisation and ensuing activity). It is therefore surprising that the tactic has historically been the least regulated of any police procedure, with challenges often emerging through the courts and the media. The concerns about the process has generally been described across two themes. First, the negative impact to the officer, which includes such issues as corruption, disciplinary problems, substance abuse, interpersonal problems, a loss of self-identity and paranoia. Secondly, there are concerns about the implications it has for police legitimacy, caused through the abuse of process. As Maguire and John (1996:319) state, 'if regulatory mechanisms lack clarity and firmness, the intense desire of detectives to catch criminals can easily lead whole units into behaviour which is unacceptable by any standard and that, in the absence of such regulation, some major scandals should almost inevitably emerge before too long'. Indeed, the main concern of this approach is the level of deception associated with undercover work, which is much greater than other covert tactics. First, the suspect is unaware of both the *purpose* and *identity* of the police; second, the process of intelligence collation allows for *'authorised criminality'*, allowing the police to engage in actions that would be a crime if found outside the context of investigation (i.e. possession of drugs, handling stolen goods). Finally, undercover work can be said to be juxtaposed with the principles of democratic policing, which relies on the rule of law and its associated values, i.e. accountability and transparency. Undercover policing therefore creates a morally ambiguous situation for the police to operate within. For example, The Metropolitan police apologised and paid compensation to at least 11 women in 2018 after they had sexual relationships with officers whilst in their undercover role (BBC, 2018). The core issue is to what level the police should be allowed to invade privacy or use trickery/entrapment. Whilst academic studies don't recommend the tactic being banned, they do argue it should be implemented more effectively.

Section 2: The use of technology and science in generating intelligence sources

In recent years advances in technology and science have enhanced intelligence across three areas: passive data intelligence sources; physical and behavioural science; and open source intelligence. These will be described below.

Passive data intelligence sources

The label 'passive data' was first used across the UK in 2005 when the investigative benefits of using vast amounts of information, captured by public and private enterprises, was recognised. Passive data relates to secondary or administrative data, generally collected by agencies other than the police. It is distinguished from other intelligence sources because it is not gathered from the targeting of a specific person or location and can sometimes be collected for purposes outside community safety. Examples of passive intelligence sources include:

- Public and private CCTV (street, garage forecourts, department stores)
- Automatic number plate recognition (ANPR) for motor vehicles
- Credit and debit card transactions
- Timed transactions at stores
- Telephone calls
- Movement through ports
- Satellite navigation systems

Perhaps the most significant facilitator of passive intelligence sources has been the increased use of smart phones which have created electronic traces in the physical environment. This electronic footprint provides a personal profile which itemises such things as mobility patterns, associates, hobbies, level of affluence and disposable income. As all of these can generate important intelligence it is worth examining some of these categories in more detail.

CCTV

The UK is recognised as a world leader in the use of CCTV when tackling crime and disorder, most of which is operated by the commercial sector. Whilst television appeared in 1936, and video recorders emerged in the 1950s, it was 1967 when the UK used CCTV to identify shoplifters (Moran, 1998). These cameras were later used to combat thefts and staff assault on the London Underground (Webb & Laycock, 1992) and vandalism on Bourne-mouth's seafront (Bannister et al., 1998). However, its popularity proliferated in 1994 when the UK government funded 585 CCTV schemes, followed by a further 680 between 1999 and 2003. These schemes have grown piecemeal and, whilst the overall number of UK cameras is unknown, estimates vary between 1.85 million (Reeve, 2011) to 5.9 million (Barrett, 2013). The UK is thought to have proportionally more cameras than most other countries and uses them across public spaces, private commercial areas, transport systems, schools and hospitals (Cahill & Norris, 2002). Although the UK is believed to comprise 5% of the world market and 20% of the European market (Market and Business Development, 2011; KeyNote, 2013), it is dwarfed by China which leads the world in using technology to monitor human behaviour. China is thought to operate 20–30 million surveillance cameras, and Klein (2008) reported they were networked and linked to biometric information and other police data during the Chinese Olympic Games.

CCTV moved on with the advent of unmanned aerial vehicles (UAVs), commonly known as drones, which involve technology solely used by the military a few years earlier. Their use in law enforcement came to the forefront in January 2013 when 65-year-old Jimmy Lee Dykes abducted a five-year-old child from a school bus in Midland City, Atlanta and killed the driver. Dykes kept the child hostage in an inaccessible underground bunker on his land and engaged in a negotiated stand-off with authorities over a six-day period. A drone carrying a covert camera allowed the police to safely survey the scene, keeping law enforcement officers safe. This type of technological advancement generally comes with ethical challenges and this is certainly true with drones. Even if used in public spaces the range of vision from a camera 4,000 feet in the air is far wider than a ground camera, meaning collateral intrusion into private areas is more likely. Whereas the police currently reassure the community that the drones will only be used for specific events such as football matches, it seems inevitable they will be used for routine patrol work in the future. Indeed, at the time of writing their use was being criticised in the UK for spying on citizens as they visited beauty spots during the coronavirus pandemic lockdown.

A further adaptation of CCTV is automatic number plate recognition (ANPR), which allows the police to photograph a vehicle's number plate and check it against police (and other agency) databases. These cameras can be used in either static or mobile form and whilst only identifying the vehicle, rather than the person using it, their use has been particularly effective in criminal investigation. Chapter 7 provides specific examples of its use.

The application of science

Physical (forensic) science

Significant developments in intelligence emerged from physical science with the search for individualisation – the process of attributing a source of forensic material to a single unique source. It started in 1686 when Professor Marcello Malphigi noticed the pattern of ridges, spirals and loops within a fingerprint could be attributed to a specific person. This breakthrough was accelerated by Emile Locard (1923, cited in Broeders, 2007:320), who famously pointed out that, 'every contact leaves a trace'. He explained that 'No one can act with the intensity that the criminal act presupposes without leaving numerous marks in his wake; either the criminal will have left traces of his identity at the scene, or by an inverse action, he will have carried indications of his stay or his actions on his body or on his clothing'. This observation opened up the use of physical science in police work, however a general lack of knowledge and equipment produced little benefit in those early days. Forensic progress was generally slow and whilst the Metropolitan Police established their first forensic laboratory in 1935, it was 30 years later that a specialist officer would routinely attend the scene of a crime (Broeders, 2007). At this time forensic information was mainly for intelligence or corroboration (blood group or glass and fibres), with the real breakthrough emerging through DNA profiling in 1984. Since then DNA techniques have improved significantly in terms of sophistication and have been supported by many other physical techniques. An example is gunshot analysis which allows scientists to match a bullet to a firearm, understand its trajectory and even listen for gunshots in urban areas. It should be emphasised that although no scientific evidence is infallible or irrefutable, it generally remains the best evidence available to the police and Courts in the 21st century. Further, even when it is insufficiently accurate to be used as court evidence, it often serves as useful intelligence.

Behavioural science – offender profiling

Social sciences, specifically behavioural sciences, have also had an impact on intelligence, and one of the most infamous has been 'offender profiling'. In essence it attempts to examine the crime scene to draw inferences about the characteristics of the offender. Some point out that offender profiling has a long history. Woodworth and Porter (1999:243) write that as 'Malleus Maleficarum' was written in the 1400s, to identify witches, it presents an early systematic approach to profiling guilty individuals. In 1876, the Italian criminologist Cesare Lombroso was perhaps the first criminologist to (wrongly) develop profiling techniques when he suggested that individuals of criminal origin could be recognised by their physical appearance (Lombroso, 1876 cited in Lombroso-Ferrero, 1972). Just over half a century later in 1956, the psychiatrist Dr James A. Brussel assisted the New York Police Department to identify the 'The Mad Bomber', an individual linked to over 30 bombings. The resulting popularity led to the FBI Behavioral Science Unit (BSU) being established in 1972, based upon the in-depth interview of 36 convicted murderers. Their typology, which separated organised from disorganised killers, explained that the former was associated with a controlled and planned crime scene, the use of restraints, and concealment of the victim. In contrast the disorganised offender often showed the opposite, illustrated by spontaneous offending (including violence); a chaotic crime scene; little discussion with the victim; and the possibility of sex following death. The FBI argued once these variables are identified they can be mapped to the characteristics of the offender. The organised offender, for example would be intelligent, confident in social and sexual interactions, live with their father and present a masculine image. The disorganised offender would show the opposite. He would live alone, be below average intelligence, lack social skills, be in unskilled occupation close to the crime, have low birth-order status; show poor hygiene and have suffered harsh/inconsistent discipline. A later review of this particular typology was found to be inaccurate when tested in an operational setting (Canter et al., 2004). Overall, the use of offender profiling, which can be generated using a variety of methods, has had mixed reviews, with its accuracy linked to the rigour of the methodology used. The approach is discussed in more detail in Chapter 7 when discussing investigative techniques.

Section 3: The rise of the internet and open source intelligence

Whilst the sciences have generated slow, but continuous knowledge development, the internet has created an exponential rise in information, which has the potential to be transformed into intelligence. The value of open source intelligence (OSINT) has been acknowledged by the intelligence community for a number of decades and was initially associated with the defence industry. Although defined by a number of organisations, the US Office of the Director of National Intelligence (2011) describes it as, 'intelligence produced from publicly available information that is collected, exploited, and disseminated in a timely manner to an appropriate audience for the purpose of addressing a specific intelligence requirement' (Section 931 of Public Law 109–163 cited in Williams & Blum, 2018:ix). Williams and Blum (2018) also distinguish between open source information (which is unclassified publicly available data) from open source intelligence. The latter is the result of a process which exploits information to endorse it as accurate, relevant, and something that can be actioned.

Open source information is wide-ranging, and whilst often free to acquire, some unpublished data can only be publicly accessed for a fee (i.e. commercial satellite imagery). Williams and Blum (2018) divide OSINT into two main categories, which are further subdivided. The first is institutionally generated information, such as news media or grey literature. News media is normally easily identified and incorporates newspapers and journals (online and offline), television and radio. In contrast, grey literature is sourced from non-media institutions and can include the public and private sector, such as governments, corporations, research establishments and academia. This type of source is mainly associated with buildings and organisations which have institutional cohesion (i.e. government departments, open accounts), and whilst efforts have been made to improve the organisation, storage and distribution of this information, it often remains ad hoc. The second category relates to individually generated data. It emanates from social media content, which can be further subdivided into long and short form – relating to its processing and usage. For example, long form social media is generated by single individuals or small groups and is extremely text heavy and often underutilised in analysis, i.e. blogs on sites such as Tumblr and Reddit. In contrast short-form individual generated content is more often examined and emanates from platforms such as Twitter, Facebook and Linked-in. This material is generally of most benefit when aggregated, although individual comments from particularly prominent individuals can be significant, i.e. a senior politician or social influencer. This type of data is particularly useful when supported by other information. For example, a single tweet, highlighting an individual's intention to protest on a particular issue or express anti-government sentiment, may be of little use. However, if many other similar tweets are found in this particular location, it takes on a new significance. The ability to conduct geo-analysis across the world's 4.3 billion IP addresses is a powerful analytic tool.

The benefits of open source information relate to it being readily accessible and generally free. However, the downsides are that it may be unreliable due to the lack of quality assurance when submitted. Commercially available tools are constantly being developed, as social media analytics evolves, to assist in gathering information from a multitude of sites instantaneously, allowing the search of names across single or a variety of social media websites simultaneously. These tools also provide support in the fields of lexical analysis, geo-spatial analysis, and network analysis. Due to the speed of change such analysis is often underutilised, especially relating to social analysis. Of course, in this process the collation and analysis of this information is processed by either human analysts or algorithms that can be subjected to bias (see Chapter 8 for further explanation).

Conclusion

This chapter serves as reference to understand the strengths and weaknesses of different types of intelligence sources. Incorporating data and intelligence from non-traditional policing sources has the potential to improve intelligence outputs for law enforcement. Later chapters will refer to how intelligence analysts can use this information both in crime reduction (Chapter 6) and criminal investigation (Chapter 7), as well as explaining the constraints in relation to their use (Chapter 3).

References

Audit Commission. (1993) *Helping with Enquiries: Tackling Crime Effectively* Vols 1 and 2. London: HMSO.

Bannister, J., Fyfe, N.R and Kearns, A. (1998) Closed Circuit Television and the City. In Norris, C., Moran, J., and Armstrong, G. (eds). *Surveillance, Closed Circuit Television and Social Control*. Aldershot: Ashgate.

Barrett, D. (2013) One surveillance camera for every 11 people in Britain, says CCTV survey. Available at http://w3.salemstate.edu/~pglasser/One_surveillance_camera_for_every_11_people_in_Britain__says_CCTV_survey_-_Telegraph.pdf [Accessed 10 June 2020].

BBC. (2018) Undercover Met Police officer sacked over relationship. Available at https://www.bbc.co.uk/news/uk-england-london-43992692 [Accessed 1 July 2020].

Broeders, A.P.A. (2007) Principles of forensic identification science. In Newburn, T., Williamson, T., and Wright, A. (eds). *Handbook of Criminal Investigation*. Cullompton: Willan.

Cahill, M. and Norris, C. (2002) On the threshold to urban panopticon? Analysing the employment of CCTV in European cities and assessing its social and political impacts. Urban Eye. RTD Project 2001–2004.

Canter, D.V., Alison, L.J., Alison, E., and Wentink, N. (2004) The organized/disorganized typology of serial murder. Myth or model? *Psychology, Public Policy, and Law*, 10: 293–320.

Clifford, B.R. and Hollin, C.R. (1981) Effects of the type of incident and the number of perpetrators on eyewitness testimony. *Journal of Applied Psychology*, 66: 364–370.

Connors, E., Lundregan, T., Miller, N. and McEwen, T. (1996) *Convicted by Juries, Exonerated by Science: Case Studies in the Use of DNA*. Washington: US Department of Justice.

Geiselman, R. E., Fisher, R. P., Firstenberg, I., Hutton, L. A., Sullivan, S., Avetissian, I., and Prosk, A. (1984) Enhancement of eyewitness memory: An empirical evaluation of the cognitive interview. *Journal of Police Science and Administration*, 12: 74–80.

HMIC (Her Majesty's Inspectorate of Constabulary). (1999) Police Integrity: securing and maintaining public confidence. Available at https://www.justiceinspectorates. gov.uk/hmicfrs/media/police-integrity-19990601.pdf [Accessed 18 May 2020].

Huff, R., Rattner, A. and Sagarin, E. (1996) *Convicted but Innocent: Wrongful Conviction and Public Policy*. Thousand Oaks (CA): Sage.

Kebbell, M.R. and Wagstaff, G.F. (1999) Face value? Evaluating the accuracy of eyewitness information. Police Research Series: Paper 102. Available at www.hom eoffice.gov.uk/rds/prgpdfs/fprs102.pdf [Accessed 12 June 2008].

Key Note. (2013) *Closed Circuit Television Market Report 2013*. London: Key Note [online]. Available at https://www.keynote.co.uk/ market-intelligence/view/product/ 10793/closed-circuit-television/chapter/1 [Accessed 2 February 2020].

Klein, N. (2008) Rolling Stone: China's All-Seeing Eye. *Council on Foreign Relations* [online] 29 May. Available at: http://www.cfr.org/china/rolling-stone-chinas-all-seein g-eye/p17048 [Accessed on 14 April 2020].

Lombroso-Ferrero, G. (1972) *Lombroso's Criminal Man*. New Jersey: Montclair.

Maguire, M. and John, T. (1996) Covert and deceptive policing in England and Wales: issues in regulation and practice. *European Journal of Crime, Criminal Law and Criminal Justice*, 4 (4): 316–334.

Market and Business Development. (2011) *UK CCTV Market Development Report* [press release] January. Available at: http://www.mbdltd.co.uk/Press-Release/CCTV. htm [Accessed 23 April 2020].

Moran, J. (1998) A brief chronology of photographic and video surveillance. In Norris, C., Moran, J. and Armstrong, G. (eds). *Surveillance, Closed Circuit Television and Social Control*. Aldershot: Ashgate.

Phillips, H. (2006) Introduction: The Human Brain. Available at https://www.news cientist.com/article/dn9969-introduction-the-human-brain/ [Accessed 18 May 2020].

Porter, S., Yuille, J. C., and Lehman, D. (1999) The nature of real, implanted, and fabricated memories for emotional childhood events: Implications for the recovered memory debate. *Law and Human Behaviour*, 23: 517–538.

Reeve, T. (2011) How many cameras in the UK? Only 1.85million says ACPO Lead on CCTV. *CCTV Image Magazine*, 28. Security Media Publishing.

The Independent. (2008) Shooting of innocent person could happen again. In *The Independent*, 7 October. Available at https://www.independent.co.uk/news/uk/crime/shoo ting-of-innocent-person-could-happen-again-954051.html [Accessed 18 May 2020].

Webb, B. and Laycock, G. (1992) Reducing crime on the London Underground: an evaluation of three pilot projects. Crime Prevention Unit Paper No 32. London: Home Office.

Williams, H.J. and Blum, I. (2018) Defining second generation open source intelligence (OSINT) for the defence enterprise. Available at https://www.rand.org/content/dam/rand/pubs/research_reports/RR1900/RR1964/RAND_RR1964.pdf [Accessed 19 May 2020].

Woodworth, M. and Porter, S. (1999) Historical foundations and current applications of criminal profiling in violent crime investigations. *Expert Advice*, 7: 241–264.

Chapter 3

Improving the intelligence process
A managerial perspective

Introduction

The previous chapter outlined the multiple sources from which intelligence can emerge. However, whilst intelligence can be a valuable commodity, this is only true when the product is gathered lawfully and in a form that can deliver on law enforcement objectives. Intelligence sources can often be associated with inherent dangers, and these dangers can be amplified if the intelligence process is not competently managed. Poor management of the intelligence process can generate scandals that have an impact much further than the locality in which they occur. Criminal Justice agencies are expected to be fair, proportionate, non-discriminatory, and transparent. If these standards aren't adhered to then trust and legitimacy in the system can suffer. This reduces the likelihood of community cooperation and increases the potential for criminal behaviour and vigilantism. An effective administration of the law is therefore essential for all genuine democracies (Council of Europe, 2000), which is why effective management of intelligence systems is so important.

To safeguard the system a variety of managerial posts exist in the intelligence community. Managers have wide ranging responsibilities that include operational and organisational performance, staff development and health and safety duties. Specific details have been developed by the College of Policing who have published a role profile for the Director of Intelligence (College of Policing, 2020a) and Intelligence Manager (College of Policing, 2020b). The purpose of this chapter is to understand the development and analysis of intelligence through a managerial perspective. It will provide a strategic understanding of the intelligence process as well as an overview of the constraints that must be adhered to if it is to remain a legitimate approach for law enforcement agencies. Specifically, the chapter will be divided into four sections:

- Section 1: Will provide an overview of different police operating models and the role intelligence has to play within them.
- Section 2: Will emphasise the critical process of maintaining standards in terms of directing, authorising, and managing intelligence.

- Section 3: Will focus on intelligence failures. It will highlight individual and organisational challenges that exist in relation to the collection, management, dissemination and actioning of intelligence.
- Section 4: Will examine the issues surrounding the well-being and professional development of staff.

Section 1: An overview of policing models

Introduction

The police have the largest budget of any Criminal Justice agency and since the late 20th century numerous recommendations have been made to explain how police services can use this finance in the most effective and efficient way. Each of these approaches interpret and emphasise the value of intelligence differently. Understanding the nuances between these approaches is important for the leader/manager/analyst, as different models require different actions within the intelligence process. The list that follows highlights some of the most prominent approaches.

The professional policing model

The professional policing model is commonly referred to as the 'traditional' or 'crime fighting' model. The police simply wait for calls from the public and deal with them on a case-by-case basis. The agency record the call, dispatch an officer to the scene, deal with the case and then move on to the next call. Whilst the use of intelligence has little or no role to play, the model is included for two reasons. First, it is the oldest model and remains in place across many police forces across the world – primarily due to its ease of implementation. Second, the reactive model has been heavily criticised since the 1970s when the benefits of proactive policing became apparent. One of the earliest was the Kansas City Preventative Patrol experiment during 1972, led by George Kelling, who argued that uncommitted time should be aligned with more targeted action (Kelling et al., 1974). This has been followed by numerous studies that show intelligence led proactive approaches are more effective and efficient.

Community policing and the evolution into reassurance policing

One of the earliest and widespread adaptations of the professional policing model was community policing. Its application can be seen across North America, Europe and Asia (i.e. Japan). Indeed, by 2000 over 90% of US police agencies reported engaging in community policing (Chappel, 2007). As the approach appears in different forms there is no agreed definition, although some specific principles do appear consistent, such as the enhancement of public trust (Tilley, 2003:315) and a focus on quality of life issues (i.e. anti-social behaviour). Intelligence products associated with this model often include community surveys, which can provide local information regarding community concerns (Skogan & Hartnett, 1997).

During 2000 an important variation of community policing emerged with the UK National Restoring Reassurance project. This followed national opinion polls which showed public concern about the rise in crime, even though it had been falling since the mid 1990s (Duffy et al., 2007). This view, replicated in other countries (Roberts & Indermaur, 2009), was linked to residents being constantly confronted by unrecorded symptoms of criminality (i.e. burnt out vehicles, vandalised street furniture, and graffiti). These 'signal crimes' disproportionately affected citizen perception of safety and changed behaviour. Further, it was discovered that other underlying 'triggers for fear' such as fly-tipping or broken glass increased these concerns whilst 'comfort factors', such as visible authority figures (i.e. police officers), or the engagement of citizen groups (i.e. Neighbourhood Watch) could reassure them (Innes & Fielding, 2002). The pilot project, implemented in eight British police forces, high-lighted the importance of community intelligence on these issues (gathered through community meetings, community leaders, and community surveys) and the use of partnerships to tackle them. The initiative not only raised public confidence but also reduced crime across the trial areas (Tuffin et al., 2006), leading to the introduction of the UK Neighbourhood Policing approach. Intelligence products included: community audits and questionnaires; visual audits of the area encompassing signal crime, triggers for fear and comfort factors; and network analysis of local communication groups and active citizenship.

Problem oriented policing

Another enduring international approach is problem oriented policing (POP), often simply referred to as problem solving. Based on the ground-breaking work of Professor Herman Goldstein (1990; 1979), who sadly passed away during the writing of this book, it argues agencies place more emphasis on the 'means' of police work (processes, structures and equipment), than the 'ends' (solving community problems). He said to provide better outcomes and deliver sustainable solutions, the police should focus on reoccurring problems of community concern, and work with partners to tackle their underlying causes, rather than responding solely to the symptoms (Scott & Kirby, 2012:4). This philosophy became synonymous with a four-stage model, known by the mnemonic SARA (Eck & Spelman, 1987). The first stage (*Scanning*) focuses on prioritising and defining the recurring problem; *Analysis*, establishes what opportunities and characteristics cause that problem to occur at a particular location and time, involving specific offenders and victims; *Response* concentrates on the implementation of a tailored intervention to prevent the incident occurring; and *Assessment* looks at evaluating the impact of the intervention. Supported by a number of criminological concepts, such as Routine Activity, Rational Choice Theory (explained in Chapter 4), SARA relies heavily on a variety of intelligence products to support the identification, analysis and assessment phases.

Intelligence-led policing and the National Intelligence Model

This is the approach that values intelligence most explicitly and has already been referred to in the introductory chapter. It emerged in the UK, prompted by concern over the (cost) effectiveness of the police. The approach was interpreted in different ways, which prompted a significant national invest-ment to create a consistent process, based on good practice. This became known as the National Intelligence Model (NIM), which was described by the newly formed National Criminal Intelligence Service (2000:11) as one that, 'involves identifying and limiting the activities of volume criminals and dangerous offenders, controlling disorder and tackling the many problems that adversely affect community safety and quality of life. The specific out-comes required are improved community safety, reduced crime rates and the control of criminality and disorder'.

The guidance document and nine volumes of supporting documents was extensive, totalling 816 pages of A4 paper (Kirby, 2013). Within that guidance it generated three critical innovations. The first conceptualised policing into three geographic levels, to allow for the seamless transfer of information and avoid duplication. Level 1 related to local policing (police divisions or com-mand units); level 2 referred to cross border issues – either between local poli-cing units or across police forces; level 3 related to relevant intelligence at a national or international level. The second major change was that the NIM provided a process in which intelligence would drive policing activity, with formal strategic and tactical assessments identifying relevant priorities. These were acted on by strategic and tactical 'Tasking and Coordinating Groups', to devise strategy and tactics to target offenders, locations, or types of crime/inci-dent at various levels. The analytical products precipitate a decision to pursue one (or more) of three options: a requirement to gather further intelligence; an enforcement-based intervention (i.e. arrest, search warrant); and/or a more preventative response (such as the use of disruption or situational crime pre-vention techniques). Underpinning this process were nine standardised intelli-gence techniques: crime pattern analysis; network analysis; criminal business profile; market profiles; subject profile analysis; risk analysis; demographic/ social trends analysis; operational assessment; and results analysis. These nine techniques were key elements of four standard intelligence products: strategic assessment, tactical assessment, problem profile and target profile (now referred to as subject profile). For the first time there were consistent national templates and guidance for how intelligence reports should be presented (ACPO, 2007).

The model was described as 'the pre-eminent intelligence model internationally' (Jones & Newburn, 2007), and elements of it became implemented across the world. However, as with many policing approaches there were implementation challenges. Cope (2004) found police officers had insufficient knowledge of both crime analysis and the intelligence process to make best use of the model. Further, there were concerns over its level of bureaucracy and mechanistic nature, which required specialist personnel and actions. In practice the NIM also over-emphasised arrest and enforcement, which as Ratcliffe (2008) shows has a limited impact in reducing crime. His example, using a representative sample of 1,000 crimes, shows only about 410 (41%) of crimes are generally reported to the police. Of these 287 (28.7%) would be recorded as a crime and 75 (7.5%) would be detected. Finally, of these detected cases only 37 (3.7%) would lead to an offender being prosecuted, and of these 21 (2.1%) would progress to a court hearing. From this, only 15 (1.5%) of cases would result in a finding of guilt, and only 4 (0.4%) would receive a custodial sentence. Ratcliffe goes on to say that even if an extra 10% of cases were prosecuted it would only raise the imprisonment rate by 0.4%, whilst requiring considerably more resources.

Compstat

Seen more commonly within the USA, Compstat (an abbreviation of computerised statistics) emerged from the 'zero-tolerance' approach, which itself was built on broken windows theory. It emphasised the importance of targeting low level offences to prevent more serious offences being committed. It therefore had intelligence processes at its core, with the approach based upon: timely and accurate computerised crime data, crime analysis and crime mapping (often displayed on large screens in police Compstat meetings); selection of appropriate tactics; the rapid deployment of police resources to the locations where crime patterns exist; and devolved decision making with associated accountability (Willis & Mastrofski, 2012). Whilst a populist approach it was criticised for its performance review procedures which made precinct commanders publicly accountable for crime levels and resulted in many being replaced (Henry, 2003:1). Willis and Mastrofski (2012:82) stressed Compstat relied upon short term enforcement-based responses, which lacked longer term sustainability. They pointed out, 'The strategies used most often were location-directed patrols, crackdowns and traffic enforcement, involving police using their traditional law enforcement powers'. They continued by saying, 'Given these findings we conclude that CompStat had reinforced, not mitigated, traditional police approaches'.

In summary, this section has illustrated that whilst the professional policing model remains widely used, reactive approaches are increasingly condemned in favour of proactive policing approaches. Proactive methods are built on an intelligence foundation, which allows the targeting of people, places and events. However, as has been illustrated, choosing a specific policing approach can require different intelligence requirements and analysis techniques.

Section 2: Directing, authorising and managing information and intelligence

Introduction

An intelligence process has a number of stages (depicted by the intelligence cycle and National Intelligence Model), overseen by an intelligence manager. Unfortunately, problems can occur throughout the process. At the outset, a misguided intelligence requirement may be set, or an inappropriate intelligence source is engaged with, resulting in irrelevant or inaccurate information. Similarly, the information may be obtained unlawfully, causing the court case to crack. Also, a poor decision may be made as to how the intelligence is used, leading to unintended consequences. In such a dynamic and complex environment, the intelligence manager plays a critical role in maintaining standards to deliver an effective, efficient and lawful intelligence process. This section will cover a number of these stages, starting first with the intelligence requirement.

Keeping your eye on the squirrel

Whilst the intelligence cycle establishes the essential things to consider when collecting, managing and disseminating intelligence it does not specify what the intelligence gathering should focus on. The intelligence requirement is normally aligned with the crime and disorder priorities of the police area. Unfortunately, in the intelligence environment, it is all too easy to depart from this initial requirement as more information is obtained. Setting appropriate outcomes and achieving the correct intelligence to deliver them is constantly affected by distractions. These temptations were noted in the Criminal Justice system as far back as the last century when Donovan (1916) educated prospective lawyers. The story has since been adapted to support police training and is revised again here to relate to the intelligence environment.

An intelligence manager advertises for a new analyst. Shortlisting five high quality applicants she takes the unusual step of speaking with them together.

MANAGER: 'I want to tell you a story about a certain farmer who was troubled with a red squirrel that got in through a hole in his barn and stole his seed corn. He resolved to kill the squirrel at the first opportunity. Seeing him go in the hole, he took his shotgun and fired; the first shot set the barn on fire.'

APPLICANT 1: 'Did the barn burn?'

MANAGER: 'And seeing the barn on fire, the farmer seized a pail of water, and ran in to put it out.'

APPLICANT 2: 'Did he put it out?'

MANAGER: 'As he passed inside, the door slammed shut and the barn was soon in full flame. Another farm worker ran into the barn with more water.'

APPLICANT 3: 'Did they all burn up?'.

MANAGER: 'An old lady came out and all was noise and confusion with everybody trying to put out the fire'.

APPLICANT 4: 'Did anyone burn up?'.

MANAGER: 'There, there, that will do. You have all shown great interest in the story.' She then looks at the remaining applicant and says, 'Now, what have you got to say?'

APPLICANT 5: (appearing uneasy), 'What became of that squirrel – that's what I want to know?'

MANAGER: 'You're the one, you've got the analyst job. You have not been switched off by the confusion and the burning barn, the hired hands and water pails; you have kept your eye on the squirrel.'

In essence it is the role of the intelligence manager to be specific about the intelligence requirement and keep staff focused on its delivery. This often takes place in an ambiguous and fast-moving arena with information on crimes and offenders constantly changing. As Donald Rumsfeld once famously said, 'Reports that say that something hasn't happened are always interesting to me, because as we know, there are known knowns; there are things we know we know. We also know there are known unknowns; that is to say we know there are some things we do not know. But there are also unknown unknowns – the ones we don't know we don't know.' As Rumsfeld highlighted both information and absence of information have significance, and this requires the intelligence manager to engage in critical and systematic thinking. It is only with this clarity and adherence to this purpose that effective intelligence gathering can be achieved.

Collecting intelligence: a legal and moral framework

It is important that standards are adhered to when directing and administering the intelligence process. The manager (as well as the analyst) need to be aware of the legal, ethical and procedural parameters that allow relevant information to be obtained and processed, and in this procedure the protection of human rights is paramount. History shows the intelligence system is associated with many breaches of human rights. To prevent such abuses an organisation needs to self-govern its activity, which should have at its core a strong ethical foundation. Ethics has been defined as 'the set of beliefs, values and standards by which people regulate their conduct' (Wright, 2007:586). Maintaining such standards can be demanding as intelligence collection can be complex, ambiguous, and generate disagreement. However, it is important the focus is on *doing the right thing*, rather than just doing the *thing right* (the technical act within the intelligence process), if an organisation's moral compass and reputation is to be maintained.

All intelligence communities provide advice and guidance on ways to collect intelligence, especially when it is captured through intrusive and covert methods. Following high-profile mistakes and scandals, nations (including the UK), have established a sizeable legal framework to dictate how law enforcement agencies should conduct themselves. For example, the UK Police and Criminal Evidence Act 1984 (known as PACE), clarified police powers in relation to the rights of a suspect and further legislation has followed. The Criminal Procedure and Investigation Act (CPIA) 1996, introduced a statutory responsibility for the disclosure of material information. This requires the prosecution to supply the defence with any information they feel can help prove the innocence of the defendant and is particularly pertinent to the intelligence community.

Perhaps the greatest driver of change in the UK has been the European Convention of Human Rights, which stimulated a variety of legislation. The most significant was the Regulation of Investigatory Powers Act 2000 (RIPA), later superseded by the Investigatory Powers Act 2016. This meant for the first time the covert world of intelligence became transparent in terms of standards and authorisation. It made apparent: in what circumstances surveillance could be used; which authorities could use surveillance powers; who could authorise the use of these powers; what use could be made of the material gained; the provision of independent judicial oversight; and a means of redress for any individual potentially harmed by the process. It also divided surveillance into five categories.

- Interception of communications (i.e. intercepting phone conversations or accessing emails).
- Intrusive surveillance which involves covert surveillance within residential premises or private vehicles. This covers visual or audible recordings within the location.
- Directed surveillance, which relates to covert surveillance generally involving the following of specific people, or recording their behaviour, in a public place.
- Covert Human Intelligence Sources (CHIS). This is highlighted in a previous section and describes a person, who under direction from a public authority, establishes or maintains a personal or other relationship in order to (covertly) use the relationship to obtain information or disclose information gained from the relationship. As well as informants it also includes undercover operatives.

- Communications data, which focuses on the record of the communication, rather than the details of the actual communication. For example, this may describe the location of the phone when the communication was made, the type of communication (i.e. email, text), as well as the time and date and how long it occurred. It can also provide information relating to the subscriber of the communications service.

Each aspect of surveillance can only be implemented if relevant authorisation from a specified person is provided. In this way the interception of a communication and intrusive surveillance requires a warrant from the UK Home Secretary or Cabinet Secretary for Justice. Other authorisations, for less intrusive surveillance, are authorised by specified senior officers within the organisation making the application. All authorisations are subject to an oversight process.

Processing and grading information

For an intelligence system to maintain its integrity it is important that information is retained appropriately, which means a sufficient reason exists for it to be held on the system. A recent example in the UK and USA relates to gang databases. It questioned whether it was sufficient to place individuals on an intelligence system just because they were seen in the company of known gang members who resided in the same residential area. Another problem occurs when old information is retained on an intelligence system as out of date intelligence can generate unintended consequences. This ranges from unfair stop and search experiences, to an early morning search warrant conducted on an innocent family who have moved into an address recently vacated by an offender.

Different countries maintain various systems to maintain the accuracy of their intelligence. In the UK (and across the developed world) a data rich world has precipitated an increase in protective legislation. In 2016 (although implemented in May 2018), Europe designed the General Data Protection Regulation (GDPR), relating to data protection and privacy. This generated the UK Data Protection Act 2018 which focused on accuracy, data retention, data security, and accountability. Because law enforcement agencies present distinctive challenges in relation to information, six principles concerning personal data exist outside the general GDPR regime (albeit broadly similar to GDPR). These explain:

1   The processing of personal data must be lawful and fair.
2   The law enforcement purpose for which personal data is collected on any occasion must be specified, explicit and legitimate, and; personal data collected must not be processed in a manner that is incompatible with the purpose for which it was originally collected.

3   Personal data processed for any of the law enforcement purposes must be adequate, relevant and not excessive in relation to the purpose for which it is processed.
4   Personal data processed for any of the law enforcement purposes must be accurate and, where necessary, kept up to date, and every reasonable step must be taken to ensure that personal data that is inaccurate, having regard to the law enforcement purpose for which it is processed, is erased or rectified without delay.
5   Personal data processed for any of the law enforcement purposes must be kept for no longer than is necessary for the purpose for which it is processed. Appropriate time limits must be established for the periodic review of the need for the continued storage of personal data for any of the law enforcement purposes.
6   Personal data processed for any of the law enforcement purposes must be processed in a manner that ensures appropriate security of the personal data, using appropriate technical or organisational measures. Appropriate security includes protection against unauthorised or unlawful processing and against accidental loss, destruction or damage.

Items of intelligence are also subjected to a government security classification model (GSC) which is used to mark the sensitivity of police information. This replaces the Government Protective Marking Scheme (GPMS) although existing GPMS grades do not have to be transferred to GSC. There are four principles that govern GSC (College of Policing, 2019):

1   There is no need to routinely mark documents or emails as OFFICIAL, as this is the default principle.
2   Where it is considered that the content needs marking, it will be marked OFFICIAL. The originator must state why it is marked as OFFICIAL, and they should consider whether further handling conditions are required.
3   Where the information is provided on a 'need to know' basis and further security control measures are required to protect the information, it must be clearly marked as OFFICIAL-SENSITIVE. Originators must state why it is marked as OFFICIAL-SENSITIVE. This must include handling conditions and network control measures.
4   SECRET/TOP SECRET are markings for sensitive/very sensitive information that justifies heightened protective measures for safeguarding purposes.

More detailed approaches are used to grade source material systems. These can be found around the world and whilst their format may differ, their general principles hold fast. These grade categories can also change over time, indeed the UK National Intelligence Model, which introduced a 5x5x5 intelligence categorisation system, has since been superseded by the 3x5x2 grading process. These codes evaluate the source it was provided from, the information given, as well as a handling code to describe dissemination. The first stage evaluates the strength of the intelligence source using three criteria: *Reliable*, where the source is believed competent and the information is generally believed to be reliable (often supported by a history of other reliable information); *Untested*, used when the source hasn't provided information before, or is anonymous (i.e. Crimestoppers) and *Not Reliable*, where reasonable concerns exist about its accuracy (and are stated). The second stage evaluates the information/intelligence itself, using five grades. These are: *Known directly to the source* (code A), who has witnessed it directly (rather than hearing about it from someone else); *Known indirectly to the source but corroborated* (B), which involves corroboration (from technical or human sources) and independent of the original information; *Known indirectly to the source* (C), and not witnessed by them. This can be supplemented by a separate risk assessment which examines how widely the intelligence should be disseminated. It is particularly relevant if the intelligence is to be disseminated out of the country and needs to be based on the grounds of substantial public interest; *Not Known* (D) when there is no means to assess the information; *Suspected to be false* (E), when the information is thought to be incorrect (again a rationale should be provided). The third and final stage provides two codes to distinguish how the information/intelligence can be shared; an important balance being the risk of sharing against the potentially greater risk of not sharing. The first code states that lawful sharing is *permitted* (code P), and for this to occur it must be associated with a policing purpose, local protocols are in place, and there is a legitimate need to receive it. Prior to designating code P, the intelligence officer should consider their legal obligations as well as the person who requests the information and what they will use it for. If shared with an agency outside the police, a lawful purpose should include:

- assist others to protect life or property
- assist to preserve order
- prevent the commission of offences
- assist others to bring offenders to justice
- linked to any duty or responsibility arising from common or statute law

The second code allows lawful sharing with conditions. Code C may therefore allow dissemination with specific conditions upon which the receiving agency is asked to observe. It may not be appropriate to disseminate all of the intelligence and the merits of redaction should be considered

As a final point it is important for intelligence managers and staff to protect intelligence sources, which means they should never unwittingly compromise their identity. For example, a single submission can provide many elements of intelligence, which can potentially expose the informant's identity. If this is the case it may need to be separated or sanitised by the manager, as the following example illustrates:

'Yesterday I met Neil Smith at 12.00hrs at the Merchants Inn. He said the day before he was round at Ian Dawson's place and he overheard him on the phone. Ian said there wouldn't be a problem. He'd got enough cash and he would take as much weed (cannabis) and coke (cocaine) as he could supply, but he didn't want any smack (heroin). Smith said the number Dawson called was 01234 56789, it was on a piece of paper on the kitchen table.'

This example clearly identifies the person speaking to the police officer was Neil Smith. If the information provided was only known by Smith this would also expose him as the informant even if he wasn't mentioned by name. The way to prevent this compromise is by submitting two intelligence reports, which omit the informants name and set out:

a   Ian Dawson is arranging to buy large quantities of cannabis and cocaine.
b   Ian Dawson has an acquaintance who is involved with the supply of cannabis, heroin and cocaine. This drug supplier uses the telephone number 0987 654321

A second example is as follows:

'Approximately 10.00hrs on Saturday 5th January 2020, the subject, Mick Turner was seen from an observation post at number 2, Central Street, Newtown, to return home driving a red BMW 3 series saloon AB58XYZ.'

This submission indicates that Richard Smith is being targeted through a covert operation, and even provides the location of the observation post. It is therefore better practice to write the intelligence report in the format set out below. Also, the inclusion of times on an intelligence report should also be considered as these can sometimes indicate the person is under covert surveillance,

'Mick Turner was driving a red BMW 3 series saloon AB58XYZ in Central Street, Newtown, at 10.00am on 5th January 2020.'

Section 3: Intelligence failure

Introduction

Although there have been many successful outcomes from intelligence analysis the irony is that much more is written about intelligence failure (James, 2016). Whilst the concept of 'intelligence failure' is widely used, there is no consensus on what the term actually means. Holman (2015) suggests the term is used incorrectly as many events which result in damaging outcomes should not be blamed on an intelligence failure. Upon reviewing the jihadist Paris attacks of 2015, he argues it can be viewed as a failure of state agencies to protect its citizens, but questions whether this failing should be aimed exclusively at the intelligence process. Often in cases of this nature whilst the strategic threat is identified, specific details concerning the when, where and who the attack involves are more difficult to establish. This is due to the variety of potential protagonists, from a variety of countries, who have the capability to conduct planned or spontaneous attacks. Collecting this detailed information from multi-agencies across different countries is extremely challenging. Whilst atrocities always generate a concern that sufficient scrutiny wasn't placed on specific individuals, these assumptions are based on the belief the information was obvious and detailed; was collected within legal/procedural parameters; and there were sufficient available resources to act upon it. In essence criticisms often suffer from hindsight bias. To summarise, the collection and analysis of information can be incredibly complex, therefore the label of intelligence failure can be somewhat simplistic and should not be the default categorisation when problems occur.

A further complexity is that although the intelligence may be of high quality, deciding what to do with it can be fraught with operational and ethical complexity, again leading to unintended consequences. One example occurred at Tottenham, London, on the 4th August 2011, when Mark Duggan (a 29-year-old British man), was in a taxicab and followed by a police surveillance team comprising firearms officers. The intelligence revealed that 15 minutes earlier he had received possession of a BBM Bruni Model 92 handgun (a replica which had been converted to fire live rounds). The decision was made to intercept the taxi in a public area and confront Mr Duggan. In the ensuing moments Duggan was shot dead by the police and a police officer was also injured (a police bullet passed through Duggan and hit the officer). The confusing and volatile situation that followed generated questions as to whether Duggan was a threat at the time of the incident and whether he was in possession of the firearm. In the aftermath a public protest escalated into riots across London and into other cities. A public inquest began on the 16 September 2013, and on the 8 January 2014 a jury with an 8–2 majority concluded Duggan's death was lawful (BBC Online, 2014).

Other commentators focus their research on how failure manifests itself. Johnston (2008:6) distinguishes intelligence errors from intelligence failure. He explains that errors are factual inaccuracies resulting from poor or missing data, whilst a failure, 'is a systemic organizational surprise resulting from incorrect, missing, discarded or inadequate hypotheses'. In essence he argues that all cited examples of intelligence failure, ranging from Pearl harbour to 9–11, have been epitomised by a central recurring theme of *surprise*. Whilst in some cases, the intelligence community are surprised by the event, it can also happen that they expect the event, but are unable to communicate or persuade those in authority to take it sufficiently seriously. A further distinction is made by James (2016) and Betts (1978) who distinguish between strategic and tactical intelligence failures. The former relates to those longer term aims, in which failures are more difficult to identify. These are more commonly associated with political or psychological factors than organisational ones. Betts (1978) argues mistakes are possible in any analytical process, due to important data being ignored or misinterpreted, or errors of judgement. It is therefore useful to distinguish mistakes into individual and organisational categories.

Individual failure

To introduce this point, consider the following two questions. First, divide 17 by 12 and multiply it by 19. Secondly, state whether you think Brexit is a good idea. Which question were you able to answer quicker? The first is a simple question which has only one unambiguous answer. However, depending on your love for numbers you might have given up, as answering the question demands a degree of cognitive effort to process the calculation. The second question is infinitely more complex, however many of us would answer it immediately. Kahneman (2011) refers to this as the difference between *slow* and *fast* time thinking. Both types of thinking are important. At times we need to make snap judgments, such as when our safety is under threat. However, when considering more complex and strategic questions, when no immediacy exists, an individual should use slow time thinking and systematically work through the necessary elements to establish a balanced and accurate answer. Unfortunately, there are many factors which prevent this systematic and objective process. This results in many of us engaging in quick time thinking, even when slow time thinking is more appropriate.

Kahneman, together with his late colleague Tversky, provided detailed understanding as to how decision making is influenced by cognitive short cuts, involving heuristics and bias (Kahneman, 2011; Kahneman and Tversky, 1973). Heuristics are often used to make decisions on ambiguous or missing information, especially when accompanied by time pressure. Common heuristics include *base rates fallacy* whereby too little weight is placed on the base, or original rate, of possibility (e.g., the probability of B occurring, given A exists). It involves the tendency for people to erroneously judge the likelihood of a situation without taking into account all the relevant data, often focusing on new information without acknowledging how this may impact on the original assumptions. A second example is the representativeness heuristic, which may influence an analyst to judge a particular characteristic or occurrence is similar to another. This permits a quick judgment, allowing the issue to be dealt with using past experience. For example, an analyst may say Jones is likely to be an organised crime offender because he/she has similar characteristics to other organised crime offenders. One final example is the availability heuristic which makes humans more likely to assess events based upon the ease they can retrieve something from their memory. This is because individuals think memories are more clearly recalled if the experience is occurring more regularly and is therefore more probable (and vice-versa). Unfortunately, this is not always the case, as studies show humans are more likely to remember anything that is recent, familiar, or distinctive. Many of these factors can come together. For example, if an analyst recently provided support on a murder, then they will be prone to use this experience to make judgements on the new case, which may be based on limited evidence (Alison & Crego, 2008).

Biases can be understood as a by-product of heuristics, they materialise from individual cognitive limitations, and can also be associated with poor decision making (Keren & Tiegen, 2004). *Belief persistence*, for example, makes a belief or opinion (such as a first-time impression) difficult to over-turn. A further phenomenon, *confirmation bias,* is also related to this as it explains how individuals search for the evidence to support their view, whilst undervaluing or ignoring evidence that refutes it. This is supported by a tendency to engage in selective information searches and the biased analysis of information. Finally, *hindsight bias* (mentioned earlier) is when individuals consider the event was predictable, but only after the incident was over. This is more likely to occur when few alternatives exist relating to the incident (i.e. police shoot suspect/don't shoot suspect) and is commonly illustrated when blame is apportioned after an event (i.e. a designated intelligence failure). All these biases are relevant to hypothesis testing, which is mentioned throughout this book.

Finally, whilst these cognitive limitations can lead to poor decision making, they should not be mistaken for incompetence. In Chapter 7, on criminal investigation, there are examples of intelligence failure through poor work rather than flawed decision making. This can occur when information isn't reported properly or house to house enquiries aren't completed correctly. An example was the Damilola Taylor case where forensic scientists systematically missed crucial evidence. As was stated, 'whereas missing one area of blood might be explicable, missing at least four areas of blood was not consistent with a careful and diligent inspection' (Rawley & Caddy, 2007:1).

Organisational failure

As well as individual failures there are many documented organisational failures. Salvatore (2018) points out a government's response to an intelligence failure is often to increase resources within intelligence hubs. The introduction of these new and inexperienced staff creates further challenge when the economy dictates human resources need to be cut, or that more has to be done with the resources available. A common response to intelligence failure has been the introduction of supra-national or intra-national hubs, which bolt on collaborative operational and information-sharing facilities. Examples of this include Europol (based in the Netherlands) and 'fusion centers' in the USA. These were strategically situated in geographic locations to collate and disseminate intelligence from disparate police agencies, due to the inability of separate law enforcement agencies to share relevant information. Whilst it was thought new intelligence tiers would improve the intelligence flow, Salvatore (2018) argues many more commentators criticise rather than endorse fusion centres at national, regional, and state level. Wardlaw (2015) says this criticism of fusion centres is for three reasons: a) the absence of a standardised model, b) mission creep, and c) underdeveloped or missing external agency partnerships.

The reason why additional tiers haven't always delivered on expectations can be diverse and mirror the myriad of problems associated with sharing information across borders and by single agencies. Sheptycki (2004) conducted research across Dutch, Swedish and Canadian police departments and identified numerous institutional problems when collecting and sharing information, which he called 'organisational pathologies'. These included: linkage blindness; too much noise in the system; duplication; institutional friction; intelligence hoarding; information silos; as well as occupational subcultures. Other commentators highlight bureaucratic organisational dynamics which rely on hierarchies, rules and procedures which can impact upon their speed and flexibility (Mastrofski, 1998; Willis et al., 2004). These factors create further difficulties with information sharing, not only because of the different languages, but also in managing data sharing agreements across international boundaries and jurisdictions, all of which have specific Criminal Justice requirements. In some cases, foreign jurisdictions are hesitant to release intelligence as they want to protect their sources or prefer to develop the information themselves.

A number of commentators also highlight the organisational culture of the intelligence community. Davies (2010), claims that British intelligence culture tends to be more integrative in nature while the US culture tends to be disintegrative. As Duyvesteyn (2011:527) observes: 'These distinctive cultures are prone to specific weak points; integrative cultures are highly sensitive to groupthink and disintegrative cultures to turf wars.' However there seems to be limited evidence for an integrative culture in any intelligence community. Davies (2002:62) notes wryly that in the mid-1990s, official committees from both the US and the UK examined each other's methods but in their final reports, '[n]either side found anything to incorporate from the other's methods, and yet neither seemed to detect that they were talking—and hence thinking—about entirely different things when they were talking about intelligence'. More importantly, commentators argue the same observation could be made even *within* national intelligence communities (Salvatore, 2018). James et al. (2017) argues a philosophy of risk aversion and information protection, often facilitated through a lack of accountability and reward, can generate an isolationist rather than an inclusive approach. This organisational culture can make the task of harmonising effective change within intelligence communities much more difficult.

This concept of *implementation failure* is an increasingly common theme in the wider law enforcement literature (Kirby, 2013). Ekblom (2012:17) supports this finding by saying, 'It seems no kind of crime prevention programme or project, and no institutional setting, is immune from implementation failure'. Most commentators suggest there are three key elements to the achievement of community safety initiatives (Wandersman, 2009; Rosenbaum, 1986). These are: a) the approach is fundamentally sound as it is based on a theoretical foundation, b) the delivery of the intervention is effective (it involves the competent planning and deployment of resources and personnel); and c) there is an evaluation to establish it was implemented correctly as well as the impact from it. Wandersman (2009), argues that there are four keys to success when delivering interventions: theory; implementation; evaluation; and resources. Hope and Murphy (1983) listed the common factors that go wrong such as: unanticipated technical difficulties; inadequate supervision of implementation; failure to co-ordinate different agencies; competing priorities; and unanticipated costs. Ekblom (2012:13) similarly highlights 'pragmatic constraints', which include resources, insufficient information, poor leadership and management. Further, system failure is often associated with limited funds; inadequate facilities; and insufficient or inadequate (i.e. poorly trained) human resources, to implement the programme with sufficient quality (Wandersman et al., 2005).

All these discussions provide further understanding on why initiatives can go wrong, which supports the view that a more extensive understanding of 'failure' would benefit law enforcement agencies. Perusing dictionary definitions of the term 'failure' discovers phrases such as 'not succeeding' or 'not doing something that you must do or are expected to do' or 'when something stops working' or 'does not work as well as expected'. Interpreting failure, using this wider description, allows a less blame driven approach, enabling resources to be more effectively transformed into positive outcomes. One method to do this is to use a logic model, which simply and graphically maps out the way in which change will occur (Public Health England, 2018). This initially details how the inputs (intelligence investment in people and resources) are transferred into outputs (measurable indicators associated with the collection, development, and dissemination of intelligence). It then explains how these outputs will be used to deliver the desired outcomes/impact (i.e. the number of terrorist attacks reduced or prevented or organised crime groups disrupted). This type of critical thinking process would examine how the intelligence is gathered and used, enabling the true cost and quality of the intelligence to be understood, thereby determining its value for money. For example, judgements could be made on the value of arresting and prosecuting an individual e.g. would it disrupt a wider criminal enterprise, or make no difference? This debate is important as intelligence development pathways are diverse. For example, open source information is inexpensive, unobtrusive and easy to access (by its definition it is open to all members of the public). In contrast intrusive surveillance often requires far greater investment in terms of its authorisation, the sophistication of the equipment used, and the need for larger teams to safeguard the operation and document intelligence. Obviously, it would be foolish to concentrate on a difficult and expensive line of intelligence development if a simpler and inexpensive method could be developed. Any such calculation on cost benefit analysis should include overt cost as well as unintended consequences, such as the impact on public trust.

In summary the term 'intelligence failure' is emotive, which assumes negative connotations and focusses a spotlight on catastrophic events, where the lack of intelligence failed to pre-warn the authorities and prevent the crime. This often generates practitioner defensiveness, rather than generating a more positive and transparent institution that learns from mistakes and fixes them quickly (Syed, 2015). Only by understanding failure can intelligence analysis be improved. A wider definition of failure, underpinned by a recognition that things can go wrong, would facilitate evaluation into the reasons for these malfunctions, thereby providing a process for continuous organisational improvement.

Section 4: The well-being and professional development of staff

Introduction

An important element of management is the care and well-being of staff. Whilst the ancient Greeks were considered to be the first to appreciate good health was created through both physical and social environments, the concept of well-being is becoming more important in contemporary society (Wright, 2012). The World Health Organization argues the aim should be 'a state of well-being in which every individual realises his or her own potential, can cope with the normal stresses of life, can work productively and fruitfully, and is able to make a contribution to her or his community' (World Health Organization, 2014). A UK Government advisor, Professor Dame Carol Black (2019) defines well-being as: 'A sense of contentment which is made up of mental health, physical health and a feeling that where you are at any time is a good place to be. That good place can, and should be, the workplace'. She goes on to argue a positive workplace can increase productivity by 25%. Whilst the topic of well-being is receiving a higher profile in policing (Hesketh & Cooper, 2019; Hesketh et al., 2015), it can still be viewed as a 'taboo' subject or one that staff find difficult to discuss openly (Soomro & Yanos, 2018). The British Safety Council (2018:19) argue that, 'the leadership of health and well-being must, unequivocally, come from the highest level' and as the access to sensitive intelligence brings a number of challenges, the manager should be aware of these potential problems.

First, access to sensitive intelligence can generate a significant number of moral issues, which can take their toll on employees. Kirby (2013) highlights a scenario where two organised crime families are in conflict with each other. A covert intelligence source indicates a principal offender from one side is intending to murder his rival. The police have three choices: do nothing; pass the information to the potential victim; or warn off the potential killer. All three possibilities have potentially negative outcomes. The dilemma in terms of warning either party could reveal an intelligence source whose life would be put in danger, or it could generate pre-emptive action by the person being threatened. The dilemma of not doing anything may generate the accusation that the police stand aside whilst a premeditated murder occurs. This conundrum has been dealt with by the Osman vs United Kingdom (1998) judgement. This court case was brought by the family of Ali Osman, shot by Paul Paget-Lewis, who alleged the authorities did not sufficiently handle the serious threat that Osman was under. Whilst the police argued they were under no obligation of care they were found in breach of article 6 of the European Convention of Human Rights (Right to a fair trial). As such 'Osman warnings' are now used when there is intelligence concerning a threat but insufficient evidence to justify a prosecution (Bird, 2018). The police now inform the victim there is intelligence of a real and immediate threat to their life. Specifically, the potential victim is visited at home and warned of the potential danger, advising them to alter their movements, temporarily move out of their home and be vigilant (Bird, 2018). The use of these warnings is increasing. During 2017, the police in England and Wales issued more than 776 Osman warnings, an increase of 14 per cent on the previous year (about half of police forces had the information available).

Second, as the intelligence community deals with sensitive information the potential risk for corruption is greater. 'Police corruption is an action or omission, a promise of action or omission, or an attempted action or omission, committed by a police officer or a group of police officers, characterised by the police officer's misuse of the official position, motivated in significant part by the achievement of personal gain' (Ivkovic, 2005:16). Whilst police corruption is not confined to one particular rank or role, it has often been linked to particular types of policing. The evolution to an intelligence-based approach has provided the police with more awareness of criminal activity. However, intelligence (especially when obtained covertly), can be difficult to convert into evidence. This inability to prosecute can lead to some police officers attempting to convict more offenders through unethical means, using techniques such as entrapment, a phenomenon known as noble cause corruption (Neyroud & Beckley, 2001).

Newburn (2013:637) provides a typology to explain the dimensions of malpractice and misconduct associated with the police. These include such activities as: *opportunistic theft* (stealing from those they are in contact with); *shakedowns* (receiving money for not taking action); *protection of illegal activities; the 'fix'* (perverting the course of justice by removing evidence); *direct criminal activities* (committing crime for personal material gain); *'flaking' or 'padding'* (planting or improving the evidence against a suspect) and *'tipoffs'* relating to inappropriate information disclosure. Police forces are increasingly highlighting that some staff are 'groomed' by those who want specific access to intelligence for criminal and financial benefit. West Midlands Police (England's largest force after the Metropolitan Police Service) has cited unauthorised disclosure of sensitive information to organised crime gangs as one of its biggest threats. Crime syndicates have been seeking information on prospective police raids, rival gangs, whether they are being investigated, and victim personal details to allow intimidation. The Police Complaints watchdog received over 613 allegations of unauthorised access and disclosure involving police between July 2013 and June 2018 (Austin, 2019).

Third, the intelligence manager is often in the middle between the analyst and the operational decision makers/consumers of the intelligence. This means the intelligence manager is critical in preparing the analyst with the skills and knowledge they need for their role. Unfortunately Harfield and Harfield (2008) concluded that 'there is enough evidence in various forms to suggest that the police service has not yet fully embraced the intelligence profession'. In fact, Evans and Kebbel (2012) argue that this evolves into a *vicious* intelligence cycle. At the start of the process, intelligence staff are poorly selected, leading to unconvincing intelligence products. This means that intelligence requirements aren't met, which makes commanders lose faith in the intelligence model. This causes them to invest fewer resources when selecting staff, which means the negative spiral continues. In summary, an analyst's competence and development are critical for both the organisation and for individual well-being, a point that will be developed further in the next chapter.

Conclusion

Intelligence managers act as guardians of the system and the people within it. Therefore, they not only protect the reputation of the approach, they allow staff to feel safe and valued at work allowing them to have access to the tools and knowledge they require. Good management significantly improves the likelihood of high-quality intelligence analysis.

References

ACPO. (2007) *Practice Advice: Introduction to Intelligence-Led Policing*. London: NPIA.

Alison, L. and Crego, J. (eds). (2008) *Policing Critical Incidents: Leadership and Critical Incident Management*. Cullompton: Willan.

Austin, J. (2019) Real line of duty: Gangsters' plans to 'infiltrate' police and 'corrupt' officers revealed. https://www.express.co.uk/news/uk/1147044/crime-news-police-west-midlands-police-line-of-duty [Accessed 27 August 2019].

BBC Online(2014)Mark Duggan inquest: Why killing was deemed lawful. Available athttps://www.bbc.co.uk/news/uk-england-london-25321711 [Accessed 19 January 2021].

Betts, R.K. (1978) Analysis, war, and decision: Why intelligence failures are inevitable. *World Politics*, 31 (1): 61–89, published by: Cambridge University Press Commentary, 14 December 2015.

Bird, S. (2018) The number of people told their lives are under threat grows, new figures show. Available at https://www.telegraph.co.uk/news/2018/06/02/number-people-told-lives-threat-grows-new-figures-show/ [Accessed 23 February 2020].

Black, Dame C. (2019) Solving the well-being puzzle. Available at https://www.politicshome.com/news/uk/social-affairs/opinion/british-safety-council/101886/dame-carol-black-solving-well-being [Accessed 8 March 2020].

British Safety Council. (2018) Not just free fruit: well-being at work. Available at https://www.britsafe.org/campaigns-policy/not-just-free-fruit-well-being-at-work/ [Accessed 12th August 2019].

Chappel, A.T. (2007) Community policing: Is field training the missing link? *Policing: An International Journal of Police Strategies and Management*, 30 (3): 498–517.

College of Policing. (2019) Intelligence management: intelligence collection, development and dissemination. Available at https://www.app.college.police.uk/app-content/intelligence-management/intelligence-cycle/ [Accessed 13th April 2020].

College of Policing. (2020a) Director of Intelligence Role Profile. Available at https://profdev.college.police.uk/professional-profile/test-6/ [Accessed 24 August 2020].

College of Policing. (2020b) Intelligence Manager Role Profile. Available at https://profdev.college.police.uk/professional-profile/test-1/ [Accessed 24 June 2020].

Cope, N. (2004) Intelligence led policing or policing led intelligence: integrating volume crime analysis into policing. *British Journal of Criminology*, 44 (2): 188–203.

Council of Europe. (2000) The role of Public Prosecution in the Criminal Justice System adopted by the Committee of Ministers of the Council of Europe, 6 October 2000.

Davies, P.H.J. (2002) Ideas of intelligence: divergent national ideas and institutions. *Harvard Intelligence Review*, 24 (3): 62–66.

Davies, P. (2010) Intelligence culture and intelligence failure in Britain and the United States. *Cambridge Review of International Affairs*, 17 (3): 495–520.

Donovan, J.W. (1916) *Kill the Squirrel: Tact in Court*. London: Sweet & Maxwell Ltd.

Duffy, B., Wake, R., Burrows, T. and Bremner, P. (2007) Closing the gaps – crime and public perceptions. Available at http//ipsos-mori.com/_assets/reports/closing-thegaps.pdf [Accessed 12 June 2020].

Duyvesteyn, I. (2011) Intelligence and strategic culture: some observations. *Intelligence and National Security*, 26 (4), 521–530, Available at https://www.tandfonline.com/doi/abs/10.1080/02684527.2011.580605 [Accessed 19 May 2020].

Eck, J.E. and Spelman, W. (1987) *Problem Solving: Problem Oriented Policing in Newport News*. Washington DC: Police Executive Research Forum.

Ekblom, P. (2012) *Crime Prevention, Security and Community Safety using the 5Is Framework*. Basingstoke: Palgrave MacMillan.

Evans, J. and Kebbell, M. (2012) Integrating intelligence into policing practice. In T. Prenzler (eds), *Policing and Security in Practice*. New York: Palgrave MacMillan.

Goldstein, H. (1979) Improving policing: a problem-oriented approach. *Crime & Delinquency*, 25 (2): 236–258.

Goldstein, H. (1990) *Problem Oriented Policing*. New York: McGraw-Hill.

Harfield, C. and Harfield, K. (2008) *Intelligence: Investigation, Community and Partnership*. Oxford: Oxford University Press.

Henry, V.E. (2003) *The Compstat Paradigm: Management Accountability in Policing, Business and the Public Sector*. Flushing, NY: Looseleaf Law Publications, Inc.

Hesketh, I. and Cooper, C. (2019) *Well-being at Work: How to Design, Implement and Evaluate an Effective Strategy*. London: Kogan Page Ltd.

Hesketh, I., Cooper, C. and Ivy, J. (2015) Leaveism and work–life integration: the thinning blue line? *Policing: A Journal of Policy and Practice*, 9 (2): 183–194.

Holman, T. (2015) Paris: An intelligence failure or a failure to understand the limits of intelligence? Available at: https://rusi.org/commentary/paris-intelligence-failure-or-fa ilure-understand-limits-intelligence [Accessed 14 May 2020].

Hope, T. and Murphy, D. (1983) The problems of implementing crime prevention: the experience of a demonstration project. *The Howard Journal of Criminal Justice*, 22: 38–50.

Innes, M. and Fielding, N. (2002) From community to communicative policing: signal crimes and the problem of police reassurance. *Sociological Research Online*, 7 (2). Available at http://www.socresonline.org.uk/7/2/Innes.html [Accessed 11 August 2019].

Ivkovic, S.K. (2005) *Fallen Blue Knights: Controlling Police Corruption*. New York: Oxford University Press.

James, A. (2016) *Understanding Police Intelligence Work*. Bristol: Polity Press.

James, A., Phythian, M., Wadie, F. and Richards, J. (2017) The road not taken: understanding barriers to the development of police intelligence practice. *The International Journal of Intelligence, Security, and Public Affairs*, 19 (2): 77–91.

Johnston, R. (2008) *Analytic Culture in U.S. Intelligence: An Ethnographic Study*. Centre for the Study of Intelligence. Washington: Government Printing Office.

Jones, T. and Newburn, T. (2007) *Policy Transfer and Criminal Justice*. Maidenhead: Open University Press.

Kahneman, D. (2011) *Thinking, Fast and Slow*. New York: Farrar, Straus and Giroux.

Kahneman, D. and Tversky, A. (1973) On the psychology of prediction. *Psychological Review*, 80: 237–251.

Kelling, G.L., Pate, T. and Dieckman, D. (1974) *The Kansas City Preventative Patrol Experiment*. Washington DC: Police Foundation.

Keren, G. and Tiegen, K. (2004) Yet another look at the heuristics and biases approach. In D. Koehler and N. Harvey (eds). *Blackwell Handbook of Judgement and Decision Making*. Oxford: Blackwell Publishing.

Kirby, S. (2013) *Effective Policing?: Implementation in Theory and Practice*. Basingstoke: Palgrave MacMillan.

Mastrofski, S. (1988) Police agency accreditation: a skeptical view. *Policing: An International Journal of Police Strategies & Management*, 21: 202–205.

National Crime Intelligence Service. (2000) *The National Intelligence Model*. London: NCIS.

Newburn, T. (2013) *Criminology*. Abingdon: Routledge.

Neyroud, P. and Beckley, A. (2001) *Policing, Ethics and Human Rights*. Cullompton: Willan.

Public Health England. (2018)Introduction to logic models. Available athttps://www. gov.uk/government/publications/evaluation-in-health-and-well-being-overview/intro duction-to-logic-models[Accessed19 January 2021].

Ratcliffe, J. (2008) *Intelligence-led Policing*. Cullompton: Willan Publishing.

Rawley, A. and Caddy, B. (2007) *Damilola Taylor: An Independent Review of Forensic Examination of Evidence by the Forensic Service*. London: Home Office.

Roberts, L.D. and Indermaur, D.W. (2009) What Australians think about crime and justice: results from the 2007 Australian Survey of Social Attitudes. In *Research and Public Policy Series*. Canberra: Australian Institute of Criminology.

Rosenbaum, D.P. (1986) *Community Crime Prevention: Does it Work?*Beverley Hills, CA: Sage Publications.

Salvatore, S.A. (2018) Fusion centre challenges: Why fusion centres have failed to meet intelligence sharing expectations. MSC thesis, Naval Postgraduate School, Monterey.

Scott, M.S. and Kirby, S. (2012) *Implementing POP. Leading, Structuring and Managing a Problem-Oriented Police Agency.* United States: Department for Justice. Available at https://popcenter.asu.edu/sites/default/files/implementing_pop.pdf [Accessed 23 September 2020].

Sheptycki, J. (2004) Organizational pathologies in police intelligence systems. *European Journal of Criminology*, 1 (3): 307–332.

Skogan, W. and Hartnett, S. (1997) *Community Policing, Chicago Style.* New York: Oxford University Press.

Soomro, S. and Yanos, P.T. (2018) Predictors of mental health stigma among police officers: the role of trauma and PTSD. *Journal of Police and Criminal Psychology*, 34: 175–183.

Syed, M. (2015) *Black Box Thinking: The Surprising Truth about Success (and why some people never learn from their mistakes).* London: John Murray Publishers.

Tilley, N. (2003) Community policing, problem oriented policing and intelligence led policing. In T. Newburn. (ed). *The Handbook of Policing.* Cullompton: Willan Publishing.

Tuffin, R., Morris, J. and Poole, A. (2006) *An Evaluation of the Impact of the National Reassurance Policing Programme.* Home Office Research Study 296. London: Home Office.

Wandersman, A. (2009) Four keys to success (Theory, Implementation, Evaluation and Resources/System Support): High hopes and challenges in participation. *American Journal of Community Psychology*, 43 (1–2):3–21.

Wandersman, A., Goodman, R.M., and Bullerfoss, F.D. (2005) Understanding coalitions and how they operate. In M. Minkler (ed). *Community Organizing and Community Building for Health*, New Brunswick, NJ: Rutgers University Press.

Wardlaw, G. (2015) Is the intelligence community changing appropriately to meet the challenges of the new security environment? Available at http://press-files.anu.edu.au/downloads/press/p319221/pdf/ch082.pdf [Accessed 19 May 2020].

Willis, J.J., Mastrofski, S.D. and Weisburd, D. (2004) Compstat and bureaucracy: a case study of challenges and opportunities for change. *Justice Quarterly*, 21 (3).

Willis, J.J. and Mastrofski, S.D. (2012) Compstat and the new penology: a paradigm shift in policing? *The British Journal of Criminology*, 52 (1): 73–92.

World Health Organization. (2014) Mental health: a state of well-being. Available at http://www.who.int/features/factfiles/mental_health/en/ [Accessed 28 November 2018].

Wright, A.(2007)Ethics and corruption. In T.Newburn, T.Williamson, and A.Wright (eds), *Handbook of Criminal Investigation*, Collompton:Willan Publishing.

Wright, E. (2012) Health and safety record breakers. Available at https://www.building.co.uk/olympic-health-and-safety-record-breakers/5036956.article. [Accessed 6 December 2019].

Wright, S. (2008) Milly: The litany of police mistakes which let her murderer escape. *Mail Online*, 26 February. Available at http://www.dailymail.co.uk/news/article-518673/Milly-The-litany-police-mistakes-let-murderer-escape-justice.html [Accessed 16 February 2013].

Chapter 4

Improving intelligence analysis

An analyst perspective

Introduction

Whereas sworn police officers are still acting as analysts in some countries, the post is normally carried out by a civilian staff member (referred to as police staff in the UK). This has a significant benefit as a UK police officer (for example) generally spends about 2–5 years in a given role before moving onto a different post. In contrast a civilian employee is selected specifically for the role, remains in the post for a considerable period, provides consistency, accrues specialist training and skill sets, as well as a detailed knowledge of systems and data sources.

Whilst the intelligence analyst has been recognised as an essential part of law enforcement for a number of decades, some argue it is still to find its footing in the UK and USA, with analysis often considered superficial (Belur & Johnson, 2016; Santos & Taylor, 2014). As Evans & Kebbell (2012:88) have pointed out, 'There can be little debate over the view that modern policing should be 'intelligence led'. However, available evidence suggests that best practice – such as the UK NIM – [has] been adopted more at the level of rhetoric and policy than in the structure and everyday practices of police organizations'. The reasons behind this concern have been multi-faceted (Keay & Kirby, 2018; Santos & Taylor, 2014). At a fundamental level concerns exist about the poor quality of the analytical output being produced (Chainey, 2012). Innes et al. (2005:39) argue that analytical products, are often 'better understood as an artefact of the data… rather than providing an accurate representation of any crime problems'. Cope (2004:188) adds that analysts are simply used as 'information translators', with their explanations insufficient to provide an understanding of a problem, thereby making it difficult to provide suitable responses or solutions. Innes et al. (2005) and Chainey (2012) suggest that if the methodologies utilised by analysts aren't sufficiently rigorous and objective, the provision of descriptive accounts simply tell the police something they already know. This approach can negatively affect the credibility of the analyst and their product. Nonetheless, whilst these concerns exist, and the role of the analyst can vary across police forces and countries, the research demonstrates that the post can deliver great benefits for law enforcement when applied properly (Ratcliffe, 2019a; Belur and Johnson, 2016). Therefore, the question is how the potential of the analyst role can be maximised to improve intelligence analysis in policing. In exploring this question the chapter will be divided into three sections.

- Section 1: Will explain the different roles analysts are asked to perform in law enforcement, together with the key characteristics and core responsibilities associated with the role.
- Section 2: Will examine the organisational environment in which the analyst operates, illustrating some of the constraints that affect analyst knowledge and skill development.
- Section 3: Will provide advice on the skills and knowledge that should be developed by the analyst, following their initial training.

Section 1: The different roles and core responsibilities of an analyst within the policing environment

This section will examine how organisations define the analyst role and establish the key characteristics and core responsibilities required by effective practitioners. A useful place to start is with the College of Policing (CoP, UK), an organisation whose purpose is to provide all staff (sworn officers and civilian staff) with the knowledge and skills they need to prevent crime, protect the public, and secure public trust. On its website the CoP sets out four role profiles associated with intelligence analysis: head of intelligence analysis, senior analyst, analyst, and professional standards analyst.

- Head of Intelligence Analysis: This is the senior management role in charge of the analysis function. It is responsible for managing and developing analysis to direct activity. The role provides advice and expertise in all analysis and intelligence matters and provides a strategic direction for analytical functions.
- The senior analyst: The person who fills this role should have highly advanced research, analysis and evaluation skills. The role manages analytical teams and specific areas of analytical business. It provides a level of quality assurance for analyst products in line with national standards, manages the introduction of new techniques and supports the intelligence manager in developing intelligence products that can best assist end users.
- The analyst: This role is generally retained within a specialist intelligence unit and provides an essential role in intelligence development targeting serious and organised criminality. Core responsibilities within this role are often derived from traditional intelligence analysis; conducting strategic, tactical and operational analysis. Historically, this role was defined by the National Intelligence Model (NIM) and associated with core training

courses, such as the NIAT (National Intelligence Analysis Training) and ANACAPA. The role is often associated with the production of evidential packages relating to criminal investigations, major incidents and for court hearings. This role is also tailored to provide assistance in specialist crime areas, for example, CSE (child sexual exploitation), robbery and, more recently, knife crime.

- Professional standards analyst: In essence this role is the same as the analyst, but the purpose of the role is to support the Professional Standards Department (PSD) and develop analytical products that relate to cases of police misconduct. Ethical considerations play a significant part within this role.

At the time of writing, these are the only analyst related role profiles posted on the CoP website. However, some police forces have developed bespoke analyst posts and others have used the analyst post generically, to conduct a variety of functions. Some of these adaptations include:

- *Performance or crime analyst.* This is often a general role, sitting within a local operational Basic Command Unit (BCU), a HQ corporate analysis function, or within a Crime Prevention department. The role is often tactical in nature, examining crime trends and assisting in crime reduction initiatives. The nature of this post is often in support of core NIM requirements that drives activity at a local operational level. This role can differ from the intelligence analyst role as it neglects intelligence work and provides insight concerning general performance (e.g. supporting national data requirements such as reducing crime or increasing detection) and describing local crime problems. Some police forces have dedicated performance analysts that concentrate on servicing internal and external data requests, e.g. Freedom of Information requests, Home Office data returns.
- *Partnership analyst* (sometimes referred to as partnership intelligence analyst). In the UK this post often sits outside the police force and within the local authority (albeit this is dependent upon how the role is funded as some local authorities fund or part-fund the post). The partnership analyst role was initially developed to support multi-agency Community Safety Partnerships, formed through the Crime and Disorder Act 1988 (sections 5–8). The role examines local crime and disorder issues, in order to develop multi-agency responses to reduce them using problem solving approaches (discussed in Chapter 3). The analyst often provides tactical and strategic analysis, in line with statutory responsibilities, based upon a variety of multi-agency data sets (explained more fully in Chapter 7).
- *Business analyst:* In wider industry, the role of a business analyst is normally centred around financial analysis, however in policing it serves a different purpose. Here its role is to provide support to corporate analysis

and performance trends (crime and disorder trends, or organisational activity). The role is closely integrated with Information Technology and engaged in data extraction and data modelling functions, therefore it can sometimes cross into a data science role (see Chapter 8).

Within the UK the most common analyst roles are referred to as either intelligence or performance analysts. Peterson (1994) noted that analyst job titles are often used interchangeably, and this is apparent in some forces which swap the terms 'intelligence', 'performance' and 'crime', when describing analysts. In the USA analysts are more clearly differentiated and their development is supported by two separate organisations. The International Association of Law Enforcement Analysts (IALEIA) represents intelligence analysts, whilst the International Association of Crime Analysts (IACA) represents crime (performance) analysts. Ratcliffe (2016) notes that crime analysts conduct analysis on what crimes are occurring and intelligence analysts conduct analysis on how and why crime is occurring.

The role of the UK analyst was first defined in the National Intelligence Model (NIM) guidance and more recently adapted by the College of Policing (CoP), which points out, 'To assist decision makers, analysts must deliver effective analysis that can be understood and acted upon' (College of Policing, 2020c). The CoP (2020b) also notes that the purpose of the analyst is to provide 'expertise through the development and use of analytical products to assist decision making at a strategic, tactical and operational level'. The following activities are listed which analysts are expected to conduct.

- Establish and interpret requirements to ensure the needs of key stakeholders are met.
- Develop and maintain relationships, internally and externally, to share data, information and analysis, where appropriate.
- Collect and evaluate data and information to support the creation of a collection plan (where applicable) and the delivery of analytical products.
- Conduct analysis at a strategic, tactical and/or operational level, identifying and using appropriate analytical tools and techniques to interpret gaps, patterns and trends, assess threat, risk and harm and make recommendations in support of decision making, prioritisation and resource allocation.
- Produce written and/or verbal briefings and presentations to stakeholders to provide a clear and concise evidence-based understanding of the subject matter, including providing advice and guidance. Be able to prepare, deliver and present analytical products for use in court proceedings, as required.
- Adhere to all legal frameworks, key working principles, policies and guidance relevant to the role.
- Maintain awareness of innovation within intelligence to ensure implementation of latest techniques and tactics, best practice, and information relevant to the role.

As with most job specifications this role profile is generic and the remainder of this chapter, will explore the skills and knowledge required by analysts, as well as the environment they operate within.

Section 2: Analysts and the internal organisational environment

Overall, the last two decades have seen the number of police analysts increase, although it is generally thought the professionalism associated with the role has not kept pace. Academic research hints at a love–hate affair between the institution of law enforcement and the analyst role, with some criticising the quality of analytical outputs (Santos & Taylor, 2014; Innes, et al., 2005). Belur and Johnson (2016) in the UK and Boba (2003) in the USA are of the view that crime analysis has not been fully assimilated into policing, noting that analysts have fought to be recognised as professional workers by their police officer colleagues. These concerns are not solely the domain of the analyst, as commentators question whether law enforcement agencies value the importance of research (Ratcliffe, 2004); the science of analysis (Chainey, 2012); the value of an analyst's output (Evans 2008; Cope 2004); or the skills associated with an analyst (Evans & Kebbell, 2012). These concerns reflect deficiencies in how the role is understood, managed and nurtured by the very organisations that crave the insight that good research and analysis can deliver. There are three issues behind these concerns.

The first relates to the strategic direction of the analyst role. Some argue that the omnicompetence required of analysts in UK law enforcement has perhaps been a factor in its stagnation. Professional development for a 'jack of all trades' approach has meant that the nature of analysis and research has been diluted. The NIM guidance also failed to recognise that analysts would be used differently and that many permutations of the role and intelligence products would evolve. An example is the number of analysts attending court and providing evidential material. The danger here is that some requests focus on presentation of evidence, a function more akin to graphic design and presentation skills than analysis. Whilst useful activity, it puts the analyst in danger of losing their expertise to simplify complex cases. This echoes what Cope (2004) described as the translation of information, rather than the provision of analysis.

Overall, there has been little consideration as to how the collective efficacy of the analyst role can be enhanced. Across the world the majority of police agencies have no co-ordinating body for analysts, resulting in role development and training becoming piecemeal and often provided outside mainstream funding. In the UK the College of Policing has proposed the IPP (Intelligence Professional Portfolio) which will hopefully be a significant step forward. Kolb (1976) notes that successful organisations require, 'an ability to explore new opportunities and learn from past successes and failures' (1976:21), and this is true for intelligence analysis. Whilst there may be a role for analysts to assist investigations and prepare evidence for court this could possibly be developed into an assistant investigator position, rather than continue to confuse the analysis landscape. There may also be scope to provide a variety of other analytic services, such as developing qualitative research projects to improve police knowledge and insight for organisational development, rather than just preparing operational briefs. In essence further clarity on how analysts should be used would be helpful.

Secondly, it should be recognised that investment to support analyst development has suffered due to the economic downturns experienced across the world since 2009. Austerity measures have negatively affected external recruitment and investment in the role (Keay & Kirby, 2018). This has meant that many forces were unable to maintain appropriate training, leaving forces to deliver ad hoc 'on the job' training. Evans (2008) may have been prophetic in his suggestion that the analyst role is vulnerable to efficiency savings as, overall, austerity measures have generally led to either fewer analysts, or existing analysts being asked to do more. Nonetheless, opportunities continue to exist for the role to develop and rise into the specialist position originally envisaged. In fact, the pressure to use finite resources more effectively and efficiently, supports the case for staff to conduct better analysis. This is illustrated with recent international interest in evidence-based policing (EBP), crime science, and problem oriented policing (POP), which places analysts at the centre of police interventions, at both organisational and operational levels.

Third, the process of recruitment, skill sets and training require scrutiny. Recruiting and selecting the right individuals into analyst posts will become increasingly important. In the UK, similar to areas of Scandinavia, a higher education degree is a pre-requisite for appointing police constables. There is also a need to consider the wider education, learning and professional development of all staff, especially in specialist services (Wood, 2019). The provision of high-quality intelligence starts with high quality people who have an aptitude for this type of work and who are valued and developed. The initial two-week NIAT or ANACAPA training course, which analysts were asked to apply in the workplace, has not kept pace with market demands. As Chapter 8 describes, in recent years there has been an exponential growth in technology and data, which has also had an impact on the analyst role. Police related IT infrastructure has often lagged behind commercial development, and generally been ignored in continuous professional development (CPD). Whilst analysts are often trained in new software systems, they are infrequently given sufficient time to fully exploit this training, more often obtaining their learning from 'on the job' experiences (Keay & Kirby, 2018). Enhanced technology skills can speed up analytical processes, from cleaning and tidying data to the visualisation of information. With more investment to train computer and data science, intelligence analysis could be greatly improved, as could the resulting outputs and insights.

However, using new technology requires the correct application of theory too. Analysts need to understand what techniques they can apply to a given situation, thereby improving their analyst tool kit. For example, using inferential statistics to analyse crime problems is not just about using a particular software package, but knowing what statistical test should be used in a given context. It should further take account of the need to obtain new skill sets to meet the demands of 'big data', machine learning and algorithms, to slice through growing data sets (this will be discussed further in Chapter 8).

Of course, these challenges should not only be tackled 'in house'. Sparrow (2016) has argued that scholarly support is a requirement to improve analysis. He argues that there is a greater need for collaboration and the wider use of different techniques and processes to improve the role. He furthers suggests the need for increased orchestration between different agencies to develop solutions for shared problems. Analysts need to be alive to this and work more collaboratively with other agencies in terms of data, intelligence and solution design. Assessing inter-agency impact, rather than the impact of a single agency, will become increasingly important.

Section 3: The critical factors affecting continued professional improvement

Assessing personal development need

Whereas the last section examined how police organisations could improve the analyst role, this section highlights the importance of continuous professional development (CPD). In essence if an analyst knows their current knowledge and skill status as well as their desired end state, then a development plan can be designed to bridge the gap. In this process, self-reflection is critical, and there exists a variety of research on the topic. Bassot (2016) explains the *conscious competence learning model*, which explains that individuals experience a four-step journey prior to learning something new. The first stage is generally 'unconscious incompetence', when the person is unaware of their lack of skills and knowledge. This moves to 'conscious incompetence' when learners become aware of their limitations. As development takes place, they become more knowledgeable and skilled, allowing them to apply their learning in practice and enter the category of 'conscious competence'. The final stage is 'unconscious competence', where the learner performs well in their role, and can use the newfound knowledge with little conscious thought.

It has also been be recognised that individuals develop particular styles when learning (Honey & Mumford, 2000; Kolb, 1984). There are *Activists*, who act first and reflect later. These individuals enjoy new experiences, focus on the present, are open minded, enthusiastic and tend not to be sceptical. Meanwhile *Reflectors* are cautious and base their decision making on a range of data. *Theorists* are more analytical and enjoy the synthesis between complex theory and their own observations. They exist as objective and rational decision makers, who pay particular attention to detail. Finally, *Pragmatists* are those who simply approach problems as a challenge which requires a solution. They like to test the efficiency and effectiveness of new ideas in practice. Each learning style has a particular advantage and there is benefit in being able to develop a variety of approaches.

A number of models help analysts critically evaluate their current position and establish the areas to develop professionally. Potter (2008) endorses the SWOT model which allows the individual to establish their own strengths and weaknesses (internal characteristics) and then assess existing external opportunities and threats. This approach has also been adapted to generate the SWAIN model, which as well as determining strengths and weaknesses asks an individual to identify aspirations, interests and needs. Figure 4.1 provides a hypothetical example of SWOT and SWAIN in practice.

Armed with these models, and prior to designing a personal development plan, the analyst needs to understand what level of skills, knowledge and experience they aspire to. Whilst there is currently limited strategic direction, a useful starting point is the College of Policing (2020b), which sets out the general skill areas expected of an analyst. These are:

Strengths	Weaknesses
• Listening skills. • Use of Microsoft Excel and PowerPoint. • Commitment.	• Lack of knowledge in research skills, specifically inferential statistics. • Lack of experience in presenting intelligence products.
Opportunities	Threats
• Opportunity to engage with local University. • Employer supporting HE qualifications. • Supportive line manager.	• Becoming overloaded with too many projects and personal development. • Focusing on quantity, rather than quality.
Aspirations	
• Completion of qualification. Improving research rigour of analytical products.	
Interests	Needs
• Serious & organized crime. • Offender behaviour and theory.	• Structured timetable for development. • Mentor.

Figure 4.1 SWOT and SWAIN examples

1 Ability to identify and scope a problem to effectively deliver analytical products.
2 Good communication skills with the ability to present information and provide recommendations to various stakeholders to ensure understanding and support decision making.
3 Ability to develop and test inferences and hypotheses and to draw evidence-based conclusions and make recommendations, in support of decision making.
4 Ability to research, analyse, and assimilate large volumes of complex data and prepare and produce concise analytical reports.
5 Skill in the use of use IT packages, systems and/or databases involved in analysing, interpreting, storing, and presenting data.
6 Ability to identify potential opportunities to enhance efficiency and/or effectiveness within own area of work.
7 Good team working skills demonstrating awareness of individual differences and providing support as required.
8 Ability to appropriately prioritise and plan their own work.
9 Ability to proactively develop effective working relationships with colleagues, partners and other stakeholders.
10 Ability to develop their own knowledge and awareness of the intelligence discipline.

Again, these points are described in general terms and require further exploration. This will be conducted using three specific headings: research skills, criminological theories, and skills and training.

Research skills

Commentators have consistently criticised analytical products for being too descriptive (Chainey 2012; Cope, 2004). In listing general skill areas, the CoP highlights the 'ability to research', which is universally accepted as a crucial area (points 3 & 4). Specifically, analysts require competency in 'research methods'. This includes the strategies, processes or techniques, required for the collection and analysis of data or evidence, which is needed to establish new information or create better insight concerning a topic. Research skills allow analysts to develop a more rigorous scientific approach which facilitates the provision of more objective and insightful intelligence products. This does not mean the role of the intelligence analyst is synonymous with that of an academic researcher, indeed it is generally accepted that whilst the academic researcher is multi-skilled in various research and analytical methodologies, the intelligence analyst is regarded as plying a tradecraft often learnt 'on the job' (Marchio, 2014). However, understanding the application of research methodologies to law enforcement can only advance the quality of intelligence analysis (Keay & Kirby, 2018). Fundamental to this approach is a research attitude (Bryman, 2016), epitomised by three steps: a) the researcher is systematic and rigorous in the research topic and methodology, which includes justifying choices and considering alternative approaches; b) the researcher is sceptical, meaning they are able to scrutinise and challenge (including self-challenge), whilst questioning the strength of supporting evidence and considering alternative explanations; and c) the researcher follows an ethical approach, following governance parameters and being mindful as to how their research has an impact on others.

Quantitative, qualitative and mixed methods approach

When a research hypothesis is formed (see below) a decision will be made as to how this can be tested and, in this process, quantitative and qualitative methodologies are often used. The decision to use qualitative or quantitative approaches (or both in mixed methodology) can only be established once the research question is established.

Quantitative approaches use numerically based data. Their purpose is to show what is happening and the frequency with which it is occurring (Sarantakos, 2005). This type of approach is growing in importance, due to the desire to find patterns within large data sets. In contrast, qualitative approaches assist in explaining why something is happening, often providing meaning by obtaining an individual's subjective view of the world (Sarantakos, 2005). This type of data is often based on individual accounts taken from sources such as interviews, focus groups, surveys, social media, and journal articles. Whilst some argue this type of approach is more subjective, there are tried and tested approaches to make the findings more representative and reliable. An example is Nvivo, a software program which assists in the analysis of unstructured text, audio, video, and image data to generate themes and patterns within the data. There is little evidence of qualitative approaches being used in intelligence analysis, although it is particularly useful when analysing community intelligence as it provides insight that crime records are unable to bring. Whatever type of data is used, the term primary data relates to data directly obtained to test the hypothesis and the term secondary data relates to data that has already been collected for another purpose.

Hypothesis testing

A critical element within research skills is hypothesis testing (see CoP point 3 above), often associated with high quality analysis and analytic reports (Chainey, 2012; Townsley et al., 2011; Heuer & Pherson, 2010). A hypothesis is an assumption, which may be true or false and which can be tested. Hypothesis testing can be similar to choosing a new suit for a wedding – a number of different outfits may need to be tried, and a number of small alterations made, before a perfect fit is found. The benefit of the approach is that it provides a focus and discipline to establishing the truth. A useful way to explain it is through the example of crime mapping, an approach synonymous with intelligence analysts, and supported by a wealth of literature and software. Ideally, mapping is used as part of the analysis process, with the map serving as the visual tool which illustrates the outcome of scientific activity. Gloria Laycock (cited in Boba, 2003:14), highlights the danger of 'blobology' where crime maps are put together reactively, with no criteria or hypothesis for the selection of the area or the crime type (see also Chainey & Ratcliffe, 2005). At a simple level the analyst can create a crime map without any hypothesis; for example, depicting where and when night-time violent crime occurs, which can be useful for briefing patrolling officers. However, a map generated under these conditions will not show the *social environment* or reflect its *social ecology* (Harris, 1999), which means it lacks understanding as to *why* the crimes are occurring in that location (Brantingham & Brantingham, 1995). This is important if the analyst is to establish the root cause of the problem and recommend more sustainable solutions (Goldstein, 1990). In this way if the analyst develops a good knowledge of the area, the map can be utilised to develop their hypotheses, i.e. violent crime increases around the transport hubs, or in the fast food area, or other congested areas at the end of licensing hours. If used in this way the map can help to support or reject the hypothesis or even suggest that the initial hypothesis needs updating or modifying. Harris (1999) points to a model called the 'hypothetic-deductive process'. This refers to the process of hypothesis generation, data collection, analysis and evaluation, which is not too dissimilar to the intelligence cycle. The process, outlined by Harris, involves the analyst in the development of hypotheses and the use of maps to help confirm/deny their suspicions, as well as assisting in the investigation of crime.

Hypothesis development is further enhanced if the analyst has knowledge of theories of crime. For example, extending the mapping example, Brantingham and Brantingham (1984:609) developed a model which postulated the 'intersection of criminal opportunities with offender's cognitive awareness space'. This argued offenders are more likely to commit offences in locations areas where criminal opportunities intersected with the areas they were familiar with. This knowledge can generate a hypothesis to be tested, and places the analyst in a stronger position to understand what data and intelligence should be gathered (McDowell, 1998).

Applying key criminological theories

Different criminological theories provide understanding as to why a crime or specific criminal behaviour takes place. Theories are categorised under many themes, such as biological, psychological, sociological, cultural or classical, and there is little consensus as to how many criminological theories actually exist. Unfortunately, no universal theory is able to explain all types of crime and it is not the purpose of this section to list all available theories. However, some theories are more commonly associated with intelligence analysis, and an understanding as to how they can be applied should be part of the analyst's core knowledge and skill set. An important point to remember is that only a small number of criminological theories have relevance to the police. For example, some sociological theories may emphasise that poverty and deprivation underpin crime and whilst these may be relevant for government policy makers, they are of less practical assistance to the police. This is because the police are unable to reverse poverty or stimulate the economy. Therefore, the theories that aid the police relate to those that assist in offender detection or identify where crime will occur as well as and ways to prevent them. Below is a summary of some key theories which, although essential for analysts, are seldom taught in initial training. A much fuller explanation of each can be found via the references provided, and their application is further discussed in later chapters.

A) ROUTINE ACTIVITY THEORY

Developed by Cohen and Felson (1979), routine activity theory states that crime is not just committed by dedicated villains but can also include the mundane actions of regular people. The theory argues that crime is a product of criminal opportunity associated with particular events, places, people and times. It argues that crime (or other policing incidents) occur when a motivated offender comes into the same place and time as a vulnerable victim, in the absence of a capable guardian. The idea of routine activity theory helped generate criminological interest as to how the environment can shape and present opportunities for criminal and anti-social behaviour. A core text in this area is *Crime and Everyday Life* originally published in 1994, currently in its 6th edition (Felson & Eckert, 2018), which inspired other theories and research in this area.

B) SOCIO-SPATIAL CRIMINOLOGY

The importance of place or location is a continuing theme in crime analysis and has already been discussed in this chapter. One of the early research findings was by Park and Burgess (1925) who argued a typical city had five concentric zones, which correlate with different levels of crime. Since that time environmental criminology has continued to develop, although Bottoms (2012:453) says it is more accurately referred to as socio-spatial criminology, which is 'the study of crime, criminality and victimization as they relate, first to particular places and secondly to the way that individuals and organisations shape their actions spatially and in doing so are in turn influenced by place-based or spatial factors'. In essence, this leads us to the same basic conclusion, that environment influences criminal behaviour. There are two central themes in this:

a   The spatial distribution of offences, and
b   The spatial distribution of offenders.

Theories relating to these principles are used to assist in both reducing and detecting crime and will be discussed in later chapters.

C) SITUATIONAL CRIME PREVENTION (SCP)

Situational crime prevention focuses on the interventions that prevent immediate opportunities for offending. It is concerned with analysing the characteristics of places where crimes occur, or are likely to occur (Clarke, 1980), then seeking to reduce the crime through altering immediate or situational factors in that environment. As Clarke (1997:4) stated, it comprises, 'opportunity-reducing measures that (1) are directed at highly specific forms of crime, (2) involve the management, design and manipulation of the immediate environment in as systematic and permanent a way as possible, (3) make crime more difficult and risky, or less rewarding and excusable as judged by a wide range of offenders'. For Clarke (and others who have developed SCP) it is the physical characteristics of the environment that are most likely to encourage or facilitate crime and therefore lead to its uneven distribution.

D) DESIGNING OUT CRIME

An important element of SCP has been the concept of *designing out crime* also referred to as CPTED (Crime Prevention Through Environmental Design) and an early pioneer was Oscar Newman (1972), who devised the concept of *defensible space*. Researching crime rates in New York, Newman found that crime was more likely to occur in high rise flats than in lower housing developments (even if occupancy rates were similar). He explained this by pointing out the higher crime rates were in areas which possessed accessible escape routes, a lack of surveillance and areas of high anonymity. This meant that criminogenic factors could be structural and 'designed out' of an area. He also described four factors associated with designing in *defensible space*. The first is generating a sense of 'territoriality' which creates ownership and makes individuals feel the space is worthy of protection. Second, 'natural surveillance' is advocated as it allows nearby residents to see what is occurring and deter potential offenders. Third there is 'image', which generates a sense of security and deters people from committing crime in the area. Finally, there is 'Milieu' which relates to other features of an area that may influence security, such as a police station, or a busy hub with a constant flow of people. However, Newman also recognised that designing in defensible space is only worthwhile if the residents are willing to play their part in preventing offending behaviour, by adopting the role of protector and denouncing crime. Further, he argued designing out crime is the responsibility of numerous agencies. This theory was tested and developed by Alice Coleman (1985) in a study of social rented housing in London which linked design with 'disorder' on social housing estates. It is supported by the 'broken windows' hypothesis (Kelling & Wilson, 1982), which was a significant part of the famous 'zero-tolerance' approach championed by Bill Bratton, Chief of New York Police. Although the broken windows theory has been subjected to some academic criticism, it states that small misdemeanours increase if they are neglected, which ultimately undermines neighbourliness and leads to physical disorder.

E) RATIONAL CHOICE THEORY

Rational choice theory considers offenders to be reasoned actors who make 'rational choices' about their behaviour (Clarke & Cornish, 1985). As such interventions can be designed to deter offenders, by making the risk of committing the crime outweigh its benefit. It is this theory, along with routine activity theory, that forms much of the basis for situational crime prevention. In fact, all theories listed in this section are inter-related and essential for understanding the basic elements of crime analysis. Rational choice theory is discussed in more detail in other chapters.

Skills and training

Most police analysts receive some introductory training when recruited. In the UK it is the National Intelligence Analyst Training (NIAT) course. The NIAT course has its origins in the original intelligence analyst course from the USA company, ANACAPA services (Peterson, 1994). NIAT incorporated requirements from the NIM to standardise training for the UK market. This situation is improving slightly with some universities and commercial organisations also offering a variety of analyst training. The analyst profile put forward by CoP (2020c) states analysts should be edu-cated to Level 6, which is undergraduate degree level (with or without honours) or have three years' experience (in the field of analysis). They are also asked to stay up to date in a number of areas, which includes such subjects as crime science (Smith & Tilley, 2005), evidence-based policing (Mitchell & Huey, 2019), police science (Weisburd & Neyroud, 2011) and problem oriented policing. Mark Evans (2008), a New Zealand police chief, argues analysts need:

1 *Awareness of current research.* This remains problematic for analysts as keeping up to date is difficult when working in busy operational environments. However, this investment is beneficial in the long term, particularly with EBP building momentum.

2   *Creative thinking to embrace new crime problems.* Analytical process is advanced through improving critical thinking skills and integration of wider analytical structures that are currently missing from many police forces (Heuer & Pherson, 2010).
3   *Have practical skills, which can be applied to real-world problems.* This capability can also improve with greater collaborative working across multi-agency and multi-skilled teams as well as operational insight.

Evans and Kebbell (2012) also note that presentation and communication are also key skills. Indeed, the College of Policing has noted that 'writing for impact' is important, whilst Chapter 8 provides further information about data visualisation. What is also apparent is that good analysis is not always conducted by a single analyst. Working in a team, whether with other analysts, intelligence specialists, academics or other agencies, can generate a better quality output. Heuer (2009) argues that structured analytical techniques enable collaboration, which opens up analysis to a variety of different sources.

A possible CPD programme

During 2018 and 2019 representatives from the N8 Policing Research Partnership (a consortium of eight universities across the north of England) delivered a CPD programme to a cohort of approximately 50 analysts from 11 different police forces. The programme was developed to deliver core ideas, training, research and data tips to improve the assimilation of rigorous scientific and academic research into policing. It also allowed analysts to improve their skills and knowledge, including new and changing technologies and data science. The programme delivered by academics, practitioners and industry leaders was modular, in an effort to reduce workplace abstractions. The CPD programme comprised the following format:

1   *Setting the scene: From analysis to data science.* (Re) defining the role of police data specialist with perspectives from analysts and academics.
2   *Analytical approaches: Problem oriented policing (POP).* This provides theoretical context and the analytical approaches that support effective problem-solving.
3   *Analytical approaches: Statistical tests.* This examined the role of data in analysis, including constructing testable hypotheses, concepts of measurement and the use of inferential statistics.
4   *Analytical approaches: Visualisation.* This session explored data visualisation and discussed concepts that support effective data driven communication.
5   *Analytical approaches: Modelling.* An introduction to statistical modelling, including commonly used statistical models, which generate insights about relationships between variables.

6 *Analytical approaches: Algorithmic decision making.* This explored the use of algorithms and machine learning, including natural language processing, which allow computers to analyse large amounts of data.
7 *Ethics and data governance.* This module examined the legal and ethical frameworks which surround research and data sharing.
8 *Futures: Predictive policing.* The final session examined how policing research contributes to the evidence base.

This programme was an interesting step forward in the development and future of the analyst role, particularly for crime and intelligence analysis. However, although universally popular with the analysts, many were not afforded the time to develop this new knowledge when back in the workplace. This has previously been noted as a common problem (Ratcliffe, 2004), as police forces often demand a quick turnaround of analytical outputs, which then reduces the quality of the product. Allowing analysts to be involved in more rigorous analysis can bring about positive change and assist the police force in applying more scientific research approaches. The organisation must allow time for new skills to be nurtured and developed. This requires line managers and senior analysts to take a key role in developing their staff and allowing the introduction of science, research and new technologies into their profile.

Supporting organisations

There are numerous websites that provide supporting information for analysts. One is PopCenter.org, which is based within the USA. Amongst their many publications available online is 'Become a Problem-Solving Analyst' (Clarke & Eck, 2003). The publication offers an excellent insight into the basic steps for crime analysis and should be regarded as essential reading. The publication also provides an insight into conducting evaluations which is perhaps one of the most overlooked exercises in law enforcement (Piza et al., 2020; Kirby, 2013). There are a number of analyst support networks that can assist analysts in developing their professionalism. In the UK they include the following.

NAWG

The National Analyst Working Group (NAWG) has been consistently striving to improve the professionalism of the analyst's role within UK police forces. The NAWG has representatives from most UK law enforcement agencies. They provide specialist advice and national direction for the analysis portfolio and often work collaboratively for the common good of continuous professional development.

LARIA

The Local Authority Research and Intelligence Association (LARIA) is a UK-based membership body largely run by public sector volunteers, predominately working at a local authority level. LARIA exists to promote continuous improvements in the quality and impact of local research and intelligence. Partnership analysts are more likely to be aware of LARIA and local authority research and analysis. It is extremely useful to work in collaboration with analysts from social care and health agencies, particularly when working on early intervention initiatives as discussed in Chapter 5.

ACIA

The Association of Crime and Intelligence Analysts (ACIA), can be accessed at https://www.acia.org.uk; it is run by volunteer members who work in the crime and intelligence arena. It has over 700 members from a variety of law enforcement agencies and related industry seeking to connect analysts in order to develop their analytical skills and progress the role through professional development, ideas and knowledge sharing. Its greatest asset is its diversity, which promotes different analytical methods and information sharing.

There are also two key associations in the USA that support and promote the analyst role.

IACA

The International Association of Crime Analysts (IACA), can be accessed at https://iaca.net. It is an American based association that provides support for crime analysts across the world. It has been helping improve analyst skills and connect valuable contacts, to help law enforcement agencies make the best use of crime analysis, and to advocate for professional standards of performance and techniques. It boasts over 4,000 members worldwide from a variety of agencies and runs an annual training conference and awards programme.

IALEIA

The International Association of Law Enforcement Analysts (IALEIA), which can be accessed at https://www.ialeia.org, has been in existence since 1981. Like IACA, it has members from law enforcement agencies across the globe and runs annual training conferences and award programmes. The purpose of IALEIA is to advance high standards of professionalism in analysis at the local, state/provincial, national, and international levels.

Conclusion

This chapter has indicated the diverse ways that analysts can be deployed by law enforcement agencies to improve intelligence analysis. As can be seen this role is open to interpretation and will vary across agencies. Nevertheless, there is a basic level of critical knowledge and skills which will enable the analyst to become more proficient in improving intelligence analysis. Whilst the basic points have been set out it is clear that an individual who is recruited to work as an analyst within law enforcement is only at the start of a long period of development.

References

Bassot, B.(2016) *The Reflective Practice Guide.* Available athttps://dl.uswr.ac.ir/bit stream/Hannan/138921/1/9781138784307.pdf[Accessed19 January 2021].

Belur, J. and Johnson, S. (2016) Is crime analysis at the heart of policing practice? A case study. *Policing and Society*: 1–19. http://www.tandfonline.com/doi/full/10.1080/10439463.2016.1262364 [Accessed 4 May 2017].

Boba, R. (2003) Problem analysis in policing. Washington: Police Foundation. Available at https://popcenter.asu.edu/sites/default/files/library/reading/pdfs/problemana lysisinpolicing.pdf [Accessed 5 May 2020].

Bottoms, A.E. (2012) Developing socio-spatial criminology. In M. Maguire, R. Morgan and R. Reiner (eds). *The Oxford Handbook of Criminology*, 5th edn. Oxford: Oxford University Press.

Brantingham, P.J. and Brantingham, P.L. (1984) *Patterns in Crime.* New York: MacMillan.

Brantingham, P.L. and Brantingham, P.J. (1995) Criminality of place: Crime generators and crime attractors. *European Journal of Criminal Policy and Research*, 3 (3): 5–26.

Bryman, A. (2016) *Social Research Methods.* Oxford: Oxford University Press.

Chainey, S. (2012) Improving the explanatory content of analysis products using hypothesis testing. *Policing: A Journal of Policy and Practice*, 6 (2): 108–121.

Chainey, S. and Ratcliffe, J. (2005) *GIS and Crime Mapping.* Chichester: John Wiley.

Clarke, R.V. (1980) Situational crime prevention: Theory and practice. *British Journal of Criminology* (20): 136–147.

Clarke R.V. (ed). (1997) *Situational Crime Prevention: Successful Case Studies*, 2nd edn. Harrow and Heston: Guilderland.

Clarke, R.V. and Cornish, D.B. (1985) Modelling offenders' decisions: A framework for research and policy. *Crime and Justice*, 6: 147–185.

Clarke, R. and Eck, J.E. (2003) *Become a Problem-Solving Analyst.* London: Jill Dando Institute.

College of Policing. (2020a) Director of Intelligence Role Profile. Available at https://p rofdev.college.police.uk/professional-profile/test-6/ [Accessed 24 August 2020].

College of Policing. (2020b) Intelligence Manager Role Profile. Available at https://p rofdev.college.police.uk/professional-profile/test-1/ [Accessed 24 June 2020].

College of Policing. (2020c) Delivering effective analysis. Available at https://www.app. college.police.uk/app-content/intelligence-management/analysis/delivering-effective-a nalysis/ [Accessed 13 April 2020].

Cohen, L. and Felson, M. (1979) Social change and crime rate trends: A routine activity approach. *American Sociological Review*, 44: 288–608.

Coleman, A.M. (1985) *Utopia on Trial: Vision and Reality in Planned Housing*. London: Hilary Shipman.

Cope, N. (2004) Intelligence led policing or policing led intelligence: Integrating volume crime analysis into policing. *British Journal of Criminology*, 44 (2): 188–203.

Evans, M. (2008) Cultural paradigms and change: A model of analysis. In C. Harfield, A. MacVean, J. Grieve, and D. Phillips (eds). *The Handbook of Intelligent Policing*. Oxford: Oxford University Press.

Evans, J. and Kebbell, M. (2012) Integrating intelligence into policing practice. In T. Prenzler (eds). *Policing and Security in Practice*. New York: Palgrave MacMillan.

Felson, M. and Eckert, M. (2018) *Crime and Everyday Life* (6th edn). Thousand Oaks: Sage.

Goldstein, H. (1990) *Problem Oriented Policing*. New York: McGraw-Hill.

Honey, P. and Mumford, A. (2000) *The Learning Styles Helpers Guide*. Maidenhead: Peter Honey Publications.

Heuer, R.J. (2009) The evolution of structured analytic techniques. Available at https://www.e-education.psu.edu/geog885/sites/www.e-education.psu.edu.geog885/files/file/Evolution_SAT_Heuer.pdf [Accessed 1 July 2020].

Heuer, R.J. and Pherson, R.H. (2010) *Structured Analytic Techniques for Intelligence Analysis*. CQ Press.

Innes, M., Fielding, N. and Cope, N. (2005) The appliance of science? The theory and practice of criminal intelligence analysis. *The British Journal of Criminology*, 45 (1): 39–57.

Keay, S. and Kirby, S. (2018) The evolution of the police analyst and the influence of evidence based-policing. *Policing: A Journal of Policy and practice*, 12 (3): 265–276.

Kelling, G.L. and Wilson, J.Q. (1982) The Police and neighbourhood safety: Broken windows. *Atlantic Monthly*.

Kelling, G.L., Pate, T., Dieckman, D. and Brown, C.E. (1974) *The Kansas City Preventive Patrol Experiment: Technical Report*. Washington, DC: Police Foundation.

Kirby, S. (2013) *Effective Policing?: Implementation in Theory and Practice*. Basingstoke: Palgrave MacMillan.

Kolb, D. (1976) Management and the learning process. *California Management Review*, 18 (3), 21–31.

Kolb, D. (1984) *Experiential Learning: Experience as a Source of Learning and Development*. New Jersey: Prentice Hall.

Marchio, J. (2014) Analytic tradecraft and the intelligence community: Enduring value, intermittent emphasis. *Intelligence and National Security*, 29 (2): 159–183.

McDowell, D. (1998) *Strategic Intelligence and Analysis: Training Manual for Analysts*. Antwerp: Istana Enterprises.

Mitchell, R. and Huey, L. (2019) *Evidence Based Policing: An Introduction*. Bristol: Policy Press.

Newman, O., (1972)*Defensible Space: People and Design in the Violent City*. London: Architectural Press.

Park, R.E. and Burgess, E.W. (1925) *The Growth of the City: An Introduction to a Research Project. The City*. University of Chicago Press.

Peterson, M. (1994) *Applications in Criminal Analysis*. Westport: Praeger.

Piza, E., Szkola, J. and Blount-Hill, K.L. (2020) How can embedded criminologists, police pracademics, and crime analysts help increase police-led program evaluations? A survey of authors cited on the evidence-based policing matrix. *Policing: A Journal of Policy and Practice.* Available at https://academic.oup.com/policing/advance-arti cle-abstract/doi/10.1093/police/paaa019/5827736?redirectedFrom=fulltext [Accessed 2 May 2020].

Potter, S. (2008) *Doing Postgraduate Research.* London: SAGE Publications.

Ratcliffe, J. (2004) Intelligence research. In J. Ratcliffe (ed.). *Strategic Thinking in Criminal Intelligence.* Sydney: Federation Press.

Ratcliffe, J. (2016) *Intelligence-led Policing.* Abingdon: Routledge.

Ratcliffe, J. (2019a) *Reducing Crime: A Companion for Police Leaders.* Oxon: Routledge.

Santos, R.B. (2014) The effectiveness of crime analysis for crime reduction: Cure of diagnosis? *Journal of Contemporary Criminal Justice,* 30 (2): 147–168.

Santos, R.B. and Taylor, B. (2014) Integration of crime analysis into police work. *Policing,* 37 (3): 501–520.

Sarantakos, S. (2005) *Social Research* (3rd edn). Hampshire: Palgrave Macmillan.

Smith, M.J. and Tilley, N. (2005) *Crime Science: New Approaches to Preventing and Detecting Crime.* Cullompton: Willan.

Sparrow, M. (2016) *Handcuffed: What Holds Policing Back and the Keys to Reform.* Washington: Brookings Institution Press.

Townsley, M., Mann, M. and Garrett, K. (2011) The missing link of crime analysis: A systematic approach to testing competing hypotheses. *Policing,* 5 (2): 158–171.

Weisburd, D. and Neyroud, P. (2011) Police science: Toward a new paradigm. *Journal of Current Issues in Crime, Issues, and Law Enforcement,* 7 (2): 227–246.

Wood, J. (2019) Private policing and public health: A neglected relationship. *Journal of Contemporary Criminal Justice,* 36 (1): 19–38.

Chapter 5

Intelligence sources and techniques for crime reduction

Introduction

Now that the book has described the framework within which intelligence analysis takes place, the next stage is to examine the knowledge and techniques currently used. Specifically, the purpose of this chapter is to outline the theories, techniques and tools used by analysts to assist in the reduction of crime and show how these approaches can be implemented in practice. The chapter will be organised in four sections, which mirror a systematic problem-solving approach.

- Section 1: Will explore the various techniques that can identify crime and incident patterns, including hot spot analysis.
- Section 2: Will describe techniques that assist the analyst understand why these patterns take place. Specifically, it will show how crime patterns are associated with the opportunities presented in everyday life, through specific locations, people, events and products.
- Section 3: Will set out the value of analysing these incidents from an offender perspective, to tailor more effective interventions.
- Section 4: Will describe different evaluation techniques, to assist the analyst understand whether the intervention has had an impact.

Section 1: Identifying the problem and where it is occurring

Introduction – crime concentrates

The Italian, Vilfredo Pareto (1848–1923) was a philosopher, sociologist, engineer and economist. He recognised that 80% of Italian land (and therefore wealth) was owned by only 20% of the population. This general principle – that most things in life are not distributed evenly – later took his name and also became known as the 80–20 principle (Sanders, 1987). In economics this general rule could explain that 20% of the workers generate 80% of the product, or that 20% of the customers create 80% of the revenue. However, the same principle is also apparent across many disciplines, in fact Pareto found the majority of his garden peas came from a minority of his plants! Although the figures are not always precise, the rule that a small number of something is associated with a disproportionate amount of something else remains constant. Using it in the field of criminology, researchers have shown that 4% of victims suffer 40% of crime (Bolling et al., 2003). Whilst 10% of offenders commit 50% of crime (Home Office, 2001), and 5% of places account for 50% of recorded crime incidents (Weisburd et al., 2004).

Whilst many factors influence the concentration of crime and disorder, a major factor is the predictability of human behaviour. If you were asked to grade yourself on a scale of 1–5, (1 that you were completely predictable and 5 completely unpredictable), what number would you choose? To help you decide, consider the following questions: What you did last Saturday, and what are you doing next Saturday? How often do you change your morning routine – including your route/transport/time to leave for work? Do you buy your clothes/food from the same shops? When you annoy friends, colleagues and family, is it the normally about the same thing? If, following these questions, you rated yourself as generally predictable, then you won't be surprised that offenders and victims show similar predictability. The fundamental characteristics that produce persistent offenders, or make victims particularly vulnerable, often remain constant over time – unless these routine behaviours can be influenced by a significant intervention. This phenomenon will be examined in more detail later, for now, the first stage of the process is for the analyst to establish the type of crime to focus on and identify where it is occurring.

Decide where to focus – frequency, risk or harm?

It has been established that crime and other incidents concentrate in time and place. However, deciding on the type of problem (i.e. crime) to be targeted is more complicated. Up until now the identification of the problem has been based upon the frequency with which it occurs (the crime or hot spot associated with the most incidents). If the analyst follows this approach then it is logical to assume that the more available a target is in a given area, the higher the number of crimes likely to be generated. However, it may be that the police prefer to target their resources on a type of crime or location that suffers the most risk (the likelihood of the crime occurring), or the crimes or areas that suffer more harm (there are fewer crimes but more serious in nature). In essence if the analyst wishes to focus on the highest volume of crime/incidents then they should simply focus on the area where the highest concentration of incidents or calls are reported. However, if the aim is to reduce risk or the level of harm, then a more sophisticated calculation is needed.

A simple way to establish whether people or places suffer heightened risk is by using a simple five step calculation (Clarke & Eck, 2005: step 27).

a   Define the event of interest (i.e. burglary; personal robbery)
b   Define the population at risk (i.e. houses in the area; people)
c   Specify the locations and times it occurs (i.e. housing estate; town centre ATMs)
d   Find data that states the number of available targets and the number of crimes that occur
e   For each of the locations, divide the number of crimes (numerator) by the number of available targets (denominator) to obtain the offence rate

Although conceptually simple, a number of factors should be considered prior to the calculation. Thought should be given to the choice of denominator, as using the number of homes is a more accurate denominator than using resident population, when contemplating risk levels for burglary. The analyst should also be mindful that further work may be needed, for example establishing the number of ATMs in the area where a robbery problem is occurring. Sometimes this type of information is difficult to obtain and in those cases proxy measures can be considered. For instance, in a vehicle crime problem the number of cars using a specific car park may be unknown, therefore the size of the car park or the number of available car parking spaces could be used instead. Be mindful that this approach is only helpful when comparing parks which have similar occupancy levels or usage.

Using risk ratios like this is particularly helpful when identifying *risky facilities* (Eck et al., 2007). For example, a ratio can be established by understanding the usage of that area against the number of crimes (i.e. 30 vehicles broken in per year in a car park that normally houses 100 cars a day would be 30/100 or 0.3). Clarke and Eck (2005) use this approach in describing a problem associated with motels in Chula Vista, California. The initial analysis showed the police received a similar number of calls to both national chain and independent motels, however the national chain motels had many more rooms. When this was factored in it was revealed the average call rate for the independent motels was 1.8 calls per room compared to 0.5 calls a room per chain motel. This approach illustrated that the independent motels were associated with a much higher risk of crime (and a proportionately higher number of calls).

These considerations can also be extended to the concept of harm. Whilst a case of shoplifting and a murder are both counted as one crime, the latter creates much more harm and consumes significantly more police resources. Over time a variety of countries have devised a variety of methodologies to calculate the level of harm. There are two models that have been developed in the UK, the first being the Cambridge Harm Index (CHI) (Sherman et al., 2016). The CHI weights crime based on sentencing structure to determine the greatest harm caused by a given crime. The CHI process 'multiplies each crime event in each crime category by the number of days in prison that crime of that category would attract if one offender were to be convicted of committing it' (Sherman et al., 2016:172). The second is the Crime Severity Score (CSS) that has been developed by the Office for National Statistics (ONS). This model attempts to illustrate the severity of a given crime by calculating the average number of days of an offender's sentence following their conviction (ONS, 2016a). When published in 2016 the ONS CSS showed that murder had the highest score (7,979 points per offence), whilst possession of cannabis possession had the lowest (3 points per offence). Aggregating all these individual crime scores it showed that the West Yorkshire police area had the highest crime severity score in the UK, one place above the Metropolitan Police, with Dyfed-Powys (Wales) in last place (ONS, 2016b).

One of the issues affecting the identification of crime problems so far has been the reliance on police data. Sometimes in areas of low community cohesion the level of intimidation prevents residents coming forward and providing information. In such situations the police have to be more proactive in obtaining data and in this a number of factors are relevant. The first is to understand that not all crime categories used by the police as performance indicators are important to the wider community. The community impact of antisocial behaviour, illustrated by such factors as discarded drug paraphernalia, broken windows and graffiti can generate fear, reduce well-being and affect the willingness of residents to protect their community. Ways to measure these concerns are discussed later in this chapter (see Community intelligence).

Making the identified problem manageable to enable problem solving (the limitations of high visibility and hot spot policing)

The section so far has discussed identifying the type of crime and its location. This is important as it allows police officers to target the problem. Areas where crime concentrates have become known as hot spots and deploying highly visible police patrols in these areas is known as hot spot policing. This approach has a proven impact and a number of research studies have provided further information on what makes hot spot policing more effective. The Koper Curve (named after its author) argues that intermittent patrol of micro-hot spots (street segments or small residential blocks), for a 10–16 minute period at least every two hours, can optimise its deterrence value (Koper, 1995). Further insight has been provided by Temple University, Philadelphia under the supervision of Professor Jerry Ratcliffe, who found increased violence reduction could be delivered with the use of foot patrol (Ratcliffe et al., 2011). They also advocate the use of offender-focussed approaches on repeat violent individuals within very specific hot spots. Police officers used a variety of targeted interventions, ranging from simple street conversations to executing warrants for recent offences. Groff et al. (2015) examined the impact of this approach on 81 violent crime hot spots by conducting a randomized control trial. After eight months the research team found offender focused approaches had significantly fewer crimes of violence than the control hot spots. However, in a parallel study Ratcliffe et al. (2015) established that the residents of those locations did not report any changes to their feeling of safety or attitude to the police. A different hot spot policing approach was evaluated by Santos and Santos (2016) which concentrated on residential burglary and theft from vehicles. This involved contacting offenders and families at their home addresses in an effort to increase their perception of risk through formal surveillance and reducing their anonymity. They did not find any significant differences in relation to the numbers of crime or arrests, although there were significantly fewer repeat arrests.

Braga et al. (2019; 2014) has stated hotspot analysis has been one of the most impactive innovations within modern policing. However, it appears that hotspot policing is even more effective when used with problem solving strategies (Braga & Bond, 2008; National Research Council, 2004). This is because using police deployments alone is resource intensive, expensive, and unlikely to provide sustainable solutions. This is due to the fact that the characteristics associated with vulnerable locations and victims, together with available offenders remains constant. In this way the problem simply returns once the effects of increased police visibility wear off. For problem solving to occur, an analytical product in relation to the hot spot needs to be specific. For example, consider the offence of burglary, which can emerge in many ways across a hot spot, including:

- Burglary via the rear, facilitated by an alleyway
- Burglary targeting Asian families, predominately for gold collections
- A burglary to steal the key for a luxury motor vehicle on the drive
- Burglary where the elderly occupant is distracted, allowing the offender to steal property
- Burglary of student multi-occupancy housing for laptops and other electronic items

In this way it is entirely possible for a range of burglaries to occur in the same geographic area, conducted by different offenders. In such locations the offences cannot be reduced by a single intervention. To understand what interventions are really needed the hot spot analysis should drill down to identify distinct (and therefore more manageable) problems. This requires more specific problem definition at street level and a useful example to explain this has been provided to the authors by Professor Gloria Laycock (University College London). The example occurred a number of years ago, when the UK experienced a significant rise in cases of personal robbery. As public anxiety grew, the government of the day decided action was needed and, following good practice, the Pareto principle was used to supply extra resources to the ten UK police forces who were suffering the majority of robberies. The challenge was then passed to an analyst (working in a large metropolitan area which suffers thousands of these crimes) to deliver an intelligence product. This needed to be sufficiently detailed to facilitate a more sustainable intervention than high visibility policing. The initial challenge for the analyst was therefore to make the identified problem more manageable. This can be achieved through two steps. First, by reducing a large geographic area to more specific and manageable locations. In this way a police force area could be divided into smaller local government areas, police operational units, or Super Output Areas. Generally speaking, the tighter the hot spot is defined, the more specific the problem definition can be. The second step is to take one of these smaller geographic areas and be specific on the type of crime to be targeted. As illustrated with burglary, official crime categories can cover a wide group of different offences and this finding was also present with personal robbery. In the example there were a variety of robbery offences that included late night snatches at town centre cash dispensers near licensed premises and knife point robberies on the transport system. Using the Pareto principle, the analyst should try and identify the category of personal robbery that has increased disproportionately and accounts for a large proportion of all robberies. In this particular example the vast majority of personal robbery offences involved victims or suspects aged 16 years or under, a category which had increased by 84% on the previous year. As such it was decided to focus police activity (and therefore the intelligence product) on this subcategory of robbery. By using these two steps the analyst is much more specific in identifying the problem to be worked upon and allows them to move forward in analysing what is actually causing the crime increase.

Different analytic techniques to identify crime concentrations

To illustrate crime concentrations analysts can utilise a number of methods, such as charts hot spot analysis, and visual audits.

a) Data visualisation and the use of charts

Once a specific geographic location for the analysis has been established (i.e. police operational area, local government area), a bar or pie chart can be used to illustrate crime distribution. This type of chart can show a visual representation of the most prevalent crime and give an immediate understanding as to where effort should be targeted. Conversely, using a bar chart with frequency on the y axis and plotting different crime categories on the x axis can show clearly the crime types which are occurring disproportionately.

Once a particular crime (or crime categories) is identified, further analysis using time series analysis (plotted using a line or bar graph) can be conducted to show how these crimes change over time. This has three benefits: it illustrates the overall trend (i.e. the incidents are increasing, reducing or remaining constant); it illustrates daily, weekly or seasonal cycles; and it can show random fluctuations, which can be created by a wide number of minor issues. Whilst comparisons are useful in establishing trends (i.e. comparing the current year with the previous year), it is important to remember aberrations are normal. For example, every four years a leap year will generate an extra day in February (therefore extra crimes). Further, bank holidays (i.e. Easter) fall at different times and certain months may incorporate more weekend days, all of which are factors that can be associated with more incidents. To establish the strength of these trends the data can be subjected to various statistical tests, such as regression analysis, which can determine the level of change and whether the trend is statistically significant or likely to have occurred by chance. It should also be remembered that sometimes it is difficult to establish when the crime actually occurs as they are discovered at a later date/time, e.g. burglary. Ratcliffe (2002) speaks of 'aoristic analysis' to better understand temporal patterns. His research has shown that by using 'start times' and 'end times' within crime data it is possible to generate a *probability* of crime occurrence. This type of analysis has shown different temporal patterns with crime hotspots and greatly improves the targeting of police resources.

b) Crime mapping and geographic information systems

Crime Pattern Theory (Brantingham & Brantingham, 1984) reveals that offence patterns are consistent with everyday movement (endorsed by routine activity theory). They argue that crimes concentrate around nodes, which are the places where people spend most of their time due to work or leisure and the pathways (roads) that connect these critical locations. These crime and incident concentrations will therefore be time dependant. So, for example a town centre hot spot will show that theft concentrates during the day, as specific stores become the target for shoplifters, and disorder during the evening as specific licensed premises/takeaways/taxi ranks become focal points for confrontation. These incidents of theft or disorder won't be distributed equally but will concentrate around certain people and locations.

The National Intelligence Model referred to in Chapter 2, explains *crime pattern analysis* as a generic term for a number of related disciplines, such as crime or incident series identification, crime trend analysis, hot spot analysis and general profile analysis. It serves as a major technique when identifying the problem and analysing its cause, having the potential to reveal linkages between offences or problems. Historically the way to illustrate geographic concentrations was by manually placing pins on maps; a cluster of pins illustrating the hot spot. During the past number of decades improvements have been made in geographic information systems (GIS), which can display these patterns in a more sophisticated way. Different shades of red are used to denote concentration at a national, regional or county level, whilst electronic points show crimes at street level. Obviously, the size and scale chosen for location will have an impact on the analysis.

c) Visual audits and community intelligence

At times police data is not available due to under-reporting. One method to illustrate non recorded incidents of crime and antisocial behaviour is to conduct a visual audit. In essence, this entails designating a specific geographic space and systematically walking through it registering every artefact of antisocial behaviour (i.e. graffiti, used condoms, broken glass etc.). This sets a baseline for the area, which allows change to be assessed at a later date. Odgers et al. (2009) provide a comprehensive process to deliver this approach with associated documentation. A further useful option is to conduct community questionnaires which can establish the level of actual crime in a specific area, rather than the amount of reported crime. There are a number of ways of conducting such a survey, however it is important that residents are both anonymous and known to be anonymous, in order to prevent possible intimidation from other residents. Such surveys can be conducted personally, by going door to door, which also presents the potential to provide crime prevention advice (again all houses in the area should be visited to prevent any suggestion of police informants). Other methods include hand delivery, with a stamped addressed envelope for return, or to conduct the project using a full postal survey.

Community intelligence can offer a different perspective on local problems. Goldstein (1979) noted that engagement with the community is essential to solution design when tackling local issues. Ratcliffe (2016) notes that community intelligence can be generated from a number of information sources within the local area, predominantly community support groups and those that reside or work there, e.g. local businesses. Even local groups on social media sites offer an insight into localised issues that can often provide police agencies with a window into community life. To improve the use of community intelligence, analysts and intelligence units will need to enhance data collection methods, and develop skills in assimilating this information that Ratcliffe (2016:87) notes as being 'abstract in nature'.

Section 2: Moving from problem identification to problem analysis

Identify the underlying opportunities that allow the problem to occur

By the time the analyst reaches this step of the process they should have in their possession a clearly defined problem. The next part of the process is to establish why that specific problem is occurring in that particular location, involving those particular people, at that particular time. In this conundrum we are assisted by routine activity theory (Cohen & Felson, 1979), which has been introduced in an earlier chapter. To reiterate, this theory argues that crime can only occur when a motivated offender comes together in the same time and space as a suitable victim in the absence of a capable guardian. This theory emphasises the importance of opportunity as it suggests crime is associated with the normal rhythms of everyday life. For example, a busy market will provide opportunities because shoppers are distracted and may leave their property insecure. In fact, it is argued even the most highly motivated offenders look for the easiest way to commit crime as they won't break a window to enter a specific house if a neighbour leaves a window open. Brantingham and Brantingham (1995) highlight that hot spots are often affected by three factors:

• Crime generators – where there is an increase of vulnerable targets;
• Crime attractors – which entice offenders into the area; and
• Crime enablers, where there exists little regulation or public management of behaviour.

Of course, all three can occur at the same time. For example, the expansion of a local university can set off a series of events to generate a crime hot spot. First, the extra courses associated with the university will bring in more students to the area, bringing with them a vast array of portable and valuable items which are desired by thieves. Second, they will be housed in an increased number of multi-occupancy buildings, which often have reduced security. Third, the influx of students will increase the number of new businesses in the night-time economy, which can be associated (dependant on their management) with increased thefts and disorder. For the analyst it is important to establish when and how the crimes actually occur, as well as their concentration pattern (weekly, daily or even hourly). Charting the frequency of incidents across days of the week and hours of the day illustrates the 'hot time periods' and enables the analyst to start forming hypotheses as to why they are occurring.

If we return to our urban robbery example, we discover that the young victims (16 years or under) show distinct offence patterns, in that the majority of offending takes place between 3pm and 5pm, between Monday and Friday. Whilst a few offences occurred outside this time (a small concentration occurred on weekdays between 8am and 9am) these were in the minority. This allows the analyst to set a very clear hypothesis that the offences are occurring immediately after the schools close for the day. Indeed, by plotting the location of offences at street level occurring midweek between 3pm and 5pm the analyst was able to see that they cluster in specific locations outside school premises, especially at transport hubs, when students converge with those from other schools. It was then that their smart phones, cash and other items of value were stolen by pupils from rival schools. Understanding this level of detail provides many more options in terms of tailoring solutions capable of providing more sustainable crime reduction.

Therefore, when conducting problem solving, 'specificity' is really important. Just as robbery is disaggregated into more specific types of crime, this process should be conducted with other crimes. Homicide for example can be distinguished into domestic and non-domestic crimes before more detailed analysis is conducted in terms of method and times of killing. Similarly, theft can be divided into numerous categories such as shoplifting, theft from the person or vehicles etc. This level of distinction makes it simpler to establish the underlying opportunities that allow the crime to occur and facilitates the design of tailored interventions. In this a useful tool is PAT.

The problem analysis triangle

Eck (2003) devised the problem analysis triangle (PAT) as an *aide-mémoire* to assist in the analysis of routine activity theory, to better understand the opportunities that facilitate the offence. The sides of the triangle are labelled offender, location and victim/target. Each one is considered in isolation to establish the factors that make: a) the victim/target susceptible to the offence taking place; b) establish what opportunities motivate the offender; and, c) understand what it is about the location that facilitates its commission. Once the dynamics across these separate elements are understood, specific interventions can be designed to attach a handler to deter the offender; a manager to protect the location; and a guardian to make the victim/target more secure. The detail surrounding this will be discussed in the next section, but for now more information will be provided for location, victim and offender.

a) Location/place

Certain locations or places are criminogenic. This could be because of their design (i.e. a house which has little security and open access to the rear); or it could be because of the way they are managed (i.e. a bar that sells alcohol to drunk customers whose manager doesn't attempt to deter violent conflict). This latter category is what Eck et al. (2007) refer to as a 'risky facility', which describes those service establishments where mismanagement facilitates crime. A typical example is a local late-night convenience store, which is a location often associated with a disproportionate level of theft and antisocial behaviour (indeed Clarke and Eck (2005), showed 6.5% of US stores suffered 65% of all robberies). Whilst the management of individual premises can generate different problems, the most common types of 'risky facilities' are traditionally:

- *Petrol stations*: Previous studies in the USA found 10% of petrol stations suffered more than 50% of drive off thefts. This has also been a perennial problem in the UK.
- *Schools:* Suffer a variety of problems both in and out of opening times. They are associated with parking problems, antisocial behaviour and theft.
- *Bus stops*: A Liverpool study showed that 9% of bus shelters were associated with over 40% of vandalism reports (Newton & Bowers, 2007).

- *Car parks*: In Nottingham a study found that one car park accounted for 25% of all the crimes across all 19 car parks (Smith et al., 2003).
- *Licensed premises and fast food establishments* are regularly associated with crime, especially violent crime and disorder.

b) Victims

Repeat victimisation is a phenomenon seen across the world. In the UK, Farrell and Pease (1993) revealed about 4% of people suffer about 40% of all crime during the course of a year. Whilst the precise level of repeat victimisation varies across different crime categories, it generally occurs reasonably quickly, often within a few weeks of the initial incident. Whilst repeat victimisation is commonplace, it can be missed by analysts because the victim doesn't report the repeat incident, or the repeat offence occurs across a variety of offence categories or different locations. It can also be influenced by the different protocols (i.e. counting periods) used to 'label' the phenomenon. Tseloni and Pease (2003) explore two explanations behind repeat victimisation. The first is the Boost account, which postulates the offender benefits from their positive experience after committing the first offence and returns to the same victim to repeat the experience. The second is the Flag explanation, which emphasises the importance of the victim, attracting different offenders due to their specific vulnerability. This vulnerability is either due to personal characteristics or because of other situational factors (they live or work in a particular location).

There is also a concept known as near repeat victimisation. This means that if someone in close proximity to the victim has similar characteristics, then they may also be at increased risk. For example, the house next to a burglary victim may have the same design and be attractive to the burglar as they already know how to gain access. Greater Manchester Police designed software to predict who was at risk and the times of increased risk. Targeting resources at these near repeat locations and utilising techniques such as super-cocooning resulted in a 38% reduction in burglary over two years (Fielding & Jones, 2012). Understanding repeat victimisation should be considered a core responsibility for anyone conducting crime analysis. Pease et al. (2018) have expressed concern that repeat victimisation has dropped from the policing agenda. Indeed, identifying repeat victimisation, against people and places, should always be a top priority in analysis.

c) Hot products

Items of stolen property also show patterns, again replicating the pareto principle. The problem analysis triangle emphasises the crime target as well as the victim, as certain items have characteristics that make them more desirable. The most commonly stolen item is cash, as it is immediately useable in a wide variety of environments and is (generally) unidentifiable. A further commonly stolen item are motor vehicles, although not all vehicles are likely to be stolen. So, vehicles stolen for the purpose of 'joy-riding' are more likely to have good acceleration, whilst those stolen and never recovered (often stolen for export) are more likely luxury status cars such as Mercedes. As Clarke and Eck (2005: step 31) argue, '[American] Domestic Station wagons, the staples of family transport, were not at risk from any form of theft. These were inexpensive, had terrible radios, and joyriders wouldn't be seen dead in them'. Clarke (1999) uses the acronym CRAVED to provide an *aide-mémoire* to understand why items are most likely to be stolen. This stands for:

- *Concealable* – Items that are easily hidden, because of their size or because they are unidentifiable, are more likely to be stolen.
- *Removable* – Items that are easily moved are frequently stolen. This includes objects that are mobile in themselves (cars, bicycles) together with smaller items that are easy to carry off (smart phones).
- *Available* – Desirable objects that are widely available are more likely to be stolen. For example, the increase of motor vehicles in the 1960s was associated with a similar increase in theft, until crime prevention interventions were designed and implemented.
- *Valuable* – Items which are obviously valuable, not just in terms of financial cost but status, are more often stolen.
- *Enjoyable* – Items that are more clearly associated with some level of enjoyment appear to be more commonly stolen. Consider the smaller number of microwave ovens stolen, compared to the many more electronic gaming consoles stolen, even though they have similar value.
- *Disposable* – Items that are easily sold on are the ones most frequently stolen.

One of the most currently 'craved' products are smart phones. During 2016 almost half a million of these items were stolen in the UK, with 60,000 thefts occurring in London. The majority of these were iPhones, stolen from young people (especially women) in the 14–24 year age group (Hodkinson, 2019). UK government analysis in 2014 shows that the majority of stolen smart phones are pick-pocketed or grabbed when briefly unattended (Home Office, 2014), although youths snatching phones, whilst riding mopeds did show a threefold increase in 2017. Smart phone thefts are an international problem and South America suffers similar problems, with Peru reporting 6,000 stolen phones a day and Argentina suffering approximately 5,000. These phones contain significant amounts of information with 10% of victims stating they had lost company data; 12% had fraudulent charges made from their bank accounts; and 9% of victims had their identity used in other frauds (Lookout, 2014).

d) Repeat offenders

An early study by Wolfgang et al. (1972) argued 5% of offenders committed 40% of crime, so why do persistent offenders exist? Outside of the causal pathways to crime Clarke and Eck (2005) argue three factors are relevant. First, offenders learn through the process of offending and use this knowledge when moving into similar crimes. Secondly, offenders learn from each other and peer groups have a strong influence. This type of communication works through numerous channels both in virtual (online) and physical environments (social networks such as prison). Indeed unusual modus operandi, such as the use of nitrogen to expand and explode ATM machines was seen to originate in Italy and spread via the internet as far away as Australia. Third it is important to understand that offenders are conscious opponents able to withdraw when their activity is obstructed, only to reappear, more educated and emboldened. Ekblom (2003) has explained that offenders and criminal justice personnel are in an *arms race* constantly evolving and looking for the upper hand. Chapter 7 describes how an offender base can influence how far he or she will travel to make the journey to crime.

Different analytic techniques to analyse crime and incidents

When initially designed, the National Intelligence Model described nine intelligence products, six of which relate to understanding why the problem occurs. These products are described as follows.

- *Network analysis:* Describes not just the linkages between people who form criminal networks, but also the significance of the links (this is covered more fully in Chapter 7).
- *Criminal business profile*: These profiles can provide detailed analysis of how criminal operations or techniques work, in the same way that a legitimate business may be explained. The application of such profiles to the problem analysis triangle will focus on the offender facet. The analysis can be used to identify key points for investigation, disruption, or highlight crime prevention and reduction opportunities.
- *Market profiles*: A market profile surveys the criminal market around a particular commodity or service 'craved' (Clarke, 1999) by offenders.
- *Subject profile analysis*: As research shows, a small number of offenders commit a disproportionate level of crime and disorder. This provides a full analysis of the offender believed to be involved in the offence(s) and should be diverse enough to be fully exploited by a multi-agency problem solving approach.
- *Risk analysis*: Risk analysis covers the duty of care in law enforcement, the requirement to manage persistently dangerous offenders and the implications of the Human Rights Act. Risk analysis therefore assesses

the scale of risk posed by offenders or organisations towards individual victims, the public at large, or agencies. Risk analysis, applied through the problem analysis triangle and other techniques illustrated throughout this book, can indicate the nature and potential impact of a proposed response.

- *Demographic/social trends analysis*: This is a technique for medium/ longer term problem solving as it is centred on demographic changes and the impact on the victim, offender and location. It also allows deeper analysis of social factors such as unemployment and homelessness. It considers the significance of population shifts, attitudes and activities. Partnership development may benefit from this technique as a predictive tool to anticipate future developments in respect of transient/migratory populations and the likely impact on the surrounding area/economy.

Section 3: Selecting an appropriate intervention

Know what works

The process so far has identified a specific problem and analysed why it is taking place. The next stage is to use this analysis and tailor an intervention to eradicate it. In this understanding 'what works' and 'why it works' can assist. A recent programme of study, conducted by University College London and the UK College of Policing, has summarised this knowledge in a toolkit to be found on the 'what works centre' website (College of Policing, 2020). One of the most significant findings was that interventions work differently in different contexts. Therefore, it is important to know what specific context the problem is occurring in and how the intervention could work in that context (referred to as the mechanism). This complexity is shown within their 'what works' evaluation model, known as EMMIE (Johnson et al., 2015), an acronym that stands for:

- *Effects* found: Did it work, if so to what degree?
- *Mechanisms:* What produced the effects, how did it work?
- *Moderators*: Was there anything that influenced the activation of the mechanism?
- *Implementation* challenges: What are the difficulties associated with introducing this approach?
- *Economy*: What are the costs and returns on the investment.

To explain mechanisms in more detail consider the example of CCTV. Studies show that CCTV is more effective in reducing vehicle crime in car parks than reducing violent crime in town centres. This can be explained by understanding the mechanism underpinning the process. CCTV acts as a deterrent because the offender knows their identity could be captured and recorded, a risk contemplated by car thieves who are more likely to choose a car park without CCTV. In contrast offenders who commit violence in town centres are often under the influence of alcohol. As such they are more likely to act on emotion and impulse, therefore less likely to consider CCTV. We therefore see that particular mechanisms work (or don't work) in different contexts.

Think like an offender

Another useful analytical technique is to consider the crime or incident from an offender's perspective. In this, three approaches are pertinent: rational choice perspective, crime script analysis and focussed deterrence.

a) Rational choice perspective

This assumes the offender makes rational decisions when committing crime although this is best considered as limited rationality. This is because cognitive process can be influenced by alcohol or other processing malfunctions (Laycock, 2005), including moods, motives, perception of opportunity, the influence of others and attitude towards risk (Bennett & Wright, 1984). Research also shows that those under the influence of drink or drugs often take greater risks when offending and are more likely to commit acts of near repeat victimisation (Quinn, 2019).

Interviews with offenders have shed some light on their decision-making process. Burglars have disclosed that specific characteristics can make them avoid one house and choose another, with deterrent factors including: large windows at the front of the property; anti-snap locks; ADT burglar alarms (which are monitored); true cul-de-sacs; as well as being overlooked by houses directly opposite (Armitage, 2018). Likewise, Quinn (2019) who interviewed 20 convicted vehicle crime offenders explained the factors that motivate them to commit crime. These include: cars with valuables on show (including work vehicles with tools); cars in less affluent areas and fewer security features, such as street lighting or CCTV; vehicles parked outside student accommodation; areas of prior successful offending; and long roads with lots of parked vehicles where few people pass by. The offenders also admitted when stealing vehicles to order, they target more expensive cars, found in more affluent areas.

Using an offender perspective allows analysts to understand why international markets for stolen smart phones continue. Many countries, including Europe, USA and South America are committed to the GSMA's International Mobile Equipment Identity Database (IMEI Db). In this the unique identity number of a stolen phone (IMEI) is registered and makes it inoperative to all countries involved in the scheme. However, Nigeria remains outside the scheme, which continues to fuel an international black market. Organised crime gangs therefore strip the phone of information before sending it for sale in countries such as Nigeria, India and Algeria. This generates a significant market in countries to which these items are in short supply, reaching a cost ten times higher than when sold in Western countries. Conservative estimates are that this market costs operators at least US $10bn a year (Hodkinson, 2019).

When devising rational choice theory, Cornish and Clarke (1986) have argued that an offender balances the level of risk and effort when committing the offence with the reward they obtain. In this way the offender can be diverted from committing the crime if the cost of doing so is greater than the benefit to be gained. To alter this balance they propose the practitioner considers five themes when devising the intervention: a) increase the effort needed by the offender to commit the offence; b) increase the risk of detection; c) reduce the reward gained from the crime; d) reduce the provocation that may surround the crime; and e) remove any excuse the offender may use to justify their actions. Each of these themes have been extended to generate a further five sub themes; this is known as the 25 techniques of Situational Crime Prevention.

Researchers have spent considerable time to populate these 25 different elements with operational examples and a small number of examples are shown below. Not all cells need to be populated, indeed the matrix should be used as a technique to increase creativity and diversity of intervention. Kirby (2018; 2013) has also used this approach in relation to reducing serious organised crime, further referred to in Chapter 7.

b) Focused deterrence

Focused deterrence, also known as the 'pulling levers' approach, benefits from using an offender perspective. This approach essentially targets known offenders and asks them to stop committing crime, whether with the support of the authorities or (if this doesn't persuade them) through enforcement action. The

Table 5.1 25 Situational crime prevention techniques (see POP Center, 2020 for further explanation)

Increase effort	Increase risk	Reduce rewards	Reduce provocation	Remove excuses
Target hardening	Extend guardianship	Conceal targets	Reduce frustration and stress	Set rules
Control access to facilities	Assist natural surveillance	Remove targets	Avoid disputes	Post instructions
Screen exits	Remove anonymity	Identify property	Reduce emotional arousal	Alert conscience
Deflect offenders	Utilise place managers	Disrupt markets	Neutralise peer pressure	Assist compliance
Control tools and weapons	Strengthen formal surveillance	Deny benefits	Discourage imitation	Control drugs and alcohol

Table 5.2 Adapted from Kirby (2013) showing how opportunities are blocked to reduce crime

	House burglary	*Football related violence*	*Shoplifting*
Increase the effort to commit the crime	Target harden the crime location by improving the security of doors and windows	Provide individuals with banning orders. Use bail conditions or civil orders to get specific offenders to report to police stations during specific games	Leave personal bags at the front of the store
Increase the risk of detection	Use overt and covert property marking	Use confidential free phone numbers for other supporters to provide information. Seats sold to named individuals	Use CCTV, and store detectives to increase surveillance
Reduce the reward from crime	Remove coin operated energy meters and replace with non-coin (token) system	Ban violent supporters from purchasing future tickets. Withdraw season tickets from convicted supporters	Tag items with security fixtures that are difficult to remove or spoil the item if illegally removed
Reduce provocation	N/A	Have filter systems to segregate opposing supporters	Move expensive and portable items (i.e. razor blades and alcohol) away from access points (Inc. emergency exits)
Remove the excuses	Use boundaries or signs to highlight areas of private ownership	Use notices and announcements to clarify a no tolerance approach to violence	Ask customers to select /use store basket

approach has been used extensively by Kennedy (2009) and others to reduce gang related crime, especially in the USA where hot spots exist for gun crime between rival gangs. Papachristos et al. (2015) point out the homicide rate in some Chicago neighbourhoods was 3,000 in every 100,000, which was much greater than the general homicide rate (5 per 100,000). He argued pedestrians in this area are at greater risk of death than they would be of activating a landmine in an Afghan war zone. Offenders are motivated in holding gang membership (even when faced with this threat) because it brings a diversity of benefits, such as: identity, credibility, protection, kinship and lifestyle. Nevertheless, Kennedy argues these gang members can be diverted from violence if the interventions are sufficiently targeted and meaningful. He says the starting point is identifying those associated with the most serious violence, who are only a small number of individuals. In Boston (similar to other areas) he found 61 groups accounted for 60% of homicides of young men under 21 years, which was 0.3% of the city's population (Kennedy et al., 1996; Kennedy, 2001). However, the gang members willing to instigate the most extreme violence account for even less, comprising 0.04% of the population (Kennedy, 2001). Kennedy (2009) found focused strategies on these individuals, which use community members, families, and Criminal Justice agencies working together, can make a significant difference. Eck and Clarke (2013) say this is because: a) it provides a direct and credible threat to the gang members involved in the violence through a range of approaches (i.e. outstanding warrants) as often the police only look to prosecute the offender who pulled the trigger; b) it provides a route out of street life through training, jobs or substance abuse support (this undermines the gang as the only legitimate lifestyle); and c) it demonstrates the community is against violence (provides a community forum to express their disapproval of the violence – especially for those close to the offenders). Braga et al. (2001) highlight the benefits of this approach in the Boston based *Operation Ceasefire* initiative, however the principles of 'focused deterrence' is widely used in other offences, such as domestic abuse.

c) Crime script analysis

This final offender-based approach was initially developed by Derek Cornish (1994). At its core it asks analysts to consider the steps that lead to an offence, setting out each element in the modus operandi. Breaking the process into these individual stages provides clearer options on what interventions can disrupt the crime process. This approach is shown in Table 5.3.

Table 5.3. Crime scripts and potential interventions

Offender actions	*Options for intervention*
Meet co-offender	Consider intelligence reports identifying associates; approach informants.
Obtain tool to break into vehicle	Control sales of items used to enter vehicles illegally (duplicate keys, slide-hammers).
Enter car park	Use of barriers or attendants; reduce access.
Loiter whilst suitable target is established	Use cameras or other formal /natural surveillance to deter people loitering.
Choose suitable vehicle	Use notices to inform owners to lock vehicles and keep valuables out of sight.
Enter vehicle using tool mentioned earlier	Improve natural and technical surveillance of car park.
Over-ride personal security of vehicle.	Encourage better design and use of security measures of car and car park.
Exit the car park	Only allow exit with use of original car park ticket; monitor the exits; activate vehicle tracking system.

The example provided is a simple one and the process can become truncated if the offence is extended (i.e. the vehicle is stolen to order or dismantled for parts). More convoluted or organised criminal actions require the involvement of many more people, some of whom need specialist knowledge or the resources to facilitate transportation or false documentation. Indeed, Hancock and Laycock (2010) have extended this type of analysis in relation to serious organised crime. They highlight its importance in attempting to rationalise the offending process by separating the temporary opportunity driven characteristics that might facilitate the crime from the longer-term infrastructure and relationships that support the offenders in seizing the opportunities. Additionally, crime script methodology can be used to develop a data collection strategy that can aid analysis (Tompson & Chainey, 2011).

Section 4: Assessing the impact

An overview

This is the final stage of the process. So far, the problem has been identified and the reasons why it is occurring have been established. This leads to a tailored evidence-based response. The question this leaves is whether the intervention has worked. There are two general types of evaluation. One is process evaluation, which examines whether the intervention was implemented as planned, and examines whether the process could be improved upon. This is useful as it can establish if implementation failure is likely to be a factor, or whether the intervention could have been introduced quicker or less expensively. The second method, and the one concentrated upon here, is an impact or outcome evaluation. The purpose of this is to establish what (if any) change has occurred to the problem, following the intervention being implemented.

An important point to remember is that not all outcome evaluations are equal. Sherman (1997) proposed a five-point Maryland Scale, which ranks the efficacy of evidence. This ranges from the least rigorous evaluation (before and after studies) to randomised controlled trials (RCTs), which attempt to replicate health-based methodologies used in drug trials. Whilst all accept RCTs are the gold standard of evaluation there remains considerable debate as to what evidence should be accepted in policing. Many consider RCTs are not always pragmatic for police interventions and they relate only to quantitative, rather than qualitative data. Further, they are expensive to conduct, in both time and resources and some would argue it is difficult to provide accurate control groups due to the diversity in people and operational context. Tilley and Laycock (2017) support 'realistic evaluation', arguing all types of evidence are suitable for evaluation provided a) that they are relevant to the question being posed and b) they are viewed in a critical manner to identify whether any bias has crept in.

Perhaps one of the most important points to be made in any evaluation is the need to be honest. There are many ways the process can be manipulated if the evaluator is motivated to show a particular result. It is always good practice to identify the evaluation criteria prior to the intervention commencing, based upon the objective. The most obvious evaluation criteria in a crime reduction initiative is that it will lead to fewer incidents, however there are many other criteria. Other more creative measurement criteria include: a reduction in the harm associated with the incidents; a reduction in the number of repeat victims; an increase in public satisfaction /confidence in the police, or a reduction in the fear of crime. Conversely more abstract or proxy indicators can also be used, such as: less truancy; fewer abandoned vehicles; financial savings; or higher property prices in the area.

Measurement is generally based upon two types of data mentioned earlier. The first is quantitative, commonly understood as numerical data, which is used to count any observable phenomenon. Qualitative data is more abstract and provides meaning, therefore the data often emanates from human perspective. Both types of data can be collected by the analyst; if the data is generated specifically for the evaluation it is known as primary data, whilst secondary data uses data which has already been collected for a different purpose (i.e. custody records, intelligence reports). The choice of which one to use is dependent on the evaluation question and sometimes a mixed method approach (that uses both quantitative and qualitative data), can be used to provide the benefits of both approaches (see Chapter 4 for further discussion). Assessment can go wrong for a number of reasons, including:

- The change would have occurred anyway without any intervention taking place, i.e. the specific offenders or victims had left the area.
- Regression to the mean. There was an uncharacteristic spike in terms of the incident and the trend naturally returns to normal.
- Seasonality. Different seasons bring an increase (or decrease) in relation to different types of incidents, i.e. summer is associated with an increase in violence. Therefore, winter months should not be compared with summer months.
- Poor choice of comparison group. The type of people chosen for the survey are unlikely to provide an accurate and objective response.
- Changing recording practice. Changes in reporting and recording approaches can compromise 'before and after' comparisons.

(Sidebottom et al., 2020)

Different analytic techniques for evaluation

When first introduced, the National Intelligence Model devoted two of its intelligence products to the process of assessment. These were used infrequently and were described as:

- *Operational assessment* which states its purpose is to provide an ongoing evaluation of the incoming information/intelligence/activity or operation.
- *Results analysis* which evaluates effectiveness of patrol strategies, crime reduction initiatives or particular methods of investigation. This is synonymous with an outcome or impact evaluation.

Evaluations are often presented using descriptive statistics (in verbal or pictorial format) as well as inferential statistics. The latter provides a more rigorous assessment as to whether the change has occurred by chance or due to the intervention. The use of evaluations cannot be underestimated as their absence means it is impossible to identify what, or if any, impact has been made. Currently analysts are rarely involved in conducting evaluations, however open source support from the crime reduction toolkit (in the UK) and the evidence-based policing matrix (in the USA) places a growing emphasis in this area.

Conclusion

This chapter has explained some of the current knowledge and techniques analysts can use when facilitating the reduction of crime. Not all of these approaches are widely understood and some are also misinterpreted or poorly implemented. However, studies show when systematically introduced, using critical thinking and research skills, they can make a significant difference in improving analysis to facilitate the reduction of crime.

References

Armitage, R. (2018) Burglars' take on crime prevention through environmental design (CPTED): reconsidering the relevance from an offender perspective. *Security Journal*, 31 (1): 285–304.

Bennett, T.H. and Wright, R. (1984) *Burglars on Burglary.* Aldershot: Gower.

Bolling, K., Clemans, S., Grant, C. and Smith, P. (2003) *British Crime Survey of England & Wales 2002–03.* http://www.esds.ac.uk/doc/5059/mrdoc/pdf/5059userguide.pdf.

Braga, A. and Bond, B. (2008) Policing crime and disorder hotspots: a randomised control trial. *Criminology*, 46 (3): 577–607.

Braga, A., Kennedy, D.M., Piehl, A.M. and Waring, E.J. (2001) *Measuring the Impact of Operation Ceasefire, in Reducing Gun Violence: The Boston Gun Project's Operation Ceasefire.* Washington DC: National Institute of Justice.

Braga, A., Papachristos, A. and Hureau, D. (2014) The effects of hotspots policing on crime: an updated systematic review and meta-analysis. *Justice Quarterly*, 31 (4): 633–663.

Braga, A., Turchan, B.S., Papachristos, A.V. and Hureau, D. (2019) Hot spots policing and crime reduction: an update of an ongoing systematic review and meta-analysis. *Journal of Experimental Criminology*, 15: 289–311.

Brantingham, P.J. and Brantingham, P.L. (1984) *Patterns in Crime.* New York: MacMillan.

Brantingham, P.L. and Brantingham, P.J. (1995) Criminality of place: crime generators and crime attractors. *European Journal of Criminal Policy and Research*, 3 (3): 5–26.

Clarke, R.V. (1999) Hot products: understanding, anticipating, and reducing demand for stolen goods. Police Research Series, Paper 112, Policing and Reducing Crime Unit, Research Development and Statistics Directorate. London: Home Office.

Clarke, R.V. and Eck, J.E. (2005) Crime analysis for problem solvers in 60 small steps. Available at http://www.ncjrs.gov/App/publications/abstract.aspx?ID=232576 [Accessed 20 May 2020].

Cohen, L. and Felson, M. (1979) Social change and crime rate trends: a routine activity approach. *American Sociological Review*, 44: 288–608.

College of Policing. (2020) What Works Centre. Available at https://whatworks.college. police.uk/toolkit/Pages/Welcome.aspx [Accessed 14 March 2020].

Cornish, D. (1994) The procedural analysis of offending and its relevance for Situational Prevention. *Crime Prevention Studies*, 3: 151–196.

Cornish, D. and Clarke, R.V. (1986) *The Reasoning Criminal: Rational Choice Perspectives on Offending*. New York: Springer-Verlag.

Eck, J.E. (2003) Police problems: The complexity of problem theory, research and evaluation. In J. Knutsson (ed.) *Problem-Oriented Policing: From Innovation to Mainstream*. Monsey (NY): Criminal Justice Press, 79–113.

Eck, J. and Clarke, R.V. (2013) *Intelligence Analysis for Problem Solvers*. Available at https://popcenter.asu.edu/sites/default/files/library/reading/PDFs/Intell-Analysis-for-ProbSolvers.pdf [Accessed 6 January 2020].

Eck, J., Clarke, R.V. and Guerette, R. (2007) Risky facilities: crime concentration in homogeneous sets of establishments and facilities. *Crime Prevention Studies*, 21: 225–264.

Ekblom, P. (2003) Organised crime and the conjunction of criminal opportunity framework. In A. Edwards and P. Gill (eds), *Transnational Organised Crime: Perspectives on Global Security*. London: Routledge.

Farrell, G. and Pease, K. (1993) Once bitten twice bitten: repeat victimisation and its implications for crime prevention. Police Research Group, Paper 46. London: Home Office.

Fielding, M. and Jones, V. (2012) 'Disrupting the optimal forager': predictive risk mapping and domestic burglary reduction in Trafford, Greater Manchester. *International Journal of Police Science & Management*, 14 (1): 30–41.

Goldstein, H. (1979) Improving policing: A problem-oriented approach. *Crime and Delinquency*, 25 (2): 236–258.

Groff, E.R., Ratcliffe, J.H., Haberman, C.P., Sorg, E.T., Joyce, N.M. and Taylor, R.B. (2015) Does what police do at hot spots matter? The Philadelphia policing tactics experiment. *Criminology*, 53(1): 23–53.

Hancock, G. and Laycock, G. (2010) Organised crime and crime scripts: prospects for disruption. In K. Bullock, R.V. Clarke and N. Tilley (eds). *Situational Prevention of Organised Crimes*. Cullompton: Willan Publishing.

Hodkinson, T. (2019) Smartphone crime is growing – How do we turn the tide? Available at https://www.trustonic.com/news/blog/smartphone-crime-turning-the-tide/ [Accessed 19 March 2020].

Home Office. (2001) *Criminal Justice: The Way Ahead*. London: Home Office.

Home Office. (2014) *Multi-Agency Working and Information Sharing Project: Final Report*. London: Home Office.

Johnson, S.D., Tilley, N. and Bowers, K.J. (2015) Introducing EMMIE: an evidence rating scale to encourage mixed-method crime prevention synthesis reviews. *Journal of Experimental Criminology*, 11 (3): 459–473.

Kennedy, D. (2001) *Don't Shoot: One Man, a Street Fellowship, and the End of Violence in Inner-city America.* New York: Bloomsbury Press.

Kennedy, D. (2009) *Deterrence and Crime Prevention: Reconsidering the Prospect of Sanction.* New York: Routledge.

Kennedy, D., Piehl, A.M., and Braga, A. (1996) Youth violence in Boston: Gun markets, serious youth offender, and a use-reduction strategy. *Law and Contemporary Problems*, 59: 147–196.

Kirby, S. (2013) *Effective Policing?: Implementation in Theory and Practice.* Basingstoke: Palgrave MacMillan.

Kirby, S. (2018) A problem-oriented account of organised crime in the UK. In G. Farrell, and A. Sidebottom (eds). *Realist Evaluation for Crime Science: Essays in Honour of Nick Tilley.* Abingdon: Routledge.

Koper, C.S. (1995) Just enough police presence: reducing crime and disorderly behaviour by optimizing patrol time in crime hot spots. *Justice Quarterly*, 12(4): 649–672.

Laycock, G. (2005) Defining Crime Science. In M.J. Smith and N. Tilley (eds). *New Approaches to Preventing and Detecting Crime*, Crime Science Series pp.3–24. Collumpton: Willan.

Lookout. (2014) Phone Theft in America: What really happens when your phone gets grabbed. Available at https://blog.lookout.com/phone-theft-in-america [Accessed 6 February 2020].

National Research Council. (2004) *Fairness and Effectiveness in Policing.* Washington DC: National Academies Press.

Newton, A. and Bowers, K.J. (2007) The geography of bus shelter damage: the influence of crime, neighbourhood characteristics and land-use. *Internet Journal of Criminology.* Available at http://www.internetjournalofcriminology.com/Newton%20and%20Bowers%20-%20The%20Geography%20of%20Bus%20Shelter%20Damage.pdf [Accessed 26 April 2020].

Odgers, C.L., Bates, C.J., Caspi, A., Sampson, R.J. and Moffit, T.E. (2009) *Systematic Social Observation Inventory – Tally of Observations in Urban Regions* (SSO i-Tour). Irvine, CA: Adaptlab publications.

ONS. (2016a) Research outputs: developing a Crime Severity Score for England and Wales using data on crimes recorded by the police. Available at https://www.ons.gov.uk/peoplepopulationandcommunity/crimeandjustice/articles/researchoutputsdevelopingacrimeseverityscoreforenglandandwalesusingdataoncrimesrecordedbythepolice/2016-11-29 [Accessed 27 August 2020].

ONS. (2016b) Crime severity score experimental statistics. Available at https://www.ons.gov.uk/peoplepopulationandcommunity/crimeandjustice/datasets/crimeseverityscoreexperimentalstatistics [Accessed 8 April 2020].

Papachristos, A.V., Braga, A.A., Piza, E. and Grossman, L.S. (2015) The company you keep? The spill-over effects of gang membership on individual gunshot victimization in a co-offending network. *Criminology*, 53 (4): 624–649.

Pease, K., Ignatans, D. and Batty, L. (2018) Whatever happened to repeat victimisation? *Crime Prevention and Community Safety*, 20 (4): 256–267.

POP Center. (2020) 25 techniques of situational prevention. Available at https://pop center.asu.edu/sites/default/files/library/25%20techniques%20grid.pdf [Accessed 6 January 2020].

Quinn, A. (2019) Vehicle crime, CPTED, and offending under the influence: a qualitative investigation of offender perceptions. *Social Sciences*, 8 (3): 88.

Ratcliffe, J. (2002) Aoristic signatures and the spatio-temporal analysis of high volume crime patterns. *Journal of Quantitative Criminology*, 18 (1): 23–43.

Ratcliffe, J.H. (2016) *Intelligence-led Policing*. Oxon: Routledge.

Ratcliffe, J.H., Groff, E.R., Sorg, E.T. and Haberman, C.P. (2015) Citizens' reactions to hot spots policing: Impacts on perceptions of crime, disorder, safety and police. *Journal of Experimental Criminology*, 11(3): 393–417.

Ratcliffe, J., Taniguchi, T., Groff, E. and Wood, J. (2011) The Philadelphia Foot Patrol Experiment: A randomized controlled trial of police patrol effectiveness in violent crime hotspots. *Criminology*, 49: 795–831.

Sanders, R. (1987) The Pareto Principle: Its use and abuse. *Journal of Services Marketing*, 1 (2): 37–40. Available at https://doi.org/10.1108/eb024706 [Accessed 15 March 2020].

Santos, R.B. and Santos, R.G. (2016) Offender-focused police intervention in residential burglary and theft from vehicle hot spots: A partially blocked randomized control trial. *Journal of Experimental Criminology, 12*:373–402.

Sherman, L.W. (1997) Policing for crime prevention. In L.W. Sherman, D. Gottfredson, D. MacKenzie, J. Eck, P. Reuter and S. Bushway (eds). *Preventing Crime: What Works, What Doesn't, What's Promising*. Washington DC: National Institute of Justice, US Department of Justice.

Sherman, L., Neyroud, P.W. and Neyroud, E. (2016) The Cambridge crime harm index: Measuring total harm from crime based on sentencing guidelines. *Policing: A Journal of Policy and Practice*, 10 (3), 171–183.

Sidebottom, A., Bullock, K., Ashby, M., Kirby, S., Armitage, R., Laycock, G. and Tilley, N. (2020) *Successful Police Problem-Solving: A Practice Guide*. Jill Dando Institute of Security and Crime Science, University College London. Practice guide. Available at https://discovery.ucl.ac.uk/id/eprint/10093612/ [Accessed 3 May 2020].

Smith, D.G., Gregson, M. and Morgan, J. (2003) Between the lines: an evaluation of the Car Park Award Scheme. Home Office Research Study 266. Available at https://pop center.asu.edu/sites/default/files/problems/parking_garage_theft/PDFs/BetweenTheLin es.pdf [Accessed 21 May 2020].

Tilley, N. and Laycock, G. (2017) The why, what, when and how of evidence-based policing. In J. Knutsson and L. Thompson (eds). *Advances in Evidence-based Policing*. Routledge.

Tompson, L. and Chainey, S. (2011) Profiling illegal waste activity: Using crime scripts as a data collection and analytical strategy. *European Journal on Criminal Policy and Research*, 17 (3): 179–201.

Tseloni, A. and Pease, K. (2003) Repeat personal victimization. 'Boosts' or 'flags'? *The British Journal of Criminology*, 43 (1): 196–212.

Weisburd, D., Bushway, S., Lum, C. and Yang, S.M. (2004) Trajectories of crime at places: a longitudinal study of street segments in the city of Seattle. *Criminology*, 42 (2): 283–322.

Wolfgang, M.E., Figlio, R.M. and Sellin, T. (1972) *Delinquency in a Birth Cohort*. Chicago: University of Chicago Press.

Chapter 6

Intelligence sources and techniques for the investigation of crime

Introduction

As was explained in the opening chapter there are many public and private sector organisations which employ staff to investigate crime, an example being insurance companies whose analysts identify fraudsters. The purpose of this chapter is to provide a greater understanding as to the role of analysis in the process of investigation. This is set out in three sections.

- Section 1: Will define criminal investigation and provide an overview of the investigative process.
- Section 2: Starts to explore aspects of intelligence that are particularly useful in investigation. This chapter concentrates on passive data and shows how it can assist in both reactive and proactive investigations.
- Section 3: Explains how behavioural sciences have become more promi-nent in generating intelligence to be used in the investigation of crime.
- Section 4: Describes a number of available analytical techniques to enhance criminal investigation.

Section 1: The investigative process

A criminal investigation is defined as:

> 'An inquiry to ascertain if an offence has been committed, to identify who is responsible, and to gather admissible evidence to be placed before a judicial authority' (UK Criminal Investigations and Procedures Act, 1996).

Reactive and proactive investigations

Investigations are commonly differentiated into reactive and proactive cate-gories and, whilst they follow similar principles, they also retain important distinctions. A reactive investigation is conducted following the report of a crime and when the offender is unknown. Then, to establish the identity of the offender, evidence is sought from both the physical crime scene and witnesses. These investigations are conducted openly, and often performed under media scrutiny, which publicises the extent of police progress. In contrast a proactive investigation normally starts with intelligence, which identifies those problematic and persistent suspect(s), who are actively involved in serious organised crime. This type of case is built on acquiring evidence against the offender and any potential crimes they may be planning in the future. This means the investigation is covert. Of course, investigations have particular nuances, so can involve both overt and covert techniques,

An example of a reactive investigation occurred during 2004 in Morecambe Bay, UK. This area was highly lucrative for cockles, a shellfish widely desired across Europe, especially Spain. Due to unusual weather conditions the shellfish had become scarce in Europe, apart from a few locations including Morecambe (UK), resulting in the price per tonne increasing from £200 to £1,300. These profits brought in many workers including those smuggled in by Chinese organised crime gangs from the Fujan province. They were packed into local accommodation and forced to work extended hours. Tragically the gang masters weren't aware of the dangerous tides, and on the fateful night the exploited workers became stranded as the tide came in, resulting in 24 deaths. The extent of the investigation was extraordinary, with 1.5m pages of documentation, 5,000 telephones and 20,000 calls and nearly 3,000 statements examined. Analysis of this information enabled analysts to link the offenders with: the area from which the deceased came; the clothing and equipment bought in China; bank accounts used to support financial transactions; the criminal involvement of the suspects, to negate the fictitious reasons they provided for being in the UK; their criminal associates and wider criminal behaviour. The investigation also found significant assets associated with the suspects which was impossible to collect through legitimate types of employment (Kirby & Penna, 2010).

A further case study, this time relating to a proactive investigation, initially started with intelligence being received that a local drug dealer was involved in the shooting of a rival. However, due to the accompanying intimidation, no witness was willing to come forward, and as such the individual became a priority subject in a proactive investigation. Intelligence analysts discovered the days and times the target was most active, and telecommunications data showed where and when the target was spending days away from his home address. Enquires, with the police from the locations he was traveling to, found he was potentially associated with drug dealers from those areas. Covert surveillance discovered he returned to these areas, using an alias to book hotel rooms, and launder money by entering various foreign currency exchanges to swap carrier bags of cash into euros. On the following day, the subject was seen to meet up with a group of known drug dealers where money and heroin were swapped. The intelligence from the surveillance operation led to other locations where other hidden assets and further evidence was discovered. He was later convicted to 21 years imprisonment.

The investigative process

An investigation generally follows eight stages, initially outlined in the UK Chief Officer Core Investigative Doctrine 2005 (ACPO, 2012). This model has stayed constant over time and continues to be endorsed by the UK College of Policing. A schematic illustration is shown below (see figure 6.1).

The rules of engagement

A criminal investigation entails a search for the truth. To try and prevent the submission of poor quality evidence, which can lead to a false conviction, all investigations take place within a legal and procedural framework. These frameworks may differ across international jurisdictions. The Criminal Justice System in the UK uses an adversarial approach which places the responsibility on the prosecution team to prove the suspect committed the offence

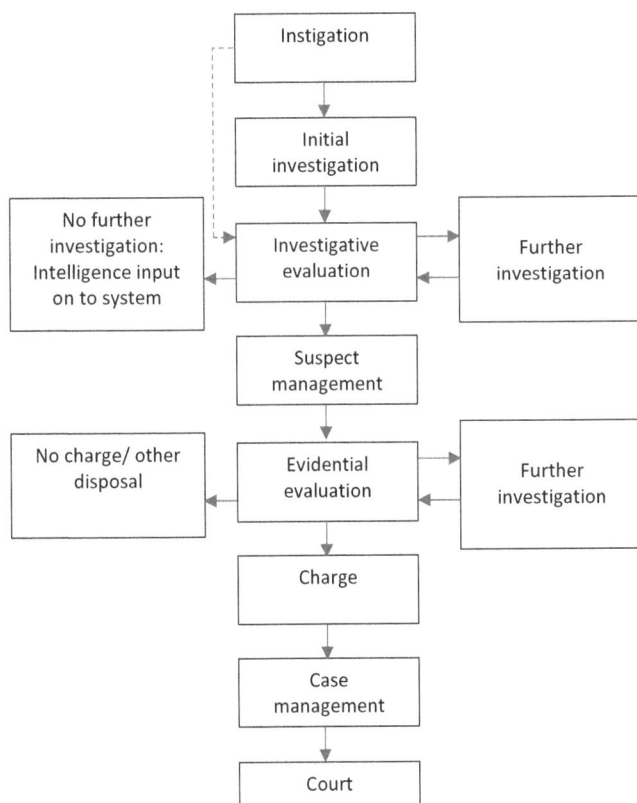

Figure 6.1 The investigation process
ACPO 2012; 2006

'beyond reasonable doubt'. This is a much higher level of proof than is found in civil court which requires guilt to be proven on the 'balance of probability'. In an adversarial system the police are asked to disclose their evidence to the defence team who can examine it before deciding whether to bring any information to refute the charge. This system differs to inquisitorial systems, seen across many other European countries, where a prosecutor or judge leads the investigation and calls witnesses in an effort to establish the truth.

A constant trade off takes place with any investigation, as lawful and procedural constraints encounter resource constraints. In the UK the Prosecution of Offences Act and Criminal Justice Act 2003 passed responsibility from the Police to the Crown Prosecution Service to decide who should be prosecuted and for what offence. In 1996 the Criminal Procedure and Investigation Act (CPIA) was introduced to define criminal investigation and the role of the investigator. It introduced a statutory disclosure process which placed a responsibility on the prosecution to reveal to the defence any relevant information which may be of material benefit to the suspect. However perhaps the most important legislation in relation to intelligence was the Regulation of Investigatory Powers Act 2000, often abbreviated as RIPA. This defined the process of covert investigation and placed it within a regulatory framework. It is important that the analyst understands the rules and procedures to be followed in an investigation, so these constraints are not breached. In this way investigators categorise information on its relevancy, reliability and admissibility (Stelfox, 2009; ACPO, 2006; ACPO, 2005). The next sections will look more closely at the types of information that assist in the investigation.

Section 2: Passive data sources

Whilst Chapter 2 described the diversity of intelligence sources, this section seeks to illustrate how these sources can be used in investigations. The use of passive intelligence sources has been of particular benefit and has been particularly effective in 'no body' murders. An example was in 2005, when David Guilfoyle went missing in Lancashire and murder was suspected. The interrogation of passive intelligence sources following his disappearance showed he had not: attended appointments; travelled abroad; spent or collected money; paid for food; phoned business colleagues or friends; or been admitted to hospital. This was sufficient to convince the investigators that he was dead and further enquiries led to a suspect being charged with his murder. Whilst the suspect thought he could not be convicted in the absence of a body, the jury were satisfied that the victim was dead, and the suspect had killed him. In 2012, many years after his conviction, the offender admitted his guilt and informed officers where the body was. The rest of this section will examine different types of passive data and explore how they can be used in an investigation.

Financial transactions

At the end of 2017, UK consumers made 13.2 billion debit card payments compared to 13.1 billion cash payments (UK Finance, 2018). The vast majority of people who own assets have both a bank account and a financial profile. All banks and financial institutions keep records to increase their profitability, reduce fraud, maintain their reputation and assist in the running of their business. Specifically, service organisations record information to:

1   Generate an invoice for payment.
2   Obtain payment (credit card or Bank mandate).
3   Deliver their goods or services.
4   Provide credit.
5   Collect information and use it for marketing.
6   Manage loyalty schemes.

Data obtained from financial and suppliers has historically been used to link people with particular items of property (i.e. they have purchased a boat or an expensive item of property). However more creative opportunities exist, for example, enquiries at a men's outfitters can provide information in relation to the size of a suspect (height, build and shoe size). It could also help in understanding whether the person owns shoes or clothes which coincide with a shoe pattern or fibres found at the scene. Much of this information can be detailed and comprise details even close acquaintances are unaware of. Identifying individual purchases exactly when they are bought provides lifestyle information. It reveals when people are most active and how they like to spend their time, providing insight in relation to their friends, enemies and even their pets. It can even provide clues as to others who were in their immediate vicinity, either when they were being victimised or engaged in offending. Locations of where the person used a debit or credit card can provide help in knowing what CCTV cameras should be checked, or whether they were in the vicinity of the crime. In summary, financial transactions can provide information relating to offenders, victims, witnesses and locations, incorporating information about assets and specific possessions, lifestyle, networks, location, and movements.

As well as commercial organisations there are other public sector agencies who hold information. These have their own guidelines for accessing information and in the UK include:

- Companies House.
- Local Authorities.
- The Department for Work and Pensions (DWP).
- The Land Registry.
- Her Majesty's Revenue and Customs.
- The United Kingdom Identity and Passport Service (IPS).

There also exist credit reference databases which allow authorised officers to examine the financial status of an individual. UK based companies include Experian, Equifax, and Call Credit, whilst the firm Dunn and Bradstreet can also provide information on such things as companies, company directors and their earnings, trading addresses, and disqualified directors. Further, CIFAS (UK's fraud prevention service) has information on multiple credit applications which are thought to be fraudulent.

CCTV

The use of CCTV has proliferated since the 1990s and its use is multi-faceted. Whilst it is used to identify the offender, it can also be used to provide alibis, by showing the suspect was somewhere else. It can also be used to persuade offenders to plead guilty and save distress to witnesses, or retain offenders in custody when they might otherwise have been bailed. CCTV often serves as a significant element of intelligence in an investigation.

There are numerous high-profile examples. In July 2005, the viewing of thousands of hours of video recordings by an intelligence analyst was critical in establishing Ramzi Mohammed, and associates, entering the London underground and failing in an attempt to detonate a bomb. A further case, in April 2010, involved a 17 year old student called Aamir Siddiqi who, on answering his door, was set upon by two men who stabbed and killed him. It transpired that Richards and Hope had been paid to kill another person and had gone to the wrong house in Cardiff. CCTV played an important role in piecing together the movements of the two offenders both before and after the crime, leading to a conviction of 40 years imprisonment (Phagura, 2012). A further example relates to the search for 5 year old April Jones in 2013. Even though the body was never found, the use of CCTV pictures was widely broadcast, which assisted in disproving a suspects' account and helping secure a conviction for murder. Even when CCTV images are insufficient to provide evidence they can provide further clues, such as suggesting where a suspect was standing to identify a search area for forensic evidence.

Whilst CCTV evidence may be available it doesn't mean to say it is used effectively. In May 2004 Kate Sheedy was knocked down by the serial killer Levi Bellfield, although it was years later when he was convicted of her attempted murder. This is because the police failed to examine the CCTV footage which would have proved his guilt; they later apologised for their error. Increasingly major investigations use dedicated teams for CCTV management – identifying relevant cameras, seizing content, viewing, recording relevant information, and ensuring evidential protocols for the processing of information are followed. It has been estimated that from a sample of 100 crime scenes, DNA would generate (on average) 2.27 detections, whilst fingerprints would lead to 3.29 detections. This means, using these techniques, a Crime Scene Investigator would obtain a detection every three days. Whilst no similar study exists for CCTV, it is felt the approach would reproduce similar levels of performance (Stelfox, 2007).

ANPR

The increase in mobility and technology has allowed CCTV to be adapted to provide automatic number plate recognition (ANPR). This can be used from static sites (i.e. petrol stations) or from mobile units (i.e. situated in vehicles), and is operated by the police, as well as other government agencies (i.e. Highways Agency) and commercial organisations (shopping centres, car parks). An ANPR camera can read the registered plate of about 3,600 vehicles per hour and provide the registered keeper details. It is also able to search the plate against local and national police and insurance databases within two seconds, being able to store the digitised image for further analysis. Whilst it captures the movements of a vehicle, rather than the person driving it, it can help:

- Identify vehicles being used to commit crime.
- Research the movements of possible suspects.
- Identify witnesses.
- Research the movements of a victim's vehicle and assist with victimology.
- Research an alibi.
- Research the movements of a target.
- Locate a vehicle and its movements for a future surveillance operation.
- Assist in a trigger or arrest plan.

ANPR intelligence can be used innovatively, and the following examples of analysis were gathered by Kirby and Turner (2007).

- *Vehicle pattern analysis:* During November 2005 Police Constable Sharon Beshenivsky was fatally shot when responding to a robbery. A witness highlighted the description of a specific vehicle and a subsequent check of the ANPR database identified this vehicle and its movement in the area before and after the incident. It was also found to be associated with other vehicles used by other suspects during the offence.
- *Geographic analysis:* Once a vehicle location is mapped it can be compared against crimes within the area, possibly correlating with a crime hotspot or being close to the scene of a serious crime. This specific technique was used to examine three armed robberies taking place in nearby towns over a three-day period. Whilst 40,000 vehicles were recorded in the area, only two were found close to all three robberies, subsequently leading to the identification of the suspects.
- *Location time analysis* can be used to assist identify stolen or cloned vehicles. For example, if ANPR identifies identical vehicles during the

same morning in Penzance and Carlisle (459 miles apart), it is likely one of the vehicles is bearing an illegal plate.

- *Sequential pattern analysis* has been used to examine the movement of a murder suspect. For example, if a vehicle normally passes through three static ANPR cameras between 7am and 8am Monday to Friday and doesn't on the day of the murder, this is worthy of further investigation.
- *Post incident analysis:* An example of this involved a serious 'road rage' incident, which took place at Heathrow Airport. Following the assault, the nearby witnesses reported seeing a 'people carrier' type vehicle. ANPR data immediately before and after the assault showed the suspect vehicle registration mark, together with other vehicles in the vicinity. This not only resulted in the quick arrest of the suspect but identified witnesses (in other vehicles close to the scene) who could describe what occurred.
- *Convoy analysis* is used to identify vehicles that may be travelling together in the commission of a crime. One example involves six burglaries where the offenders stole the keys of high-performance vehicles and used them to drive the vehicles away. ANPR analysis showed three of the stolen vehicles used a particular route to leave the county. The analysis then examined whether any accompanying vehicles were present, five minutes before and five minutes after the stolen vehicles were seen. On these three occasions a specific vehicle was seen to be travelling in the same direction within one minute and was also found to be in the vicinity of the other three burglaries. The analysts suggested the vehicle was being used as transportation for the burglars and following a further burglary, police officers were deployed to the registered owner's address. He was later arrested, and two other stolen vehicles were found.

Telecommunications data

Communications data is gathered by service providers for the purposes of charging and monitoring the use of the network. If the phone belonging to a suspect is identified, their communications data can be highly valuable to the police. Even though the content of the communication is not disclosed, it can help identify who communicates with each other. It can also identify when, where, and what time the phone was used. The analysis of communications data has become significant within the intelligence arena. Intelligence gained through smart phones is becoming increasingly rich and supports 'big data' analysis (see Chapter 8). Whilst smart phones contain details of calls that will be time and date stamped they may be geo-tagged, via a variety of social media apps. As social media grows and smart phones are used as personal computers, the potential for intelligence is expected to continue.

Suspicious Activity Reports (Elmer database)

The Proceeds of Crime Act 2002 (Part 7), together with the Terrorism Act 2000 dictates those in the regulated sector are to submit a Suspicious Activity Report (SAR), if they know or suspect a person is engaged in terrorist financing or money laundering. Whist there has been criticism that these reports aren't sufficiently scrutinised, the National Crime Agency state that SARs intelligence has been critical in 'locating sex offenders, tracing murder suspects, identifying subjects suspected of being involved in watching indecent footage of children online and showing the movement of young women being trafficked into the UK to work in the sex industry'. They also assist in providing intelligence to the UK's strategic threat assessment to identify new trends either at a geographic level or in relation to a particular theme. At a tactical level, multiple SARs relating to the same individual or company can identify new targets for cash seizures or confiscation orders. They can also provide information regarding assets, bank details and aliases that can assist current investigations or form the impetus to instigate new ones. These reports are open to checks by police forces who have access to the Elmer database, which is provided for this purpose.

Terrorism Act passenger data

The increased availability of data about international travel generates the opportunity to detect crime, which often involves cross border activity. Schedule 7 (paragraph 17) of the Terrorism Act 2000 provides a power for an examining officer to apply to the owners of specified ships or aircraft in writing for details of passengers, crew or cargo. This must be supplied as soon as reasonably practicable.

Accessing different forms of data

These examples show that passive data is helpful when investigating crime, however gathering such information is not always straightforward. First there is the challenge of identifying who has possession of the information and secondly, it must be legitimately obtained, so that it can be used in the investigation. Identifying the owner of the information has become more problematic since the increase of consumer choice. For example, in September 2019, Ofgem (UK) disclosed there were 61 active gas and electricity suppliers. This ability to change service providers, whether it be insurance, banks or network provider has led to outsourcing, in the form of call centres, customer care, servicing and marketing. For example, Tesco outsource their mobile phone service to O2 (except in Hungary where they use Vodafone and in Ireland where they use '3'). This process can create complications in knowing who is authorised to release information.

Authorisation to release information is governed by legal procedure. The main principle is that owners of passive data are obligated to provide information when it assists in the investigation of crime, however this must be compliant with human rights. For example, the Proceeds of Crime Act 2002 can only generate orders which relate to the seizure or confiscation of assets, or money laundering investigations. A wider power is when the investigator requests personal data under provisions of the Data Protection Act 1998. However, this can only be released if the information is required for:

- The prevention or detection of crime;
- The apprehension or prosecution of offenders (section 29 (3)); or
- For reasons of national security (section 28) to the extent that non-disclosure of the requested information would be likely to prejudice one or more of those same purposes.

In relation to requests for information from banks and other financial institutions the information is categorised into open and closed data and can be obtained with a court production order. Information will usually be divulged to a financial investigator if one or more of the following criteria are met:

- Where disclosure is compulsory by law;
- Where there is a duty to the public to disclose;
- Where the interests of the bank require disclosure;
- Where the disclosure is made by the express or implied consent of the customer.

Communications data (telephone subscribers, itemised billing etc.) and electronically encrypted data (passwords, access codes etc.), can be obtained with the appropriate RIPA authorisation. Communications data is defined in section 21 of RIPA 'as any traffic data comprised in or attached to a communication'. This does not provide the content but information concerning how and when the information is delivered. Passive data, which is not covert, falls outside the directed surveillance definition.

In summary this section has started to illustrate the enormous potential of desk-based investigation. The power of open source information has recently been shown in investigative journalism, specifically the Salisbury poisoning case where Sergei Skripal a former Russian intelligence officer, and his daughter, were poisoned with Novichok. A group of investigative journalists, including Eliot Higgins, who use the web name 'Bellingcat', poured over the wealth of available information. A corrupt Russian market has made it possible to get public access to car registrations, telephone information and passport photographs. Using a photograph of the suspect released by the UK authorities the journalist traced one of the suspects to a military academy, from which they found his real identity. This and other recent examples suggest that new opportunities are now possible within police analysis, if sufficient emphasis and investment is placed into open source innovation.

Section 3: The behavioural sciences

Science has provided considerable assistance to the investigation of crime, from the early days of fingerprinting to the more advanced techniques of DNA analysis. However significant research has also been invested in behavioural sciences, especially in relation to offender behaviour and management. This section provides further detail on how a small number of these intelligence innovations have been used.

Offender profiling

Since the 1970s offender profiling has emerged as a widespread intelligence tool to assist reactive and proactive investigations. As highlighted in Chapter 2, this technique examines crime scene behaviour and uses that information to draw conclusions as to the offender's characteristics and background. In the UK there are a cadre of accredited Behavioural Investigative Advisors (BIAs), who have professional experience in this field. The main reasons for using the approach is to reduce the list of suspects (i.e. by age or geographic location) or by proposing new avenues for investigators to explore. However, history shows caution is needed in the use of this information. Pioneered by the FBI Behavioral Science Unit (BSU), who based their analysis on the interviewing of 36 incarcerated murderers, they said that murderers could be categorised into organised and disorganised killers. However, this typology was later tested by Canter et al. (2004) who found this dichotomy could not be verified in an operational setting.

Investigators (and analysts) when using such advice therefore need to know the methodology and expertise that the profiler bases his/her opinion on. Offender profiles, unlike other intelligence products, are not graded in terms of accuracy, therefore it is important to understand their efficacy. This was highlighted in the UK when Rachel Nickell was brutally attacked on Wimbledon Common. The Metropolitan Police turned to a clinical psychologist, Paul Britton, whose analysis played a significant part in linking Colin Stagg to the subsequent profile. The Police asked him for further advice when deploying a female undercover police officer to approach Mr Stagg. Whilst the suspect never admitted any involvement he was charged with the offence and remained in custody for 13 months whilst awaiting trial. The case was dismissed by the judge who was extremely critical of police action. Some 16 years later Robert Napper, a man with a history of violent and sexual attacks on young women, pleaded guilty to the killing, due to the finding of DNA evidence. Although he was flagged to the police on a number of occasions, these investigative opportunities were missed, and Napper went on to kill another woman and her four-year-old daughter a year after the Wimbledon attack. The failing in relation to Colin Stagg case was commented upon by Ormerod and Sturman (2005), who highlighted three police failures. First, the Criminal Procedures and Investigations Act 1996 (CPIA) stipulates the crime (and not the offender) should be investigated; meaning there is also an obligation to also examine information that disproves a suspect's involvement. In this particular case a specific suspect was pursued in an effort to obtain a confession and the investigators exhibited clear confirmation bias. Secondly, the profile can only suggest the type of person who could be associated with the crime. This means that there are people who fit the profile who won't have committed it and people who didn't fit the profile who could possibly have done it. As the prosecution must prove the case beyond reasonable doubt an offender profile is not sufficiently rigorous to identify the offender. Finally, for a finding to be admitted as scientific evidence it must be generally accepted in the scientific community, a standard which has not been reached by offender profiling. All these factors mean that offender profiles can only be used for intelligence purposes and not for evidence, a finding supported by similar cases in the USA.

Notwithstanding these criticisms, it is also accurate to say the work on offender profiling has improved significantly since the early days of research. Many universities across the UK run specialist post graduate courses on investigative psychology and the staff who run these courses also conduct their own research and supervise doctoral students. As such research has been conducted on large databases of offenders and this information has been tested against psychological principles to provide excellent insights. This increased use of applied psychology has improved intelligence analysis, as the next section shows.

The journey to crime

Canter (2007) has argued that the most objective and observable aspect of any crime is where it occurs. The criminogenic nature of place was highlighted far back by Shaw and McKay (1942) who pointed out that crime was most frequent in 'zones of transition'. This suggested inner city areas, which experience constantly changing and diverse residents, experience crime as a natural by-product of economic deprivation and poor social cohesion. Houchin (2005) looked at the Scottish male prison population on one date in 2003 and found that a quarter of the prison population lived in just 53 of the 1,232 (4%) local government wards (cited in Bottoms 2012:561). Therefore, the offender studies show very clearly that crime is patterned according to the environment and where offenders, especially persistent offenders, live. Further, as discussed in the previous chapter, Brantingham and Brantingham (1984) explained, through Crime Pattern theory, that crime follows the natural mobility patterns surrounding individual bases. These nodes, which include home, work and leisure bases are areas where the crime is more likely to take place, as are the pathways between these nodes.

These ideas have been extended by others including Canter and Youngs (2009), who summarise the geographic principles influencing offence locations. Offence distribution reflects an offenders' internal map as locations are associated with individual life stories and a personal 'narrative'. Understanding the processes that take an offender to a given location can be used to assist with investigative strategies. Perhaps the most important finding in criminal psychogeography is 'propinquity' which relates to the spatial proximity of the offending in relation to an offender base (generally the offender's residence). The discussion about how individuals make their 'journey to crime' argues that general offenders have an optimal range of offending and commit crimes close to their home or other base (Rossmo, 2000), despite the many and varied opportunities available to them (see Repetto, 1974). Wiles and Costello (2000), who interviewed acquisitive crime offenders, discovered that even when they committed offences further afield from their home base, these decisions were influenced by acquaintances they had in that area. They also found that whilst conscious choices influenced location choice (i.e. staying away from places where they think they will be recognised or offending in places where targets are more available), there will also be subconscious underlying patterns. These can be influenced by the perceived level of security and the amount of time spent in a specific area.

Distance decay explains that the further an offender strays from their base, the less likely they are to commit an offence. This is due to a number of factors, which includes their desire to offend in familiar areas and areas they feel safe in. Travel is also affected by a buffer or safety zone which relates to the minimum distance they will travel from home before they feel they can safely offend (i.e. won't be easily identified). In this Phillips (1980) found offending did not occur within half a mile of their home for fear of being recognised. Wiles and Costello (2000) found, on average, offenders travel 1.93m from their home to commit a crime. So, each offender has an offending range, between their shortest distance and the longest distance they are willing to travel to commit crime. Individual patterns can vary for a number of reasons. For example, some studies show older offenders travel further. Offender resources are also a factor, as an offender who targets a particular victim may have to travel further. Other influences include mental buffers, which involve emotional or physical cues. Examples include significant boundaries such as rivers, main roads, or parks, which can influence the offenders mental map of the area and unconsciously reduce the chance of them crossing those borders to offend (Canter, 2007). Temporal buffers are also observed as serial offenders often stay away from their most recent offence. Using this information, a useful method for analysts is to draw a circle connecting the two offences furthest away from each other, as the offender is likely to have their base within this area (Canter & Gregory, 1994). This has become known as the circle or marauder hypothesis and a number of studies across various offence categories show this occurs with a high degree of probability. Rossmo (2000) has stated that the offence and body dump sites of serial killers can be associated with the circle hypothesis. However, another type of offending pattern can also appear. This is seen if the offender legitimately travels to a specific area of population density (i.e. for work or to find a specific type of victim). This is referred to as the windscreen model and the plotting of crimes shows a cluster pattern around a specific location. Like other elements of behavioural science, it should be accepted this type of research does not tell the investigator exactly where the offender lives, although it provides a systematic way to prioritise suspects or enquiries.

Section 3: Investigative analysis techniques

So far, this chapter has provided both theory and other material to help analysts use intelligence to identify offender characteristics. As with the last chapter this section proposes some specific techniques that can be used by analysts to illustrate connections and patterns in the data. Often within investigations the plethora of information can generate ambiguity or inconsistency. Visually portrayed information can be used to communicate information much more clearly. Analysts can assist by showing emerging trends in relation to certain types of criminal behaviour; the locations in which those offences occur (hot spots); the links between incidents and offenders; and the common characteristics across crimes. There are a number of core intelligence techniques and products that can assist investigators in this approach.

Technique 1: Analysts thinking like investigators

Stelfox (2009) argues it is important that those engaged in the investigation of crime have an investigative mindset. In this he specifically highlights the 5WH acronym – who, what, where, when, why and how, as a useful template to evaluate what is known and unknown in the investigation. This tool, which can be supported by the use of hypothesis testing, is set out in Table 6.1.

Technique 2: Sequence of events analysis

Establishing what occurs, and when it occurs, can be conducted using sequence of events analysis. This should be established in the early stages of an investigation to illustrate how events have unfolded and the relationship between different occurrences and the involvement of individuals. By detailing the information in this way, it assists hypothesis testing and highlights gaps in knowledge, thereby directing further intelligence gathering.

Sequence of events analysis can be displayed as a simple timed narrative or illustrated in an event chart. If the latter is used this should be clear and

Table 6.1 5WH analysis (Who, What, When, Where, Why and How)

5WH categories	What is known	What is not known
Who: Can the main individuals be identified? This involves establishing who the victim(s), witnesses, suspect(s) and associates are. If a specific identification cannot be made are there details, for example a description, which can assist in saying who they are, or linking them with the behaviour of another individual highlighted in the case. Further can this specific behaviour or these characteristics point to a specific individual?		
What: Can it be explained what has happened both immediately before, during and immediately after the crime has occurred.		
Where: Is it clear where the crime took place. Have any other locations which facilitate the offence commission, either immediately before (i.e. preparation), or immediately after (evidence disposal) been identified? Does it appear that the locations have been chosen or are random? How important is that location to the commission of the offence – does it house a particularly desirable or vulnerable individual or group? Has the location been victimised previously?		
When: How did the actions take place over time. Analysts can make particular use of timelines to organise the chronology of what took place. This is particularly useful in establishing clarity, to understand the logistics surrounding the offence and to make sense of ambiguous, inaccurate or conflicting information.		
Why: What was the motivation to commit this type of offence. Why did it happen at this specific location, involving this particular victim, at this particular time?		
How: This question requires deeper analysis than the *what* question. It provides further detail by establishing what skill or expert knowledge was used by the offender. For example, did the offender have to gain entry by some sort of deception, or was the offence committed by bypassing security measures such as alarms or CCTV?		

accurate as well as being simple and to the point. Particular events should be captured through the use of specific symbols (i.e. circles/rectangles) with short descriptions. Connecting lines indicate the relationship between these events, with arrows showing the time flow. Throughout, the date and time of the event is associated with its description (UNODC, 2011). Currently computer software packages allow these complex charts to be designed, whereby the horizontal scale (x) is used to depict time and the vertical scale (y) can be divided into specific themes, depicting people, vehicles or telephones.

Technique 3: (Crime) pattern analysis and GIS

Whilst pattern analysis can emerge in many forms including graphs and tables, one of the most common ways has been through GIS (geographic information systems). This approach has been discussed in previous chapters. It is important in the detection of crime as plotting specific offences can provide significant insight such as indicating the most likely area a serial offender will be based. Similarly, it can also be illuminating in a single offence of homicide to plot all relevant locations, i.e. victim base, murder scene, and any disposition sites (body/weapon/vehicle). This can show offender mobility patterns and suggest possible residential base.

Technique 4: Comparative case analysis (CCA)

When a series of offences take place, it is useful to establish if any (or all) are committed by the same offender or group of offenders. Linking crimes has a number of benefits as it helps focus resources and allows evidence and clues to be pooled, thereby assisting in the suspect search. To undertake comparative case analysis a simple matrix (offence variables across the top and individual cases down the side) can be designed. Variables can include description and characteristics of the offender/victim/location as well as the behaviour during the offence (i.e. modus operandi), and forensic evidence. A simple content analysis indicating whether these variables are present or absent shows the similarity or differences between each case. It is important the analyst does not just seek to prove the connection and is aware of the heuristics and biases mentioned earlier. The analyst must also be aware that the dynamics of a specific offence may change offender behaviour in some way. For example, if a victim is particularly aggressive in defending themselves, the offender may also increase their level of violence to subdue the victim. In the short example below (an actual CCA would be conducted using many variables), cases 1 and 2 appear similar. The fact that an isolated area is chosen indicates the offender is targeting this type of location, supported by the offender leaving the scene in the same direction as he arrived.

Table 6.2 Comparative case analysis example

	Female victim	Urban location	Isolated area	Spoke to victim prior to attack	Blitz attack	Left in same direction as approach
Case 1	x		x	x		x
Case 2	x		x	x		x
Case 3	x	x			x	

Technique 5: Hypothesis testing

The development of a working hypothesis is crucial in the investigation of crime. Already discussed in Chapter 4 it is useful to comment on this approach again as it can test the relevance of existing information and direct the search for further information. When conducting this process it is important that biases do not affect judgement. A renowned example, which illustrates confirmation bias in hypothesis testing, is the 2–4–6 game. If you were presented with these specific three numbers and asked to a) choose the next number and b) guess the rule that governs the three-number sequence, what would you propose? Peter Wason (1960) found only 21% of people were accurate, a finding which has been consistently replicated. Many suggest the next number is 8 and when informed this is correct are confident to propose the underlying rule is an increase of 2. Unfortunately, this is not the rule, indeed the correct rule simply states the numbers increase in ascending order (not that they increase consistently by 2), so the number 8 was correct but not because of the reason most people think. This is relevant to hypothesis testing because we have a bias towards confirming, rather than disconfirming, our hypothesis.

A technique known as the analysis of competing hypotheses (ACH) (Heuer, 1999) can be used to provide a more objective approach to hypothesis testing and reduce common cognitive biases. It also provides an audit trail which lists previous considerations and conclusions. Whilst the early stages would probably be conducted by a single analyst, a longer-term investigation, which generates numerous hypotheses, can benefit from a number of analysts working together as a group. This assists in ensuring all the information is systematically considered, as well as preventing anything that can assist, or derail the investigation, being missed. It also helps make sure that any possibilities are considered as a whole, rather than being considered in isolation.

The way in which ACH is conducted is with a simple matrix. The hypotheses are written across the top and along the side is listed any relevant evidence to be factored into the evaluation. As well as known facts and assumptions being included it should also highlight missing factors (i.e. no forensic evidence on the weapon) which can be used to negate particular hypotheses. The analyst(s) should then ask the question: 'If this hypothesis were true, how likely would this evidence be?' A score is then assigned for each piece of information and totalled for each hypothesis. As with any type of comparative analysis, if a particular piece of information is consistent with all the hypotheses then it does not serve to differentiate and should be withdrawn. When the analysts have reduced the number of likely hypotheses, they should consider how strong their lead hypothesis is and whether or not the judgement would still stand if items of evidence were incorrect. They should then use their conclusions to improve their analytical assessment and determine what information needs to be developed further. Recently Dhami et al.

(2019) conducted an evaluation of ACH, using 50 analysts some of which used the specific matrix and some who did not (allocated randomly). The study found mixed evidence for the ability of the model to reduce confirmation bias, although the study also pointed out not all analysts adhered completely to the procedures.

Technique 6: Generating and evaluating scenarios

Scenario planning assists the analyst in objectively considering the implications of particular actions and can also be used in crime reduction initiatives. This provides decision makers with a transparent process to consider the impact of contingencies and provide evidence to support their predictions. In this process the analyst can also flag factors which can serve as early warning signs of a particular phenomenon occurring. Scenario planning is particularly useful when a range of potential decisions exist. One actual case, involving one of the authors, relates to a series of aggravated burglaries (burglary involving weapons), on large pub/restaurants, with the premises being attacked shortly after closing time on busy weekends. Four offenders were committing these offences and the investigators initially found minor evidence in relation to two of them. The dilemma was whether to arrest the two offenders or to continue the investigation in the hope of harvesting more evidence. The scenario planning explored issues such as evidence being found/ disposed of, offences continuing, offenders being warned/displaced. Of course, the complexity of some situations makes it difficult to establish all scenarios, although systematically highlighting the most obvious routes and implications allows a logical decision to be made. In this case it was to arrest the offenders and during the searches of the premises additional evidence was found which resulted in their later convictions.

There are other approaches which generate more sophisticated techniques around scenario planning. These methods involve: quadrant crunching, force field analysis, cone of plausibility, red teaming and backcasting. An example of quadrant crunching, as shown below, uses the 5WH technique to break down different factors. This example, adapted from a CoP example discloses a prominent protestor is due to be released from prison, immediately prior to a high-profile event taking place. He is known to engage in illegal protest as well as engaging in and inciting others to commit violence. If he is released and other protestors are willing to travel, then a protest may occur, however, if he is kept in prison and other protestors are not willing to travel, it is less likely that a protest will occur. Figure 6.2 shows how this would be set out.

A further technique, force field analysis, emanated from the social psychologist Kurt Lewin (1951), who argued that behaviour (of an organisation or individual) is affected by numerous factors. The strength of any particular factor at any particular time will influence their movement in a particular direction. This process therefore identifies and evaluates the power of these

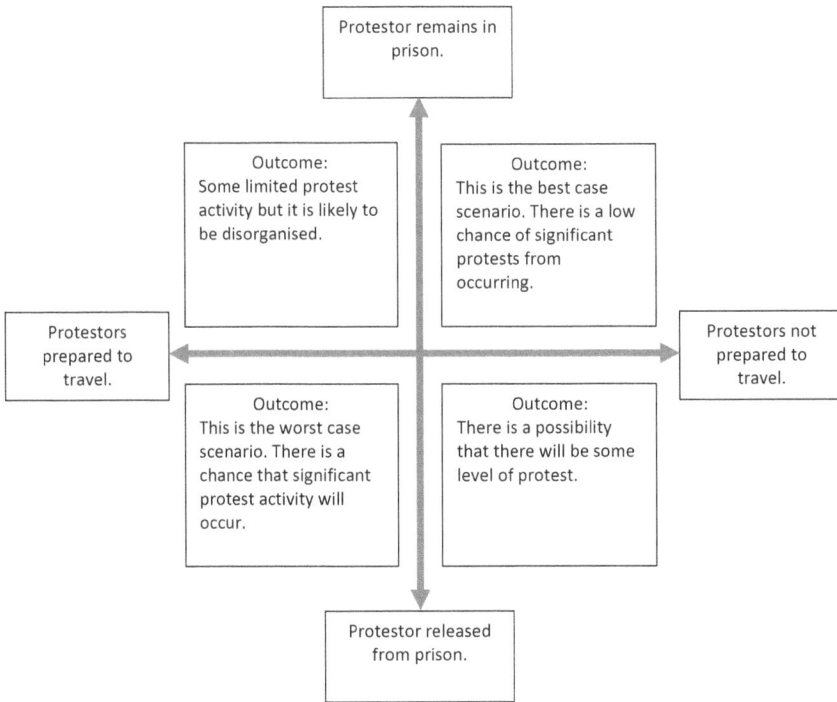

Figure 6.2 Quadrant crunching diagram
Adapted from the College of Policing, 2020

factors and establishes whether a particular intervention is likely to stabilise or destabilise this movement. As specific interventions are implemented, the process can be updated to establish the current status and consider what drivers are now serving as the greatest influence. In practice the key drivers should be considered in turn and assigned scores (i.e. 1 weakest and 5 strongest).

The final three techniques in scenario planning are as follows. The first is the cone of plausibility, which generates the most plausible scenarios at a specific time or following a specific intervention. This emphasis on plausibility assists credibility when the analyst presents the results. The red teaming technique requires the analyst putting themselves into the shoes of the suspect (or group) to consider the threat from this perspective. It requires in-depth knowledge of the group and the ability to generate specific questions (i.e. how I would respond if I were the principal offender? What would my immediate priorities be? What would my immediate concerns be? And how would I respond to them?). Using an offender perspective can provide greater insight and fill intelligence gaps. Finally, an evaluation technique to consider is backcasting, which is helpful when a particular scenario is expected, and measures are put in place to mitigate the threat. The analyst is asked to think about specific likely outcomes and the timeframes in which they occur. A timeline is then set out based on the expected key events, together with the assumptions underpinning them. Using this method potential precursor events can be highlighted, which provide pinch points to assess their plausibility and methods to reduce their occurrence.

Technique 7: Network and social network analysis

During a criminal investigation many people, locations, organisations, buildings, vehicles and events are identified. One of the tasks for the analyst may be to establish whether these people, or other factors, are connected, and if so, how? For example, in an Organised Crime Group (OCG) questions may include: who are the principal and peripheral offenders? Who launders the money; what premises do they operate from; which port do they use to export their products? Or, the questions could surround a murder investigation, for example to ascertain whom a suspect has been in contact with, and what premises and locations they visit.

Network analysis utilises any data pertaining to a network, be it an IT network, a telecommunications network, railroad network, or social network. It highlights network nodes and the existence or absence of links between them. It can show the association between such things as people, groups, vehicles, companies, addresses, and communications data, showing hierarchies, levels of contact, and levels of influence. As well as showing criminal associations it can illustrate the suspect's associations and interests outside of crime. This information can build a picture concerning where criminal proceeds are being disposed of or illustrate legitimate elements of their business. Whilst these links can be evidence in themselves, they can also establish intelligence gaps, or show where opportunities can be exploited, to obtain evidence or disrupt criminal behaviour.

Social networks analysis (SNA) is slightly different, in that the nodes being examined relate exclusively to people (individuals, teams or organisations). Examples of current social networks might involve Facebook, Twitter, an organisation's formal email network, or even informal networks that take place (e.g. those who meet in the canteen for lunch). However, in a law enforcement setting social network analysis can help develop an understanding of criminal networks, methods of targeting these groups and the management of post-police activity within the network, i.e. how policing impacts on the network and how the network might respond (Burcher & Whelan, 2018). Social network analysis is a quantitative sociological approach. It provides the means to visualise large amounts of data, and through statistical measures uncovers the roles of actors in a network (Freeman, 2004; Klerks, 2002). Contacts can be shown through phone calls, witness accounts (of meetings and conversations between individuals), and sightings through CCTV or ANPR. SNA is normally produced in three ways.

The first is an association chart (also known as link chart or network chart) produced manually by the analyst from available intelligence sources. A second approach is facilitated by computer software, with some well-known examples being Analyst's Notebook (IBM), Netmap, COPLINK or Link explorer. These generate a visual overview of the links and give an indication as to the density level. More recently other software development has been able to provide visual representation of interpersonal relations in group settings. This technique is also referred to as a sociogram, and as the process is based on mathematical computations it provides a more objective means to highlight core actors, structures and subgroups.

Eck and Clarke (2013) highlight three major concepts in identifying network positions, a) degree centrality, which relates to the role the node plays and whether this is critical to the network; b) closeness centrality, which refers to how physically close a node is to other actors, as well as their importance in facilitating tasks and moving resources across the network; and c) betweenness centrality, which relates to their role in connecting others. Ianni and Reuss-Ianni (1990) explain that network structure can establish whether the whole group is closely or loosely connected, whether they are open to other contacts or whether particular cliques or subgroups are evident. In this way network density can be divided into network, clique, and cluster. Their connectedness can be established by direct and indirect contacts between individual members. One of the operational benefits is that the analysis can show weak points in the network, which assists investigators make informed decisions about where to target their efforts. For instance, should they disrupt collaborations, or arrest those at the centre or on the periphery of the network?

Empirical studies in the field have described the benefits and concerns with social networks analysis. Bright (2015) and others argue SNA is crucial in identifying key offenders, particularly those who often seem invisible, such as brokers. Bright et al. (2017) also found targeting this role generated the most significant disruption. They argued that combining SNA with crime script analysis assists analysts to understand how resources are exchanged between co-offenders throughout the crime event (Bright et al., 2017). However, there are some limitations associated with the approach. Rostami and Mondani (2015) found that SNA results differed in terms of the number of nodes and centrality values, depending on the information source. They found surveillance information produced networks where the surveillance subjects had the highest centrality values, possibly caused through selection bias in the surveillance data. They deduced that multiple sources of information add more value to SNA as it reduces the level of bias. This view is supported by Campana (2016), who agrees selection bias can generate a network based upon the targets of an operation and can be misleading due to missing information. A review in relation to SNA use in police investigations was provided by the UK Home Office who trained analysts in its use and then invited them to analyse a Manchester based street gang (Gunnell et al., 2016). From a core group of five gang members the analysts highlighted connections with a further 137 individuals. The process was useful in identifying the crimes associated with the individuals, specifically drug related, and established an association between two gangs which previously had been missed (Gunnell et al., 2016). The practitioners were supportive of the approach as it allowed a more objective analytical process.

Conclusion

This chapter has demonstrated the importance of the analyst within the investigation of crime, especially serious crime. It has explained that rules (legislation and procedure) govern the way crimes are investigated, and therefore how information is harvested. Even with these constraints the information generated in an investigation can be enormous. A significant challenge for the analyst is to find patterns within this information and clarify the who, what, when, where, why, and how. This chapter has shown a variety of theories and techniques which explain how the interaction between offender, victim, place and time can be analysed.

The information and techniques outlined in this chapter have been used to successfully convict many offenders of serious crimes. However, analysts can only work with the information they are given and this can be flawed. This has less to do with the techniques, and more to do with flawed decision making (Nicol et al., 2004; Smith, 2003). Whilst this has been discussed previously it deserves to be commented upon again as analysts must be aware of human fallibility. An example relates to Milly Dowler, who was initially reported missing at 7pm on the 21 March 2002, when she didn't arrive home after school. Six months later her body was found some distance away, hidden in woodland. Levi Bellfield was convicted of her murder nine years later. When the case was reviewed, it was discovered the day before she went missing a man was reported trying to entice a 12-year-old schoolgirl into his red car. The police operator registered it as a suspicious incident and passed it to the local intelligence office, but neither highlighted it as significant to the investigation team. This was a significant mistake, as during that time Bellfield was living with his girlfriend close to the area and using her red car, which was reported stolen 24 hours after Milly went missing. A further failing was the officers conducting house to house enquiries knocked on Bellfield's door ten times but did not receive a response. When they finally obtained access, they found new tenants resident in the flat, but did not attempt to identify the previous occupants (Wright, 2008).

References

ACPO. (2005) *Major Incident Room Standardised Administrative Procedures (MIRSAP)*. Wyboston: NCPE.
ACPO. (2006) *Murder Investigation Manual*. Wyboston: NCPE.

ACPO. (2012) *Practice Advice on Core Investigative Doctrine* (2nd edn) London: NPIA.

Bottoms, A.E. (2012) *Developing Socio-Spatial Criminology.* In M. Maguire, R. Morgan, and R. Reiner (eds). *The Oxford Handbook of Criminology*, 5th edn. Oxford: Oxford University Press.

Brantingham, P.J. and Brantingham, P.L. (1984) *Patterns in Crime.* New York: MacMillan.

Bright, D.A. (2015) Identifying key actors in drug trafficking networks. In G. Bichler and A. Malm (eds). *Disrupting Criminal Networks: Network Analysis in Crime Prevention.* First Forum Press.

Bright, D., Greenhill, C., Britz, T., Ritter, A. and Morselli, C. (2017) Criminal network vulnerabilities and adaptations. *Global Crime*, 18 (4): 424–441.

Burcher, M and Whelan, C. (2018) Social network analysis as a tool for criminal intelligence: understanding its potential from the perspectives of intelligence analysts. *Trends in Organised Crime*, 21: 278–294.

Campana, P. (2016) Explaining criminal networks: Strategies and potential pitfalls. *Methodological Innovations*, 9. Available at: https://www.repository.cam.ac.uk/handle/1810/256297 [Accessed 13 September 2019].

Canter, D.V. (2007) *Mapping Murder: The Secrets of Geographical Profiling.* Virgin Books.

Canter, D., Alison, L.J., Alison, E. and Wentink, N. (2004) The organized/disorganized typologies of serial murder: myth or model? *Psychology, Public Policy and Law*, 10: 7–36.

Canter, D. and Gregory, A. (1994) Identifying the residential location of serial rapists. *Journal of the Forensic Science Society*, 34: 169–175.

Canter, D.V. and Youngs, D. (2009) *Investigative Psychology: Offender Profiling and the Analysis of Criminal Action.* Sussex (UK): John Wiley & Sons Ltd.

College of Policing. (2020) Delivering effective analysis. Available at https://www.app.college.police.uk/app-content/intelligence-management/analysis/delivering-effective-analysis/ [Accessed 13 April 2020].

Dhami, M.K., Belton, I.K. and Mandel, D.R. (2019) The 'analysis of competing hypotheses' in intelligence analysis. *Applied Cognitive Psychology*, 33 (6): 1–11.

Eck, J. and Clarke, R.V. (2013) Intelligence analysis for problem solvers. Available at https://popcenter.asu.edu/sites/default/files/library/reading/PDFs/Intell-Analysis-for-ProbSolvers.pdf [Accessed 6 January 2020].

Freeman, L.C. (2004) The development of social network analysis: a study in the sociology of science. *Administrative Science Quarterly*, 50 (1): 148–151.

Gunnell, D., Hillier, J. and Blakeborough, L. (2016) *Social Network Analysis of an Urban Street Gang Using Police Intelligence.* Data Research Report 89, London: Home Office.

Heuer, R.J. (1999) *Psychology of Intelligence Analysis.* Washington (DC): Center for the Study of Intelligence.

Houchin, R. (2005) *Social Exclusion and Imprisonment in Scotland.* Glasgow: Glasgow Caledonian University.

Ianni, F.A.J. and Reuss-Ianni, E. (1990) Network analysis in criminal intelligence analysis. In P. Andrews and M. Peterson (eds). *Criminal Intelligence Analysis.* Loomis (CA): Palmer Enterprises.

Kirby. S. and Penna, S. (2010) Policing mobile criminality: towards a situational crime prevention approach to organised crime. In K. Bullock, R.V. Clarke and N. Tilley (eds). *Situational Prevention of Organised Crimes.* Cullompton: Willan Publishing.

Kirby, S. and Turner, G. (2007) The use of ANPR in Major Crime Investigation. *Journal of Homicide and Major Incident Investigation*, 3 (2): 35–42.

Klerks, P. (2002) The network paradigm applied to criminal organisations: Theoretical nitpicking or a relevant doctrine for investigators? Recent developments in the Netherlands. *Connections*, 24 (3): 53–65.

Lewin, K. (1951) *Field Theory in Social Science: Selected Theoretical Papers*, (ed.) D. Cartwright. New York: Harper & Row.

Nicol, C., Innes, M., Gee, D. and Feist, A. (2004) *Reviewing Murder Investigations: An Analysis of Progress Reviews from Six Police Forces.* London: Home Office.

Ormerod, D. and Sturman, J. (2005) Working with the courts: advice for expert witnesses. In L. Alison (ed.). *The Forensic Psychologists Casebook: Psychological Profiling and Criminal Investigation.* Cullompton: Willan Publishing.

Phagura, S. (2012) Teenager 'battered to death on his doorstep by heroin addict hit-men who had got the wrong house'. *Daily Mail* [online] 12 September. Available at http:// www.dailymail.co.uk/news/article-2202167/Aamir-Siddiqi-Teenager-battered-dea th-doorstep-heroin-addict-hitmen-wrong- house.html#ixzz2mQc26Hwl [Accessed 5 September 2019].

Phillips, P.D. (1980) Characteristics and typology of the journey to crime. In D.E. Georges-Abeyie and K.E. Harries (eds). *Crime: A Spatial Perspective.* New York: Columbia University Press.

Repetto, T.A. (1974) *Residential Crime.* Cambridge (MA): Ballinger.

Rossmo, D.K. (2000) *Geographic Profiling.* Boca Raton, FL: CRC Press.

Rostami, A. and Mondani, H. (2015) The complexity of crime network data: A case study of its consequences for crime control and the study of networks. *PLoS ONE*, 10 (3): 1–20. Available at https://doi.org/10.1371/journal.pone.0119309 [Accessed 11 November 2019].

Shaw, C. and McKay, M. (1942) *Juvenile Delinquency and Urban Areas.* Chicago: University of Chicago Press.

Smith, Dame J. (2003) *The Shipman Inquiry, Second Report: The Police Investigation of March 1988.* London: HMSO.

Stelfox, P. (2007) Foreword. *The Journal of Homicide and Major Incident Investigation*, 3 (2), Wyboston: NPIA.

Stelfox, P. (2009) *Criminal Investigation: An Introduction to Principles and Practice.* Cullompton: Willan Publishing.

UK Finance. (2018) Convenience of debit card payments puts cash in second place. Available at https://www.ukfinance.org.uk/press/press-releases/convenience-debit-ca rd-payments-puts-cash-second-place [Accessed 14 March 2020].

UNODC. (2011) *Criminal Intelligence: Manual for Analysts.* Available at https://www. unodc.org/documents/organized-crime/Law-Enforcement/Criminal_Intelligence_ for_Analysts.pdf [Accessed 15 August 2011].

Wason, P.C. (1960) On the failure to eliminate hypotheses in a conceptual task. *The Quarterly Journal of Experimental Psychology*, 12 (3): 129–140.

Wiles, P. and Costello, A. (2000) *The 'Road to Nowhere': The Evidence for Travelling Criminals.* Home Office Research Study 207. London: Home Office.

Wright, S. (2008) Milly: The litany of police mistakes which let her murderer escape. *Mail Online* 26 February. Available at http://www.dailymail.co.uk/news/article-518673/Milly-The-litany-police-mistakes-let-murderer-escape-justice.html [Accessed 16 February 2013].

Chapter 7

The multi-agency partnership environment

Introduction

Whilst police-centric intelligence can provide significant benefits, the terms *partnership* and *multi-agency* started to emerge more frequently as it became apparent the police cannot reduce crime and disorder on their own. Studies have shown crime and policing problems are associated with a diverse range of social factors, such as inequality, poverty, and residential location (Currie, 1985; Ehrlich, 1975). Further, those who live in areas that experience a high degree of negative environmental incivility (noisy parties, loud music, itinerants or drunks in public spaces, youths on street corners, graffiti, and litter), experience an elevated fear of crime (Robinson et al., 2003). These underlying factors cannot be impacted upon by the police acting alone. In the UK, the importance of partners was officially recognised by the Morgan Report (Morgan, 1991), with the term community safety introduced to emphasise the wider social and situational aspects of crime, as well as the fear associated with it. The report emphasised the need to widen the responsibility for tackling crime, by embracing local government and community members. However, whilst partnership working and crime analysis are both well documented in the literature, there is little discussion on how the two converge. This chapter explores this interplay across four sections:

- Section 1: Defines multi-agency partnership working, and explains the reasons why it has grown in prominence;
- Section 2: Explores how different partnerships generate different strategies and follow different structures, all of which have an impact on intelligence analysts;
- Section 3: Provides examples of partnership intelligence;
- Section 4: Provides a conclusion, highlighting the most prominent areas that practitioners need to be aware of when engaging with intelligence approaches for multi-agency solutions.

Section 1: What multi-agency partnership working is, and why it is important

Partnership working in this context has been defined as 'a co-operative relationship between two or more organisations to achieve a common goal' (Berry et al., 2011:1). It requires individuals or organisations, who are normally independent of each other, to collaborate in order to deliver satisfactory outcomes for both themselves and the community. This often utilises different services, agencies and teams of professionals, who work between themselves and other practitioners to provide services in a timely manner (Connelly, 2013).

There are two reasons for the rise in popularity of multi-agency working. The first relates to the benefits it brings for the service user. This is because many community safety issues are complex, comprising multi-faceted issues, which single agencies are unable to tackle effectively on their own. As Goldstein (1990) has argued, police enforcement powers are relatively ineffective as they can only tackle the symptoms of the problem, rather than their causes. Schuller (2013) argues a 'convergence of disciplines' leads agencies to provide more sustainable solutions, as they provide those needing help with a more tailored approach using the most relevant service. Whilst multi-agency responses are often associated with marginalised individuals who find themselves the focus of numerous agencies, they can also be used to tackle problem places and events. The second benefit is felt by the agencies themselves. Public sector budgets across the world are under considerable pressure, therefore merging resources avoids duplication and reduces cost. In practice the ability to fuse resources is aided because crime concentrates around particular people and places, with crime hot spots consistently associated with areas of unemployment, poor health and poor educational outcomes. This phenomenon was illustrated within the UK 'Troubled Families' initiative. In this project, the selected individuals generated scrutiny not just from the police, but from housing, employment, education and social services. Sharing information on the people and places who generate activity across numerous agencies reduces duplication, demand and cost.

In essence whilst a newly designed holistic public sector could be formed around 'client need' rather than traditional silo-based services, in lieu of any such change, multi-agency partnerships appear the best way forward. It is also important to recognise that police forces inhabit a unique place in partnership working. As a 24/7 immediate response service, free at the point of delivery, they are on the front line when people and places hit crisis point. They have the benefit of viewing incidents as they happen, in the context they take place, being able to use significant discretion and broker public services (Bartkowiak-Théron and Asquith, 2012).

Section 2: Strategy and structure in multi agency intelligence analysis

Whilst partnership working is simple in theory, its implementation is more difficult as it brings together agencies with different priorities (Atkinson et al., 2005), and wide variations in cultural practice (Barnes, 2008; Horwath & Morrison, 2007). This means, partnership working can often produce procedural conflict rather than a cohesive team response (Robinson & Cottrell, 2005). To alleviate this tension requires awareness and compromise, which includes agreeing on who leads, what the objectives are, and who holds accountability. It also requires clarity over logistical issues, including: inter-operability; funding (possibly shared budgets); buildings and facilities; appropriate training; managerial support; time devoted to the activity; and agreed operating protocols (Sloper, 2004).

Partnerships can occur in both informal and formal settings. Informal ad hoc partnerships are often problem based, being formed to tackle immediate and specific concerns by practitioners who face the problem. An example would be a police officer working with those from a local school, housing association and residents committee to tackle anti-social behaviour in the area. The benefits of informal partnerships include being flexible, outcome oriented and inexpensive to run. An analyst used to assist in this type of partnership would provide very specific intelligence products, relating to the people, places and times associated with the problem. In contrast formal partnerships are generally more rigid and bureaucratic, although they can endure beyond the individuals who established the affiliation and beyond a single problem. Similarly, they are more likely to be financially supported, with some formal UK partnerships (such as Community Safety Partnerships) assigning full time intelligence analysts to the group. These formal partnerships differ in terms of strategy and structure, and these factors shape the expectations of the intelligence analyst. The role of the analyst in strategic partnerships is more diverse, and includes devising problem and subject profiles, examining demographic trends and evaluating initiatives.

Those involved in formal partnerships can favour very different approaches. Whilst some partnerships simply come together to be more efficient when reacting to complaints, others are more proactive and form to prevent the problem occurring or becoming worse. Even then there are three dominant strategies in prevention, which require different types of intelligence analysis. The first is known as a primary or upstream approach, aiming to prevent or minimise the risk of the problem arising in the first place. This generally involves delivery of the intervention to the wider population, rather than targeting a specific group. Secondary approaches, referred to as midstream or early intervention, focus on those individuals/groups/locations who are at an increased risk, again in an attempt to prevent the problem occurring. Finally, a tertiary or downstream approach targets those people and places where a chronic problem already exists. It seeks to provide remedial treatment to reduce the intensity of the problem.

The dilemma for the policy maker is this. The further upstream the intervention, the more potential for reducing harm and cost. However, it is far more difficult to show resources are targeted correctly when a longer time period is required to illustrate the impact. In essence primary interventions are often more expensive and difficult to evaluate. This is because they deliver universal services which also include those people and places who are unlikely to be problematic. Secondary interventions (referred to as midstream or early intervention) also generate mixed reviews. Whilst there is some evidence that early intervention approaches for young children can benefit future well-being and development (Campbell et al., 2014; Gutman & Schoon, 2013; Dearden et al., 2011; Gregg & Goodman, 2010), there are others who question the efficacy of early intervention, especially in relation to community safety (Gilles et al., 2017; Allen, 2011). Some argue that labelling individuals at an early age can heighten their profile and lead to greater engagement with the Criminal Justice System. Unintended consequences can also be compounded by inaccurate risk factors which identify the wrong individuals for early intervention (known as false positives) or neglect those who should have been identified (false negatives).

Because of these dilemmas the most common police prevention initiatives focus on tertiary or downstream problems. These focus on easily identifiable sub-populations of victims/offenders who are most likely to suffer future victimisation/offending (Pridemore & Berg, 2016; Zayfert, 2012; Farrell et al., 2005). David Kennedy (director of the US National Network for Safe Communities) advocates this approach in relation to violence reduction. While accepting the principles of early intervention, he argues that although many problems underpin crime (i.e. racism, segregation, deprivation, failed education, dysfunctional families, mental health, addiction), local communities remain fundamentally healthy. He cites a Boston community (population of 284,000) which suffered 50 youth homicides in one year within its 1,500 gang members. Subtracting the 1,500 gang members he argues this equates to 282,500 members of the community who don't require any intervention. He also reminds us of the many well-meaning interventions, through history, for 'at risk' groups which have made the problem worse. He concludes by arguing that proactive partnership working should only focus on those individuals who are suffering acute problems and who engage in serious violence. This tertiary approach is particularly relevant to those who experience a disproportionate amount of assistance from public sector services. Such individuals are often associated with specific demographic, employment, health and lifestyle characteristics which generate repeat calls.

Once a formal partnership clarifies its strategy, it should design an appropriate structure to facilitate its operational activity. Different countries follow different formats. In the USA, for example, local mayors often have responsibility for a variety of agencies and are therefore in a position to co-ordinate them. Although the UK does not follow this mayoral approach (other than in major cities), it remains in a unique position due to the Crime and Disorder Act 1998, which requires Community Safety Partnerships (originally known as Crime and Disorder Reduction Partnerships) to be formed. This legislation, later extended by Section 97 Police Reform Act 2002, dictates that 'responsible authorities' (local government authority, police, probation, fire, and health) must work together to formally identify, prioritise, and tackle local issues of crime, harm and disorder. In each local government area this partnership is asked to conduct an annual strategic assessment and formulate a strategy to reduce its incidence by coordinating a partnership response and monitoring progress. In practice these partnerships often employ dedicated analyst teams to direct their activity and monitor the impact. This innovative legislation also acted as a catalyst for other formal partnerships to emerge across the UK. For example, the Health and Well-being boards became a lawful requirement from 2013 and paved the way for the introduction of joint strategic needs assessments (JSNA) and joint health and well-being strategies for local communities (Department of Health, 2011). All were epitomised by the need to involve local communities. As well as these strategic legislative partnerships there also exist a wide variety of other formal partnerships.

Information sharing

Whilst one of the most significant benefits of partnership working relates to the sharing of information, this also remains as one of its biggest challenges (Pinkney et al., 2008) and deserves further discussion. It is evident that information sharing is easier when fewer barriers exist for the collection, storage and communication of electronic data. Trevillion (2001) suggested that integrated information systems can generate bridges, facilitating the flow of communication, which allow agencies to move away from lone working to collective decision making. However, partnership information sharing is difficult as public sector information processes are normally constructed for the purpose of internal administration, rather than client need. This means that silos of information form, designed around: geographical jurisdiction (national, regional, local); agency (i.e. health, police, social services), and role (custody, hospital, outreach). Each of these information silos can be built on separate hardware and software systems, which create compatibility issues. To overcome the challenge of information sharing, four operational models are generally observed:

a   *Dedicated co-located multi-agency teams* based upon geography. An early UK example is seen with Youth Offending Teams, formed as a result of the Crime and Disorder Act 1988. They comprise representatives from the police, social work, and probation, to provide multi-agency information and intervention. This format was replicated by a variety of voluntary partnerships, one of which is the Multi-Agency Safeguarding Hub (MASH). This was formed in the UK in 2011 to deliver multi agency risk assessment and intervention for those at risk of violent or sexual abuse. These teams were formed in response to previous agency failure in the safeguarding of children and young people (Dunne & Finlay, 2016). Often co-located in a central hub they either table their own information, or request/respond to specific information from other agencies (Cheminais, 2009). Partners include the police, Adult Services, Health, Mental Health, Child Social Services, Education Workers, Youth Offending Team, Probation Services, and Fire Service. Their practice is normally facilitated through a formal information sharing agreement (Hanson et al., 2015). Many staff are complimentary about the process, which they say increases high quality, accurate and timely safeguarding responses to deliver positive results (Home Office, 2014; Cullinan, 2013). However, others argue they can become overly bureaucratic, often deferring decisions (Shorrock et al., 2020). A similar partnership model can be seen in US Fusion Centres or Europol (discussed in Chapter 3). Over time, within the UK, this model has evolved into locally based 'place-based partnerships'. Here local police officers come together with a variety of practitioners from other agencies to handle general incidents surrounding community safety.

b   *A 'lead professional' model* (other terms are used) is where a specific individual, from the agencies involved, is made accountable as the co-ordinating case worker. This person has the benefit of immediate access to a virtual multi-agency team. Whilst the practitioners remain in their normal work environments, they meet for case conferences and provide relevant organisational information to assist with the problem.

c   *Information sharing agreements.* In this model partners continue to work from their own agency, but they have general agreements in place to share information with other specific agencies on specific topics. This information sharing is most often done manually but bespoke electronic systems are increasingly being used. An example of this is PAM, a commercial system that provides a bespoke software platform to share information concerning serious organised crime, between partner agencies in the UK. This uses a secure platform which is shared between invited partners, to highlight trends, work on specific problems, and feedback the outcomes of their interventions.

d   *Live-time integrated information sharing systems* is an approach currently being developed across the world, albeit with limited success. This allows one agency to directly view the information system of another agency (or part of their system). Whilst extremely challenging to implement, this provides the most fundamental approach to multi-agency working as it allows partners to search information on a live system outside their own organisation (within parameters and security measures). It also provides the potential to warehouse information from a number of systems to provide insight into new patterns and trends.

In summary to this section there are many formal and informal partnerships in place, which incorporate voluntary, private and public sectors. Further, there is also a growing appetite for police agencies to work more closely with academic institutions (Mitchell & Huey, 2019), as Evidence-Based Policing (EBP) gains traction. However, aggregating and synthesising information across a multi-agency environment remains challenging. Therefore, those working in the intelligence arena (intelligence officers, researchers, analysts, etc.) should understand the type of data that can be collected and how it can provide insight. Quite often intelligence products suffer from being 'data-led' and are criticised for not providing new understanding (Keay & Kirby, 2018a). The challenge for analysts is therefore to understand their data sources so that they can use them more effectively to provide operational and strategic insight.

Section 3: Multi-agency partnership intelligence working in action

Whilst the discussion so far has explained different models and conceptual approaches, it is helpful to understand how multi-agency ideas can work in practice. The following section provides some examples.

a) The Vulnerable Localities Index

The mapping of hotspots allows resources to be directed in a more effective way (Chainey & Ratcliffe, 2005), however this almost exclusively relies on police data, which can result in short term enforcement-based responses. Efforts have been made to integrate police and partnership data within geographic mapping systems and one of the most successful was developed by the JDI Centre (University College London) and a UK national police agency (Centrex) to identify neighbourhoods at risk of decline (Jill Dando Institute, 2003). The process places secondary data from partners into a pre-designed Microsoft Excel template, which is known as the Vulnerable Localities Index (VLI) and is outlined on the JDI website (Tompson, 2012). The VLI model uses Super Output Areas (SOAs), as a unit of calculation, which comprise aggregated smaller Output Areas (OAs) sharing a coterminous boundary. The three data sources, which generate its six scores, comprise the following.

- *Crime data:* 'burglary dwelling' and 'criminal damage to a dwelling'. Incidents are accessed from police data sources. Each OA and SOA has a unique identifier code that links all the data and enables the counts to be directly inserted into the VLI template. Once within the template the data can be converted into crime rates by dividing the crime count with the number of households in the specified area.

- *Deprivation data*: Levels of income and unemployment are taken from the Indices of Multiple Deprivation (IMD). This data is only available at SOA level and the raw index score is already formatted allowing it to be put in its original form into the VLI template.
- *Census data*: The first relates to educational attainment, defined by individuals whose highest qualification is less than 5 GCSEs grade A* to C, shown as a proportion of the whole geographical area. The second index refers to the percentage of young people, aged between 15 and 24 years, who reside in the area.

The final VLI score is calculated by adding the average of the six individual index scores, across the geographic areas. These are categorised in bands (0–80; 80–120; 120–160; 160–200; 200+) and uploaded into a GIS to provide visual representation. The system can be tailored to individual requirements, for example it can include factors such as the number of offenders living in the area, broader crime issues, or other partnership data (i.e. health, fire, and housing) not previously considered in the original VLI equation. Reece-Smith and Kirby (2012) explain how the approach was used in Merseyside, which showed that 29 SOAs emerged as vulnerable localities, with an index score of 200(+). Whilst these areas comprised only 2% of the land mass they accounted for 22% of the most serious violent crime, 13% of all crime and 13% of robberies, 12% of all firearm discharges, and 11% of knife crime. The citizens living in these 29 areas, when compared with the rest of Merseyside, were therefore: 7 times more likely to be a victim of more serious violent crime; 4 times more likely to be a victim of robbery, firearm discharge or assault with less serious injury; and 3 times more likely to be a victim of house burglary, serious acquisitive crime or knife crime. The study found practitioners were complimentary of the process, saying the VLI was easy to use as the data was readily available and analysts required little training to use it. Further analysis of the 29 areas, using other aspects of partnership data, found higher levels of child obesity, lower educational attainment, higher levels of families on benefits, and poorer life expectancy. This approach engaged partners more effectively on these hotspots than police data alone.

b) Partnership Intelligence Assessment

A further example involved the Lancashire Constabulary together with the Lancashire County Council Community Safety Partnership analysis team developing the Partnership Intelligence Assessment. Its aim was to merge aspects of the NIM problem profile with the Joint Strategic Needs Assessment (JSNA) process. Recognising the drawbacks of the traditional problem profile in a partnership setting, the team looked to elements of the JSNA process to improve collaboration, engagement and problem understanding, thereby improving the analytical output. The first of these assessments was to examine child sexual exploitation (CSE). UK Police forces had been locked in a cycle of producing a CSE problem profile every six months. It was feared with this regularity that the law of diminishing returns would set in, that is the more often the profile was produced, the less value it would have. Problem profiles were not only descriptive but heavily reliant on police data. Whilst using wider data streams initially caused some consternation this was negated through new data sharing agreements, use of appropriate legislation and strong communication between the key agencies. The work involved cross-referencing a sample of CSE referrals to the police with information from education, social care and public health. The aim was to examine the results and compare them using the *needs analysis triangle*, a technique used within Lancashire County Council Public Health JSNA work. The needs analysis triangle is based upon Bradshaw's (1972) ideas around a taxonomy of social need. It is used to identify and gather data and information about samples and populations which can then be used to identify 'at risk' communities or groups from their use of support services. The final assessment was able to demonstrate new information regarding contributory factors and highlight the key agencies essential in tackling CSE and safeguarding vulnerable members of the community

Analysis like this helps push the boundaries previously set by a traditional problem profile approach. As already noted, chronic problems go far beyond a policing response and multi-agency working not only requires engagement, communication and data sharing but also the use of common terminology. Ironically, this is what the NIM set out to achieve with its original objectives, but its terminology focussed on law enforcement related matters. One of the benefits of merging different processes in this example was the shift from crime-related terms to ones around harm and health. This has been seen in epidemiological criminology, which has explored the synergy between crime, criminal justice and public health. Akers and Lanier (2009) note that members of public health and criminal justice disciplines often work with the same marginalised populations (e.g. people at high risk of drug use, health issues, etc.) but do not necessarily work in a coordinated fashion to tackle the shared problem (Akers & Lanier, 2009). Bartkowiak-Théron and Asquith (2017) note that services, particularly health and the police, come together to manage operational threats but struggle to develop shared strategic policies. If intelligence analysis is to improve across disciplines and look to new ways in multi-agency working, then this approach can act as a foundation for that work. It particularly examines crime from the victim's perspective, using a public health perspective, to assess victims' vulnerability (Waltermaurer & Akers, 2013).

c) Super users – high intensity callers who require police assistance

International studies show approximately 80% of all police calls relate to incidents other than crime, with a recent UK study finding this figure to be

83% (College of Policing, 2015). Herman Goldstein (1977:35) pointed out that one of the numerous non crime objectives for the police was to 'assist those who cannot care for themselves: the intoxicated, the addicted, the mentally ill, the physically disabled, the old, and the young'. In recent years this type of demand has increased for the police due to the fact that, whilst public service budgets have been reducing, police continue to provide 24/7 access. Helping vulnerable people can reduce overall demand, prevent individuals becoming involved in more serious crime or incidents (as victims or offenders), and save public resources. The latter was famously illustrated by Malcom Gladwell (2006), in the case of 'Million-dollar Murray'. Murray Barr, was a US military veteran who, returning from active service, became homeless on the streets of Reno, Nevada. Described as a bear of a man, he was an alcoholic and, whilst extremely popular when sober, his personality changed when drunk, leading to him being regularly arrested or hospitalised. He received his nickname from two Reno police officers who calculated the cost of his behaviour to the state. Making the final calculation they said, 'It cost us one million dollars *not to* do something about Murray'. This dilemma has generated a growth of literature examining vulnerable populations that impact upon policing services (Keay & Kirby, 2018b; Asquith et al., 2017). In the UK (and there is no reason to believe this is not replicated in other developed countries) specific individuals will call the police up to 100 times a month, with many others calling 50 times each month. These individuals also call other services, especially ambulance, mental health and social services (Kirby, 2020).

In this specific UK example, police analysts from one agency identified 1,352 high volume callers associated with 15 factors. Three themes were particularly prominent as being associated with demand. The first related to *elderly people*, who contacted the police as a result of abuse (relationship issues), dementia or loneliness (becoming confused or just wanting to talk to someone). Secondly was the theme of *alcohol*, which seemed to be associated with self-harm, domestic violence and mental health issues. The third related to *young people*, some of whom were open to exploitation by others. Understanding the static and dynamic risk factors which generate high volume calls allows a variety of agencies to come together and devise sustainable action plans to prevent the need for police assistance. A 'lead professional' chosen from one of the partner agencies co-ordinates the multi-agency response. In this particular example the agencies included: local government services (including adult and child services); Fire & Rescue Service; Ambulance Services; Health Services; volunteer schemes; Youth Offending Team; and Probation Service. Staff at the local university were also asked to assist with the evaluation. The initiative is best illustrated with a couple of case studies. One example was an alcoholic suffering severe personality disorder who regularly contacted police, ambulance and mental health services, threatening to commit suicide. On arrival the caller would be aggressive and verbally abusive. The multi-agency analysis found this behaviour was linked to significant childhood trauma, which required a longer-term approach using a variety of partner agencies. When these issues were tackled, he stopped calling. Another example, which had continued over many years, involved a woman who lived with her two sons (one disabled and both alcohol dependent), her grandson and one of her son's girlfriends. All the family experienced abuse from her husband, who was suffering from dementia. Again, this more detailed analysis provided the information to apply a more sustainable solution. In essence the project illustrates that analysis can identify the most vulnerable, which dominant issues should be tackled, as well as highlighting much needed policy changes and training. The evaluation for a representative group of 259 callers, showed clear operational benefits with calls being reduced by 26% (n=2892) for the six months following the intervention (p <.01). It was further discovered that those with a mental health issue were most likely to benefit from an intervention (Kirby, 2020).

d) Organised crime – UK

There have been many partnership initiatives in relation to organised crime. During 2017 it was estimated 5,866 organised crime groups (OCGs), comprising 39,414 active offenders were active in the UK (NCA, 2018). Organised crime is a subject which focuses the attention of many intelligence analysts, who often explore ways to detect and convict offenders. However as 85% of offenders are considered recidivists (Sproat, 2012), the use of preventative approaches requiring multi-agency involvement is also needed. The benefits of information sharing in this area are widely acknowledged as many partners have access to a diversity of community intelligence which can be used to disrupt serious and organised crime offenders. Good practice is associated with four components: (i) the identification of appropriate organised crime targets; (ii) engagement of partners; (iii) sharing of information between partners; and (iv) partnership activity based on shared information (Van Staden et al., 2011). There are many good examples of how partners can impact upon organised crime and a number are provided below.

The first example is situated in Manchester UK, an area of 2.55million people, and no stranger to organised criminality. The *Scuttler gangs* were prevalent around the city in the latter part of the 19th century (BBC, 2014), and during 2012 the city became the centre of an OCG dispute leading to the murder of two police officers. *Programme Challenger*, a dedicated multi-agency team was instigated and one of the work strands was Project Engage, which sought to: 'Identify those at risk of, or vulnerable to, involvement in SOC using local intelligence; and to develop interventions that would prevent their ongoing involvement'. This project brought representatives from a wide variety of agencies, including: Police; Local Authority services (Community Safety; Children Services; Early Help); Education; Housing Association; Health; Department of Work & Pensions; Independent Youth services;

Voluntary Sector. A six-stage process was instigated with the emphasis being on intelligence analysis. This included identification of 33 young people on the periphery of SOC followed by a 'deep dive', which involved all agencies providing detailed information to profile the young person, their behaviour, and any previous intervention. The analysis showed the participants' history to be incredibly complex, being enticed into a criminal lifestyle through financial and social rewards, coupled with the cultural need to conform to peer loyalty and non-co-operation with authority figures. One specific case study shows the level of this challenge. In this case a specialist youth worker engaged with a number of young men to facilitate their co-operation. The plan was to use a well-established education programme to help them improve basic educational standards. This would lead to them being accepted on a vocational skills course which could provide a recognised construction qualification and access to apprenticeship programmes. However, whilst simple in theory the plan was more difficult in practice as the skills programme meant travelling from one area of Manchester to another and crossing territorial gang boundaries. Eventually an individual was conveyed to the skills centre by taxi, however on one visit he was recognised by a rival gang member who fetched others to retaliate for a prior dispute. The young man wasn't present, but the training centre understandably declined to take any others from the project. A further challenge related to the difficulty in monitoring change. The impact analysis found some limited benefits from the scheme, but argued turning around such complex lifestyles required a longer intervention (Boulton et al., 2019).

e) Other examples in organised crime

The use of a multi-agency approach to SOC is replicated across the UK. One such example involves Essex and Kent police forces who work with 10–15 partner agencies (HMIC, 2017a). Kent Police hold workshops with partner organisations including, community safety partnership managers, Kent Fire and Rescue Service, Trading Standards, Public Health England, Medway Unitary Authority, and HM Prison Service (HMIC, 2017b). The two also work together in the gathering and use of partner agency intelligence, particularly HMRC and Border Force (HMIC, 2017f) investing financially in a joint serious crime directorate to enhance their capability. The forces run joint operations, which include partner agencies, to disrupt OCGs (HMIC, 2017f). A further example is seen in Lancashire (UK) where a dedicated IT platform (PAM) is used to share SOC information across partner agencies. Following licensee training on the subject of Human Trafficking and Modern-Day Slavery, a local hotel contacted the Police to voice their suspicions. This identified a male and female who, as part of an OCG, had control of a Romanian sex worker and had been active in the North East region before coming to Lancashire. This intelligence was later passed to the National Crime Agency. The final example in this section comes from a police force which runs joint management meetings with partner agencies on Organised Crime Groups. In one particular meeting the Environment Agency highlighted that one of the police monitored groups were also involved in fly-tipping. The police deployed their surveillance team based on the intelligence supplied by the partner agency and the gang were followed and later imprisoned for illegal fly-tipping.

Conclusion

This chapter has shown that for any analyst working in a multi-agency environment there are fresh challenges. First, as a multi-agency partnership has multiple aims and objectives, it is helpful for the analyst to know the outcomes the partners are trying to achieve as it will affect the intelligence requirement. Specifically:

a   At what level of the problem (people and places) should the analysis concentrate – at a strategic or tactical level?
b   Does the partnership generally plan to deliver interventions reactively or be prevention led? If preventative, what level will this be: primary, secondary, or tertiary?
c   What partners are involved and why? What intelligence can they provide surrounding the problem?
d   Will all partners be sharing information and be willing to engage in the proposed interventions?

Further, within any partnership activity there are likely to be individual projects targeting specific people, places and events. It is useful for the analyst to know which agency will be leading the project (and who will take operational decisions during the analysis), as well as operational decisions for response proposals and accountability structure. Unless the analyst has a specific point of contact, from which to take instructions, decision making can be ambiguous. Finally, on the subject of information sharing, the analyst should be aware of the following questions.

a   What information should be shared and why?
b   On what grounds can it legitimately be shared?
c   What model will be used to share the information – is this feasible in practical terms and what resources will be required to support it?

If these factors are understood and followed then intelligence analysis can be improved.

References

Akers, T. and Lanier, M. (2009) 'Epidemiological criminology': coming full circle. *American Journal of Public Health*, 99 (3): 397–402.

Allen, G. (2011) *Early Intervention: The Next Steps*. HM Government. Available at: https://www.gov.uk/government/uploads/...data/.../early-intervention-next-steps2. pdf2 [Accessed 7 February 2017].

Asquith, N., Bartkowiak-Theron, I. and Roberts, K. (2017) *Policing Encounters with Vulnerability*. Sydney: Palgrave.

Atkinson, M., Doherty, P. and Kinder, K. (2005) Multi-agency working: models, challenges and key factors for success. *Journal of Early Childhood Research*, 3 (1): 7–17.

Barnes, P. (2008) Multi-agency working: what are the perspectives of SENCos and parents regarding its development and implementation? *British Journal of Special Education*, 35 (4): 230–240.

Bartkowiak-Théron, I. and Asquith, N. (2012) The extraordinary intricacies of policing vulnerability. *Australasian Policing: A Journal of Professional Practice and Research*, 4 (2): 43–49.

Bartkowiak-Théron, I. and Asquith, N. (2017) Conceptual divides and practice synergies in law enforcement and public health: some lessons from policing vulnerability in Australia. *Policing and Society: An International Journal of Research and Policy*, 27 (3): 276–288.

BBC. (2014) The Scuttlers of Manchester. Available at http://www.bbc.co.uk/manche ster/content/articles/2008/10/20/201008_scuttlers_interview_feature.shtml [accessed on 24 August 2020].

Berry, G., Briggs, P., Erol, R. and van Staden, L. (2011) *The Effectiveness of Partnership Working in a Crime and Disorder Context*. Home Office Research Report 52, London: Home Office.

Boulton, L., Phythian, R. and Kirby, S. (2019) Diverting young men from gangs: a qualitative evaluation. *Policing: An International Journal of Police Strategies and Management*, 42 (5): 887.

Bradshaw, J. (1972) The concept of social need. In G. McLachlan (ed.). *Problems and Progress*. Oxford: Oxford University Press.

Campbell, F., Conti, G., Heckman, J.J., Moon, S.H., Pinto, R., Pungello, E. and Pan, Y. (2014) Early childhood investments substantially boost adult health. *Science*, 343 (6178): 1478–1485.

Chainey, S. and Ratcliffe, J. (2005) *GIS and Crime Mapping*. Chichester: John Wiley.

Cheminais, R. (2009) *Effective multi-agency partnerships: Putting every child matters into practice*. London: SAGE.

College of Policing. (2015) *College of Policing Analysis: Estimating Demand on the Police Service*. Online report. Available at: http://www.college.police.uk/documents/ demand_report_21_1_15.pdf. [Accessed 1 February 2020].

Connelly, G. (2013) *Multi agency working*. In T.G. K. Bryce, W.M. Humes, D. Gillies and A. Kennedy (eds). *Scottish Education*. Edinburgh: Edinburgh University Press.

Currie, E. (1985) *Confronting Crime: An American Challenge*. New York: Pantheon.

Cullinan, M. (2013) *Lancashire Improving Futures Programme*. Available at www.lanca shirechildrenstrust.org.uk/web/viewdoc.asp?id=103050 [Accessed 18 June 2015].

Dearden, L., Sibieta, L. and Sylva, K. (2011) The socio-economic gradient in early child outcomes: evidence from the Millennium Cohort Study (No. 11, 03). IFS Working Papers.

Department of Health. (2011) Joint Strategic Needs Assessment and joint health and well-being strategies explained. Available at: https://assets.publishing.service.gov.uk/government/uploads/system/uploads/attachment_data/file/215261/dh_131733.pdf [Accessed 2 March 2020].

Dunne, J.F. and Finlay, F. (2016) Multi-agency safeguarding hub – a new way of working. *Archives of Disease in Childhood*, 101 (1): A369–A370.

Ehrlich, I. (1975) On the Relation between Education and Crime. In F.T. Juster (ed.). *Education, Income and Human Behaviour*. New York: McGraw-Hill.

Farrell, G., Tseloni, A. and Pease, K. (2005) Repeat victimisation in the ICVS and NCVS. *Crime Prevention and Community Safety*, 7 (3): 7–18.

Gilles, V., Edwards, R. and Horsley, N. (2017) *Changing the Politics of Early Intervention: Who's Saving Children and Why?* Bristol: Policy Press.

Gladwell, M. (2006) Million Dollar Murray. *The New Yorker*. Available at https://www.newyorker.com/magazine/2006/02/13/million-dollar-murray [Accessed 20 May 2020].

Goldstein, H. (1977) *Policing a free society*. University of Wisconsin Legal Studies Research Paper No. 1349 Cambridge (MA): Ballinger Pub. Co. Available at http://ssrn.com/abstract=2596883 [Accessed 6 May 2020].

Goldstein, H. (1990) *Problem Oriented Policing*. New York: McGraw-Hill.

Gregg, P. and Goodman, A. (2010) *Children's Educational Outcomes: The Role of Attitudes and Behaviours, from Early Childhood to Late Adolescence*. Centre for Market and Public Organisation: University of Bristol and Institute for Fiscal Studies.

Gutman, L.M. and Schoon, I. (2013) *The Impact of Non-cognitive Skills on Outcomes for Young People*. London: Education Empowerment Foundations.

Hanson, J., Carwardine, J., Chapman, P., Ross, D. and Massey, K. and Bamford, N. (2015) *Safeguarding Annual Report 2014–2015*. Preston: East Lancashire CCGs.

HMIC. (2017s) *PEEL: Police Effectiveness 2016. An Inspection of Essex Police.* Available at: https://www.justiceinspectorates.gov.uk/hmic/publications/peel-police-effectiveness-2016-essex/[Accessed 10 May 2017].

HMIC. (2017b) *PEEL: Police Effectiveness 2016. An Inspection of Kent Police.* Available at: https://www.justiceinspectorates.gov.uk/hmic/publications/peel-police-effectiveness-2016-kent/[Accessed 10 May 2017].

Home Office. (2014) *Multi-Agency Working and Information Sharing Project: Final Report*. London: Home Office.

Horwath, J. and Morrison, T. (2007) Collaboration, integration and change in children's services: critical issues and key ingredients. *Child abuse and neglect*, 31(1): 55–69.

Jill Dando Institute. (2003) *Vulnerable Localities Index Excel Template*. Available at http://www.ucl.ac.uk/scs/research-consultancy/geographical-analysis/VLI (Accessed 18 July 2012)

Keay, S. and Kirby, S. (2018a) The evolution of the police analyst and the influence of evidence based-policing. *Policing: A Journal of Policy and Practice*, 12 (3): 265–276.

Keay, S. and Kirby, S. (2018b) Defining vulnerability: from the conceptual to the operational. *Policing: A Journal of Policy and Practice*, 12 (4): 428–438.

Kirby, S. (2020) Repeat callers to police in Lancashire, UK. In M.S. Scott and R.V. Clarke (eds). *Problem-Oriented Policing: Successful Case Studies*. London: Routledge.

Mitchell, R. and Huey, L. (2019) *Evidence Based Policing: An Introduction.* Bristol: Policy Press.

Morgan, J. (1991) *Safer Communities: The Local Delivery of Crime Prevention through the Partnership Approach.* London: Home Office.

NCA. (2018) *National Strategic Assessment of Organised Crime.* Available at https://na tionalcrimeagency.gov.uk/who-we-are/publications/173-national-strategic-assessm ent-of-serious-and-organised-crime-2018/file [Accessed 20 September 2020].

Pinkney, L., Penhale, B., Manthorpe, J., Perkins, N., Reid, D. and Hussein, S. (2008) Voices from the frontline: social work practitioners' perceptions of multi-agency working in adult protection in England and Wales. *Journal of Adult Protection*, 10 (4): 12–24.

Pridemore, W.A. and Berg, M.T. (2016) What is past is prologue: A population-based case-control study of repeat victimization, premature mortality, and homicide. *Aggressive Behavior*, 43 (2): 176–189.

Reece-Smith, R. and Kirby, S. (2012) Exploring the VLI, for identifying priority neighbourhoods in the context of multi-agency community safety initiatives. *Policing: A Journal of Policy and Practice*, 7 (1): 42–52.

Robinson, J.B., Lawton, B.A., Taylor, R.B., and Perkins, D.D. (2003) Multilevel longitudinal impacts of incivilities: fear of crime, expected safety and block satisfaction. *Journal of Quantitative Criminology*, 19 (3), 237–274.

Robinson, M. and Cottrell, D. (2005) Health professionals in multi-disciplinary and multi-agency teams: Changing professional practice. *Journal of Interprofessional Care*, 19 (6): 547–560.

Schuller, N. (2013) Is crime a question of health? *Safer Communities*, 12 (2): 86–96.

Shorrock, S., McManus, M. and Kirby, S. (2020) Profile of repeat victimisation within multi-agency referral. *International Review of Victimology*, 26 (3): 332–343.

Sloper, P. (2004) Facilitators and barriers for co-ordinated multi-agency services. *Child: Care, Health and Development*, 30 (6): 571–580.

Sproat, P.A. (2012) Phoney war or appeasement? The policing of organised crime in the UK, Trends. *Organised Crime*, 15 (4): 313–330.

Tompson, L. (2012) *Vulnerable Localities Index.* JDI Brief Series. London: UCL Jill Dando Centre. Available at https://www.ucl.ac.uk/jdibrief/analysis/Vulnerable-Loca lities-Index [Accessed 27 April 2020].

Trevillion, S. (2001) Building partnership through communities. In D. Taylor (ed.). *Breaking Down Barriers: Reviewing Partnership Practice.* University of Brighton: Health and Social Policy Research Centre.

Van Staden, L., Leahy-Harland, S. and Gottschalk, E. (2011) *Tackling Organised Crime through a Partnership Approach at the Local Level: A Process Evaluation.* Home Office Research Report 46. London: Home Office.

Waltermaurer, E. and Akers, T. (2013) *Epidemiological Criminology: Theory to Practice.* Oxon: Routledge.

Zayfert, C. (2012) Cognitive behavioural conceptualisation of traumatization. In M.P. Duckworth and V.M. and Follette (eds). *Retraumatization: Assessment, Treatment and Prevention.* New York: Routledge.

Chapter 8

The increasing influence of data in intelligence analysis

Introduction

The onset of the 20th century brought a relentless march of new technologies, software, computer applications (apps), and social media platforms. Following the US Department of Defense development of the internet in the 1970s a plethora of technological advances appeared, including fibre optic cables, microprocessors and the World Wide Web. This allowed services, goods and information to be transferred much more quickly across both physical and virtual environments. By the 1990s the world became connected as never before, influenced by global corporations such as Microsoft, Apple, Facebook, and Amazon. This 'data explosion' (Bramer, 2016:1) came to define society as the 'Information Age', emphasising the importance of accessing and controlling information.

Marr (2018) illustrates this exponential rise of data, explaining that 2.5 quintillion bytes of data are created on a daily basis, a figure which will increase due to the popularity of the Internet of Things (IoT). Some 90% of all the world's data has been generated over the previous two years, with over 3.7 billion of the global population using the internet to generate five billion internet searches a day (Google alone processes 40,000 searches a second). For each minute on social media, Snapchat shares half a million photos; four million YouTube videos are viewed; and nearly half a million comments are posted on Twitter. Similarly, Facebook (as the largest social media platform) has two billion active users (307 million across Europe), who upload 300 million photographs a day and half a million comments a minute. On top of this, the global population send 16 million text messages and 156 million emails a minute. The internet is changing the structure of society, with access to services and increasingly online experience, epitomised by the gig economy, of which Uber provides 14 million trips each day. The future suggests more of the same, with the IoT remotely connecting smart devices to enhance lifestyle experiences, e.g. remote access to home appliances such as heating. During 2018, eight million people were reportedly using voice control on a monthly basis and this number is expected to increase.

Whilst technology has helped improve methods to explore and analyse data, there is limited evidence to show how it has improved police effectiveness (Ariel, 2019). This is due to the challenges associated with its use, as the ability to select appropriate data and technology is complex, and in some cases controversial (Ferguson, 2017; Koper et al., 2014). Whilst the police generally lag behind commercial enterprise in the use of technology, advances can assist in the identification of crime and the design of policing responses. This chapter explores a number of the issues surrounding data management within the police organisation.

- Section 1: Will initially look at how the police obtain data, before explaining the terms big data, artificial intelligence, machine learning and data visualisation.
- Section 2: Will explore how law enforcement use these themes in an operational setting, and the challenges of doing so.
- Section 3: Will explore how police agencies and crime analysts can exploit current and future data opportunities to improve operational outcomes.

Section 1: The police use of data and the emergence of big data

A data rich environment

When explaining how the police service collects and uses data, it is helpful to describe some basic information. The majority of police data can be classed as 'process-generated data' which serves administrative rather than research purposes (Diekman, 2009:653 cited in Von Gunten et al., 2014), and the quality of this data is affected by two points. First, 'discretionary procedures' determine whether individuals (be they victims, witnesses or police officers) decide to report or record an incident, as often this does not always occur. Secondly, institutional practices determine how this data is actually categorised (May, 2001). These two issues therefore influence the type of data that is collected, the format in which it is kept, and the ability to retrieve it. It means that whilst the police and other public sector bodies harvest a considerable amount of information it isn't always valuable or accessible.

A further factor is that police related information is often gathered routinely for no specific purpose, which can create unnecessary bureaucracy. A national review by Berry (2010:2) reported that 'one third of effort is either over-engineered, duplicated or adds no additional value', arguing that 'old bureaucracy is quickly replaced by new demands for data and information'. Within the UK the majority of information is historically requested for 'top down' performance measures and targets, being mandated by the Home Office and HMICFRS (Her Majesties Inspectorate of Constabularies and Fire and Rescue Services). Whilst some believe this scrutiny can provide benefits (Hibberd, 2015), other commentators believe it can generate dysfunctional organisational behaviour

(Guilfoyle, 2015), which diverts practitioner creativity from improving performance to trying to meet targets (Seddon, 2008). Whilst a policy change in 2010 brought the end of the performance target regimes in England and Wales, these were replaced by statutory data returns and ADRs (annual data requirements) (Home Office, 2020). This required the continued collection and submission of specific data, mostly related to notifiable offences, conducted by internal Police Corporate Development or Performance Management Departments. Whilst the data was often in support of specific projects run by the Home Office or National Crime Agency, and whilst it has relaxed the need for other intelligence data collection plans, it remains burdensome for police forces to manage. National automated methods for collecting this type of data, which would cease the need for local effort, is possible in theory, yet appropriate software solutions are not in place. This means police researchers and analysts continue to be engaged in laborious data collection and data cleaning, rather than using the time for more valuable and targeted operational and organisational research.

It is also useful to point out that previous and existing data management projects have often courted controversy and failed to deliver on expectations. A typical example was a Home Office project to provide mobile data units, at a cost of £80m, which failed to deliver its aim of saving 30 minutes per officer per shift (Berry, 2010). In a BBC news article, Waterhouse (2019) more recently highlighted a commonly used UK IT system (Athena), which has cost nine police forces £35m, over the past ten years. The system has been described as problematic and is said to hinder the ability of officers to detect crime, enabling offenders to evade justice. Whilst the news article focused on Derbyshire Police, other forces (Cambridgeshire, Kent, Norfolk, Suffolk, Warwickshire and West Mercia) were also reported as experiencing similar problems.

Data management is complex. In a data rich world, choices have to be made concerning the type of information to be collected and for what purpose. When the term big data is used in conjunction with crime data, it does not necessarily mean a collection of single crime incidents; it may also include a series of data attributes that link to a variety of other incidents. For example, in the UK most crime records will also be associated with further incident information. There may be details or identification numbers attached to one or more of these records with a variety of different data points. Therefore, the complexity can increase as one record links to another (incident, vehicle, premises, people) and often these associated data sets can sit in unconnected servers, bespoke systems, locations, and departments with restricted access. The ability to cut across different records and databases is a valuable asset to analysts as it provides an improved data return and improves knowledge when examining problems, such as crime series or repeat victimisation (Pease et al., 2018). Stanko (2008) argues analysts should make sure they explore as much of the existing police data as possible, before mourning over missing data. Wheeler (2020) also believes that police administrative data should be used more and is concerned there is a lack of knowledge about the data actually collected. Data management could be improved by more rigorous hypotheses-led approaches to identify the actual data needed to test the questions being asked. This more rigorous approach may require existing data to be recoded, which could generate more insight.

The emergence of data science and the data scientist

Kearns and Muir (2019:6) define data-driven policing as 'the acquisition, analysis and use of a wide variety of digitised data sources to inform decision making, improve processes and increase actionable intelligence for all personnel within a police service, whether they be operating at the front line or in positions of strategic leadership'. This assistance can include identifying or diagnosing operational or organisational problems; assessing and deciding the most appropriate course of actions; providing appropriate information to partners; directing daily activity; and assisting organisational culture and motivation. McAleer et al. (2018:137) summarise this by saying it makes decision making 'more targeted, with attention appropriately and efficiently directed; more tailored, so that responses fit divergent needs; more nimble, able to adjust quickly to changing circumstances; and more experimental, with real time testing of how problems respond to different strategies'. This can bring transparency to the use of public funds and also increase effectiveness and efficiency.

Whilst the origins of data science are often aligned to a mathematician called John W. Tukey in 1962, it is commonly thought D.J. Patil and Jeff Hammerbacher are the people who popularised the term in 2008. The advent of large and diverse databases (big data), converged with improvements in technology that allowed data-led decision making, which was of great commercial benefit. As this unstructured and complex data, often involving diverse sources such as mobile phones, internet searches and social media, was time-consuming to analyse, commercial companies were more likely to outsource analysis. This requirement created a new profession of data scientist, whose practitioners relied upon multi-disciplinary skills such as computing, mathematics and statistics. This quickly developing field is expected to become more popular and dictate more sophisticated techniques as data scientists are asked to interpret an increasing amount of data (University of Wisconsin, 2017).

New techniques allow the user to probe huge databases very quickly, which a human would be incapable of manually completing in an entire lifetime. The role of the data scientist is to abstract these findings and communicate them in a format that can be used by decision makers (Banton, 2019). Specifically, these findings are often used in predictive analytics, which calculates future patterns of behaviour, based on what has occurred in the past. Some argue there are five stages to data science. These include the *Capturing* of the information (data acquisition, data entry, signal reception, data extraction);

followed by the *Maintenance* of the data (data warehousing, data cleansing, data staging, data processing, data architecture). This then moves on to the *Processing* of the data (data mining, clustering/classification, data modelling, data summarisation) and its *Analysis* (exploratory/confirmatory, predictive analysis, regression, text mining, qualitative analysis). Finally, there is the *Communication* of the data (data reporting, data visualisation, business intelligence, decision making) (Berkeley School of Information, 2020). Some of these terms are outlined in more depth below and often overlap.

Big data

Generally, there is no consensus as to how the term big data should be defined. The *Oxford English Dictionary* (OED) defines big data as 'data of a very large size, typically to the extent that its manipulation and management present significant logistical challenges'. Boyd and Crawford (2012), state that 'big' data cannot be defined purely in terms of the size of a dataset, but rather the 'capacity to search, aggregate, and cross-reference large data sets'. Ferguson (2017) discusses big data in terms of information gained through the normal patterns of how we all live. He notes that, 'big data comes from you' (Ferguson, 2017:9) as people use smart phones, have smart homes, store cards, credit cards, etc., and all of which leave a digital trace, therefore the comings and goings of everyday life can be tracked. Big data is therefore understood as large and complex data sources that traditional data processing techniques are unable to process. Laney (2001) is credited with an early and enduring explanation of the concept. He explains it as data that has greater variety, arriving in increasing volumes and with ever higher velocity. This became known as the three Vs, which are worthy of further explanation. In relation to the first V, big data is involved in the processing of high volumes of data, some of which will be structured (numerical data), and some unstructured (i.e. Twitter feed, web pages or sensor-enabled equipment of unknown value). Velocity relates to the speed the data is received. The faster the data is received, i.e. streaming directly into a memory source, the quicker it can be processed, which is important as certain intelligence products are required to work in real time. The final V relates to variety, which describes the growth of increasingly diverse formats of unstructured and semi-structured data, such as text, and audio, associated with increased challenges when deriving meaning. In recent years it is argued that two more Vs have materialised: value and veracity. The increased importance of data driven decision making, has generated reductions in cost (storage, analysis, and improved processing speeds). This has allowed more accuracy and efficiency when developing data driven products or solutions. However, the phenomenon of false news has also highlighted the importance of honest data, which requires due diligence before it is accepted. Whilst the term 'big data' is generally associated with commercial business it is pervasive in police discussions, especially in relation to analysis. Ferguson (2017:8) suggests that big data 'is a short-hand term for the collection and analysis of large data sets with the goal to reveal hidden patterns or insights' and goes on to argue that the tools of big data are also tools for law enforcement and surveillance. Similarly, the UK Policing Vision 2025 (NPCC, 2016) refers to the importance of a more accurate understanding of policing demand. It suggests this can be assisted by finding joint technological solutions to improve data sharing and data analysis (including forecasting).

Artificial intelligence

Artificial intelligence (AI) is linked with machine learning and the concept is reasonably straightforward. The start of the process requires a commissioner (individual or group) who specify a clear, but limited, question(s) for the data to answer. Software developers then write a code, which allows the machine (computer) to establish the optimal way to answer the question. This process is invisible to a human observer and relies on algorithms which enable the machine to learn throughout its experience (in the form of calculations), leading to the identification of patterns within these vast databases (The Information Commissioner's Office—ICO, 2020). Boosted by the processing capability of IT, coupled with the reduced cost of data storage, the results have been astounding. In 2018, a group of US universities ran a competition to test whether 20 lawyers were more effective at spotting contract loopholes than a machine using artificial intelligence. The AI found 94% of the mistakes compared with 85% success rate of the lawyers, however the machine was able to complete the task in 26 seconds, whilst the lawyers took 92 minutes (Petit, 2018).

There are concerns surrounding artificial intelligence. Its ability to manipulate human behaviour can be seen in everyday life, epitomised by the online content selection algorithms used by Twitter, Facebook and Google. These interact with online users over considerable periods, examining their selection history, identifying existing patterns, and proposing new products for an individual to purchase or information to view. This data manipulation is thought to be used by others to influence political opinion and elections through monitoring individual political interest and forwarding selected information to their attention (which can include fake news). A study conducted by the company DuckDuckGo (Paul, 2018) examined the use of specific key word searches on the devices of 87 people. When an individual entered the search term 'vaccination' nearly all the computer search engines in the study (92%) returned similar results, however for the term 'immigration' it was 63% and for 'gun control' it was 59%. This suggested that algorithms are able to monitor search terms more aligned to political interests, and direct users to specific information. This provides the potential to maintain and endorse an individual's current views, generating confirmation bias. Epstein and Robertson (2015) refer to this as the Search Engine

Manipulation Effect (SEME). They provide five separate pieces of evidence, from two countries, to show how presenting biased search rankings can change the voting preferences of undecided voters by at least 20%. This level of change can be higher in certain demographic groups and the biased search rankings can be presented to the user without their knowledge.

Machine learning

Machine learning (ML) is a critical element of artificial intelligence as it needs computational power to process the scientific algorithms and statistical models which are able to work from patterns and inference. When these are used to find solutions to business problems the process can also be described as predictive analytics. Babuta (2017:3) explains 'The theories underlying machine learning are statistical, and therefore ML algorithms deal with probabilistic classifications or predictions, not certainties, and generalisations from particular observations'. This leads to the concern that any system supported by machine learning will duplicate human biases as they will be written into the system. For example, if a particular subsection of the community is targeted in relation to a particular crime, the algorithm will highlight that this group is posing an increased risk. Based on this information the police are more likely to target this group once more, which in turn leads to a self-fulfilling prophecy (Buranyi, 2017). Angwin et al. (2016) established that a sentencing algorithm used by a US court to highlight the risk of repeat offending was disproportionately affected by ethnicity, with only 20% of those identified as being likely to commit violence actually doing so. At the time of writing, UK education has been under scrutiny for A-Level and GCSE gradings following the controversial use of an algorithm.

Data visualisation

Any data findings need to be conveyed effectively to the user and in this process visualisation through charts, graphs and maps consistently improve understanding. Crime data visualisation is seen as a 'must have' for law enforcement (Walker & Drawve, 2018). Data visualisation has previously emphasised crime mapping, association charts and sequence of events, with the latter two being key topics on basic analyst training (Anacapa in the USA and NIAT in the UK). This visualisation has been useful for intelligence briefings, as long as the process adds meaning to assist decision-making. Indeed, over the past decade crime mapping has developed as part of the analytical process, rather than being an end in itself (Chainey & Ratcliffe, 2005). High-quality publications exist to improve the use of crime mapping by analysts (Chainey & Ratcliffe, 2005; Santos, 2014), which explain how the process can be used to test ideas and hypotheses, rather than simply displaying dots on a map. These publications increase understanding on such subjects as what makes a hot spot 'hot' and 'cluster significance' (Grubesic & Murray, 2001). For example, is it the time of the event that creates the hot spot and if so, how might this determine resource allocation? These questions (and others) support hypotheses generation, which lead to more productive analysis, leading to a better quality intelligence product. Unfortunately, whilst there is evidence of clear benefits in the academic literature of GIS (Geographic Information System), its potential remains underutilised.

One further point is that although a number of software providers offer numerous ways to display real time data, this can only be done if an IT infrastructure can link the data with the visualisation software. It is obviously beneficial to quickly see how many crimes are occurring, at a particular time and place, however this software often generates licensing costs. At the time this chapter was being written there was considerable work being undertaken by HMICFRS, to develop a national data visualisation process for the national inspection framework, known as PEEL, through the use of Microsoft Power BI (other software solutions are available!) The idea being that the data from each police force could be visualised by all.

Big data and ethics

Analysis of historical crime data can, in theory, bring many benefits. It can provide insight to make decisions about patrol deployment (Bennet Moses & Chan, 2016), and recommend which crimes should be investigated or filed. It can also predict where and when the next crime will occur, or whether a sex offender is likely to reoffend. However, the use of big data to assist in these decisions can be controversial.

The police in most developed countries operate on a consent-based relationship, underpinned by trust (Bottoms & Tankebe, 2012; Jackson & Bradford, 2010; Tyler, 2004). This means that any activity, including the use of technology and data, must be perceived to be fair and just (Bradford et al., 2018; Tyler, 2006). The concern is that new data led approaches often emerge prior to guidance, protocols, and legislation to guarantee this legitimacy. As such the inability to maintain trust has been highlighted as the downside to data-led policing approaches (Meijer & Wessels, 2019; Grace, 2019; Završnik, 2019). The main concern occurs because algorithms work on mathematical calculations, which cannot be considered neutral as they can entrench pre-existing bias. Further, they are unable to take into account the current context or ethics of a situation in the same way that human decision making can (Couchman, 2019). This is an ambiguous area and there is little research looking at the efficacy of these algorithms on real world scenarios (Bennet Moses & Chan, 2016). This makes it really important to differentiate between decisions based on systems and those generated by humans (London Police Ethics Panel, 2019).

Big data and predictive analytics are used by most large retailers, and an example which highlights the ethics of this was provided by the US based superstore, Target (Duhigg, 2012). The store chain wanted to identify new mothers, who normally buy their items (baby milk to toys) from a variety of stores as they wished to entice them to purchase everything from Target. This was seen as a particular opportunity as the period surrounding pregnancy is when consumers are particularly susceptible to changing consumer allegiance and purchasing behaviour. Target therefore asked one of their statisticians to identify pregnant women without their knowledge, in order to send them marketing material. Data analysis found the purchase of approximately 25 products (ranging from supplements to scent free soap), could indicate different stages of pregnancy and allow an individual pregnancy prediction score to be allocated. This was linked to their customer ID number, which also provided information as to how they responded to marketing (i.e. response to discount vouchers). The ethical issues were underlined a year after these marketing changes when a man complained to the Minneapolis store manager that his high school daughter had been sent discount coupons for baby items. He angrily asked if the store was encouraging her to get pregnant. The manager apologised at the time and rang back a week later, to reiterate his contrition. It was at this stage the man confessed that his daughter had revealed she was pregnant but had been keeping it from him. In essence individual electronic footprints can generate extremely detailed profiles. Other insights, such as sexual orientation, can be easily established through online purchases, social media associates and browsing sites. Whilst the majority of this online analysis is made in good faith to make life easier, this type of sensitive information is open to abuse.

A specific ethical concern regarding technology and data in the policing environment has been Live Facial Recognition software (LFR), the purpose of which is to automatically scan crowds of people and analyse biometric facial data to confirm matches against subjects of interest (Denham, 2019; Fussey & Murray, 2019). It raises a number of ethical issues which include: the right to privacy (many people who have their image collected and analysed are citizens going about their lawful business); accuracy and bias within algorithms and machine learning process (accuracy is thought to differ in terms of ethnicity); and the lack of specific legislation to cover its use. This was challenged in the case Bridges vs South Wales Police, where the police were challenged under Human Rights Act 1998, Data Protection Act 2018, and Equality Act 2010. The police initially defended the challenge successfully due to their actions which included not retaining the data of images scanned in the area. However, the High Court said their decision should not be interpreted as blanket authorisation for other areas to use it in all circumstances. In August 2020 this decision was overturned on appeal and the use of LFR was deemed to be unlawful. However the Court of Appeal based its ruling not on the fact that the use of LFR was disproportionate but that there was no clear guidance on when it should be used; who could be placed on a watchlist; the lack of sufficiently robust data protection impact statement in place; and the absence of reasonable steps to establish if the software had a gender or racial bias. It is expected that LFR will continue to be used in the UK, as it is in other countries, following further safeguards being introduced.

As with other chapters it is also prudent to highlight implementation failure, which has further been illustrated with Body Worn Video (BWV). This is generally reported as a technology that can improve public and police behaviour (Brucato, 2015; Rowe, 2007), assist analysis, and help in the audit of police compliance (HMIC, 2013). However, this relies on it being used appropriately and there are many reports of it not being switched on, being inappropriately switched off, or damaged (*Washington Post*, 2016). This means that analysts should always be aware of the reliability of their data as well as the absence of data.

Section 2: Exploring how big data and associated techniques have been used in a police operational setting

The analysis of large amounts of data is viewed as a means to identify solutions and predict future patterns, although the capability to evaluate huge amounts of data remains challenging (Kumar & Nagpal, 2018). Reviews on the police use of big data are extremely limited in both the UK (Babuta, 2017) and the USA (Ridgeway, 2018). Babuta (2017) argues that in the UK, the approach is seen across three areas: The National DNA database; mass surveillance; and predictive policing. All three are supported by a number of national databases. The Police National Computer (PNC) has 12.2m personal records, 62.6m vehicle records, and 58.5m driver records, the *Ident1* system contains 7m fingerprint records, and the National (UK) DNA database has over 5m records on file. Finally, there is the Police National Database (PND), designed to interrogate 220 databases from individual police forces, potentially holding approximately 3.5 billion records (Babuta, 2017).

Policy makers and police leaders are often interested in predicting future crimes and how demand impacts on police resources. Babuta (2017) explains that police use of big data is severely limited due to the diverse, fragmented, and incompatible nature of police databases. Indeed, even digital information is regularly confined to manual searches, although the knowledge is available to design automatic analysis software. This reduces the ability to exploit wide-ranging surveillance information, which is often unstructured (i.e. video imagery or voice recording). Previous attempts to predict where crime will occur, using systems such as PredPol and CompStat, have failed to gain long term traction, although the topic continues to generate research (Ratcliffe et al., 2020). The most notable aspect of predictive policing concerns hotspots and a systematic review shows the positive benefits of targeting these areas (Braga et al., 2019). However, the approach currently predicts future offending in a given area rather than providing particular insight into the type of crime, suggesting the term 'forecasting' rather than 'prediction' provides a more accurate explanation (Ratcliffe, 2019). Meijer and Wessels (2019) conducted a systematic review of the available research around predictive policing initiatives, finding it to be supported by strong arguments and anecdotal evidence, rather than an evidence base of systematic empirical research. Nevertheless, efforts to generate data driven predictions continue and in the UK police forces are being asked by the Home Office to develop Force Management Statements (FMS) (HMICFRS, 2018). These are comprehensive documents, known to exceed 150 pages, aiming to assess the capability and capacity of the police force in dealing with demand at a strategic level over the next 3–5 years. They examine four basic areas (HMICFRS, 2019:10):

1   Establish the gap between current demand and demand expected in the next four years.
2   Establish the current status of the workforce and other assets: including performance, condition, capacity, capability, serviceability, wellbeing and security of supply.
3   Explain what will be done to enable the workforce and associated assets to meet future anticipated demand. For example changing the skills of the workforce, investing in new ICT, or improving work processes.
4   Describe the type and level of future demand the force is concerned it will not be able to meet (having made the changes and efficiencies in step 3).

Coupled with this there are many other projects involving the police and wider Criminal Justice sector, working with partners, especially academia, eager to use data mining techniques on large databases. There are many ad hoc examples of big data projects. In 2018 the Lancashire Constabulary worked with Leeds University on a project that used machine learning to identify hate speech on Twitter (Leeds Institute for Data Analytics, 2018). This research provided Lancashire Constabulary with a clearer picture of victim and offender profiles, as well as where and when the incidents were occurring, allowing resources to be allocated more effectively. The learning from this project has been used to re-focus a multi-agency response in tackling hate crime and has emphasised the importance of accurate crime recording and the application of appropriate analytical techniques. Secondly, Durham Constabulary (2020), in collaboration with the University of Cambridge, also used an algorithmic approach in their HART model (Harm Assessment Risk Tool), to support officer decision making regarding re-offending risk. This supports the Constabulary Checkpoint programme which aims to reduce reoffending by providing tailor-made interventions to tackle underlying issues such as mental health and substance abuse. The intention is to divert suitable offenders rather than perpetuate their offending by bringing them into the Criminal Justice System (Durham Constabulary, 2020). The use of the algorithm for HART is said to be experimental and 'subject to ongoing assessment and validation' (Oswald et al., 2018:225). Finally, in a similar vein, Kent Constabulary has been working with University of Cambridge in the development of EBIT (Evidence-Based Investigatory Tool), to produce a probability score of a crime's solvability. Eight factors were found to influence the solvability of an investigation and these factors form the basis of the algorithm applied to other unsolved cases to assess the likelihood of a resolution. Not all crimes are used in the algorithm (hate crimes, domestic abuse or crimes involving vulnerable people are excluded). The aim is to reduce officer time investigating cases that are unlikely to generate a positive outcome and to redirect their efforts more productively. Yet despite the potential learning that this approach can have, the use of the algorithm has attracted criticism, not just in relation to EBIT (Howgego, 2019) but also nationally (Grace, 2019) and further afield (Miró-Llinares, 2020; Završnik, 2019).

Again, the concerns are that these algorithms contain the bias which is implicit within existing recorded data (Ferguson, 2017). Recorded data is an extension of how police officers and police staff decide to report and record crimes and incidents. Ferguson (2017) refers to this as 'black data', although the concept is not uniquely linked to black people. He argues that 'black data exposes how all marginalised communities face a growing threat from big data policing systems' (Ferguson, 2017:5). Therefore, any bias in any recorded data will be amplified by an algorithm. Over time this bias should (hopefully) work its way out of the system, possibly through the application of improved computer science techniques. However, currently this presents a challenge to any police force looking to exploit technology, such as machine learning or AI. Ethical considerations will continue to run alongside the narrative for increased investment on this type of technology. Police forces need to ensure that ethical considerations are taken into account and projects can stand up to external scrutiny, similar to those 'checks and balances' recognised by Durham in the example above.

In summarising this section, Oswald et al. (2018:224) noted that 14% of forces responding to a UK FOI request 'did use some form of computational or algorithmic intelligence analysis or decision-making software'. However, the use of algorithms and machine learning within policing appears to be in a developmental stage in the UK and USA. There are no national programmes or standards in respect of their use, and they are instigated on a case by case basis, often in collaboration with a specialist partner agency.

Section 3: The challenges for police forces and intelligence analysts in maximising the potential of data

Role and responsibilities of the analyst

To establish the role of the police analyst in the use of data it is useful to review three different approaches: data science, crime analysis, and crime science. The characteristics of each approach are summarised in Figure 8.4.

Data science:	Crime analysis:	Crime science:
Data capture Data Maintenance Data Processing Data Analysis Data Communication (Berkely School of Information, 2020).	Identify / explain crime and incidents to support strategic and tactical deployment of resources to prevent and detect crime (Pearce, 2008).	The application of scientific methods to the study of crime and security problems with the aim of reducing harm (Cockbain & Laycock, 2017).

Figure 8.1 Elements of science within law enforcement analysis

Although these three categories can be compatible, each has its own emphasis. Data science emphasises the use of big data, which has predominantly been used in the commercial sector, and requires specialist skills to process and interpret large datasets. The crime analysis approach focuses exclusively on improving decision making for law enforcement personnel, although not specifying the means in which this is achieved it mentions such techniques as crime pattern analysis. Finally, crime science places the emphasis on using scientific methods to analyse data and information, to assist decision making. As its name suggests it focuses on crime, although it is also a suitable approach for those agencies which exist outside law enforcement (i.e. government, architects, social services). In essence, crime science pursues a similar approach to crime analysis but asks that the analyst conduct the role using a more rigorous research-based methodology, whilst in contrast a data science approach requires a more radical departure from current practice.

A data science approach, which exploits big data, requires a direct link between data users (analysts) and the police IT department, more specifically the data modellers (or data scientists). Data modelling relates to the design and building of databases. The aim is to ensure that all data within the database is organised logically and physically to improve extraction and manipulation. To simplify this discussion for law enforcement there are two elements at play. The first is in relation to the data management, in essence its identification, collection, and extraction. This can be achieved in a variety of ways, but requires a person with the skills, knowledge and experience in database structure, programming languages, data extraction and data modelling or data science. These skills are needed at the beginning of the process, to ensure that data is collected and stored appropriately, allowing easier extraction in the future. The second element relates to analysis, which is the interpretation of data to make it meaningful for decision makers. Whilst traditional police analyst skills serve as a good foundation, newer skills are required to meet the changing environment. It is unclear whether it is possible, or even desirable, for staff to cover the continuum between data science and crime science. Other approaches would be to divide the skill sets across employees or work in collaboration with academics and other specialist organisations. In understanding this further it is useful to break this process down into its various stages to help assess where analyst skills and training should focus. The model below sets out the skill sets required by analysts, which cover the basic tenants of data collection, modelling, extraction, analysis and visualisation (see Figure 8.2).

Most police analysts have a level of data analysis and visualisation skills. Often this will depend on their individual background, employer, role responsibilities and training opportunities. In contrast many analysts will have little or no knowledge and skills in the early stages of the process (data collection, modelling and extraction). This is often performed within the IT structure, either in the business analysis or the data science arena, and the linking of all these aspects is rare.

This confusion is often reflected in the numerous prefixes to the analyst role: criminal intelligence analyst, performance analyst, partnership analyst, major investigation analyst, business and data analyst, to name but a few. The responsibilities of these roles can vary from force to force. Some police forces have looked to develop existing analyst roles and move them towards data science, whereas other forces have kept the roles separate, maintaining data science within their IT infrastructure. So, should intelligence and crime analysts become data scientists? Should organisations invest in the recruitment of specialist data scientists, or would it be more effective if police forces were to work in collaboration with externally based data scientists? The answers to these questions have a significant bearing on the strategic direction of a police force, as well as affecting the structure and role of analyst posts. It is therefore incumbent on individual organisations to examine what structure best suits their organisation and deliver this through appropriate investment. This may pose some organisational challenges due to the resources being held between intelligence and IT departments. Further, there are also obvious inefficiencies for national institutional development if individual law enforcement agencies make these decisions in a piecemeal and fragmented way.

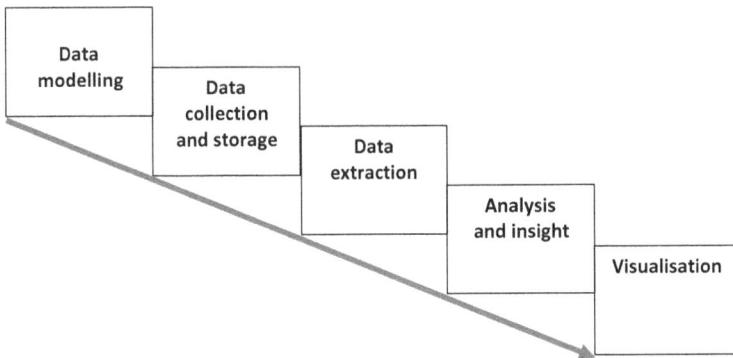

Figure 8.2 From data collection to data visualisation

Conclusion

'Datafication' is a term used by Mayer-Schönberger and Cukier (2013) referring to the use and transformation of data by the organisation. It is not simply about 'lots of data', but understanding what data is held and its value, as well as how the organisation can analyse it more effectively. As they argue, data is much more than the simple digitisation of information. The use of big data, machine learning and algorithms is changing the nature of established intelligence protocols and criminal justice procedures (Završnik, 2019), and their obvious potential is being commonly discussed in policing (Fox et al., 2019). However, police chiefs need to ensure that they do not become seduced by the science and recognise that new technologies should enhance analysis rather than replace it. Walker and Drawve (2019:235) draw on the four myths identified by Perry et al. (2013):

- Myth 1: the computer actually knows the future.
- Myth2: the computer will do everything for you.
- Myth 3: you need a high-powered and expensive model.
- Myth 4: accurate predictions automatically lead to crime reductions.

Walker and Drawve (2019) explain that these myths present problems for analysts, especially when police officers believe them. It is simply not the case that predictive computer systems reduce the requirement for analysts. Whilst new software solutions, apps and technologies provide new approaches for police forces, a key ingredient continues to be a trained and knowledgeable analyst who is aware of the techniques to use and when to use them. This means that investment is required, not just in the technology, but also in the knowledge and skills of analysts, so they can be used. This evolution may mean an increase in collaborations with other institutions, such as academia, where specialist data science skills can be explored. Current frailties are particularly exposed when external researchers request data or conduct analysis of existing data, as data mining skills such as SSMS, SRS, R or Python are rare. The latter two systems are particularly problematic as open source software is not permitted beyond police IT firewalls, despite them being free and increasingly used in academia.

A further change is the growing emphasis on data visualisation, with many police forces (at this time) adopting programs such as Microsoft Power BI, Clikview or Tableau to present their information. Guilfoyle (2015) has noted that officers have become transfixed with presenting data in a visual form as opposed to understanding what it really means. He, and others, argue that this has often misinformed decision making and devalues the analytical process (Chainey, 2012; Cope, 2004). Whilst data visualisation techniques can influence the audience before a word has been read (Archambault et al., 2015), if there is insufficient analysis it provides little insight (Few, 2004).

Ultimately there is little doubt that there will be increased demand for the manipulation of large data sets. The success of investigative journalists in international incidents (i.e. Salisbury poisonings – see Chapter 7) has shown the power that digital analysis can have. More locally, an opportunity for a new approach to data collection, analysis and presentation could start with Force Management Statements (FMS) in England and Wales, as this provides an opportunity to rethink the data collection framework in a policing context. It would be appropriate that police analysts and academics are involved in discussions to redefine data collection frameworks as this would improve the analysis surrounding crimes, incidents, and other calls for service. Collecting the right data will enhance the introduction of technological solutions, which provide insight to improve policing services. A 'systems thinking' perspective is especially useful in this context to consider the challenges associated with police demand. Whatever route law enforcement agencies navigate it is ultimately required that analysts become more skilled if they are to deliver the existing potential that technology and data provides. Rigorous science is still missing from much of police analysis. National oversight agencies, practitioners and their leaders all share a responsibility to promulgate innovative practice, and develop working partnerships for sharing skills, knowledge and experience. Pease and Roach (2017) have argued that experience is just as important in personal development and Evans (2008:112) has noted that analysts should view continuous professional development as a priority, emphasising the importance of staying up to date with research, being creative and street smart to solve real world problems.

References

Angwin J., Larson, J., Mattu, S. and Kirchner, L. (2016) Machine Bias. *ProPublica*, 23 May 2016. Available at https://www.propublica.org/article/machine-bias-risk-a ssessments-in-criminal-sentencing [Accessed 22 March 2020].

Archambault, S., Helouvry, S., Strohl, B. and Williams, G. (2015) Data visualisation as a communication tool. *Library Hi-Tech News*, 32 (2): 1–9.

Ariel, B. (2019) Technology in policing. In D. Weisburd and A. Braga (eds). *Police Innovation: Contrasting Perspectives*. Cambridge University Press.

Babuta, A. (2017) *Big Data and Policing: An Assessment of Law Enforcement Requirements, Expectations and Priorities*. Available at https://rusi.org/sites/default/files/ 201709_rusi_big_data_and_policing_babuta_web.pdf, [Accessed 22 March 2020].

Banton, C. (2019) Data Science. Available at https://www.investopedia.com/terms/d/da ta-science.asp [Accessed 23 May 2020].

Bennett Moses, L. and Chan, J. (2016) Algorithmic prediction in policing: Assumptions, evaluation and accountability. *Policing and Society*, 28 (7): 806–822.

Berkeley School of Information. (2020) What is Data Science. Available at https://data science.berkeley.edu/about/what-is-data-science/ [Accessed 23 May 2020].

Berry, J. (2010) *Criminal Justice Units and Case Building: Reducing Bureaucracy in Policing*. London: Home Office.

Bottoms, A. and Tankebe, J. (2012) Beyond Procedural Justice: A dialogue approach to legitimacy in Criminal Justice. *Journal of Criminal Law and Criminology*, 102 (1), 119–170.

Boyd, D. and Crawford, C. (2012) Critical questions for big data: provocations for a cultural, technological, and scholarly phenomenon. *Information, Communication & Society*, 15 (5): 663.

Bradford, B., Jackson, J. and Hough, M. (2018) Trust in Justice. In E. Uslaner (ed.). *The Oxford Handbook of Social and Political Trust*. Oxford: Oxford University Press.

Braga, A., Turchan, B.S., Papachristos, A.V. and Hureau, D. (2019) Hot spots policing and crime reduction: an update of an ongoing systematic review and meta-analysis. *Journal of Experimental Criminology*, 15: 289–311.

Bramer, M. (2016) *Principles of Data Mining* (3rd edn). London: Springer.

Brucato, B. (2015) The new transparency: Police violence in the context of ubiquitous surveillance. *Media and Communication*, 3 (3): 455–473.

Buranyi, S. (2017) Rise of the racist robots – How AI is learning all our worst impulses. *The Guardian*, 8 August 2017.

Chainey, S. (2012) Improving the explanatory content of analysis products using hypothesis testing. *Policing: A Journal of Policy and Practice*, 6 (2): 108–121.

Chainey, S. and Ratcliffe, J. (2005) *GIS and Crime Mapping*. Chichester: John Wiley.

Connelly, G. (2013) Multi agency working. In T.G.K. Bryce, W.M. Humes, D. Gillies and A. Kennedy (eds). *Scottish Education*. Edinburgh: Edinburgh University Press.

Cope, N. (2004) Intelligence led Policing or policing led intelligence: integrating volume crime analysis into policing. *British Journal of Criminology*, 44 (2): 188–203.

Couchman, H. (2019) *Policing by Machine: Predictive Policing and the Threat to our Rights*. London: Liberty. Available at https://www.libertyhumanrights.org.uk/wp -content/uploads/2020/02/LIB-11-Predictive-Policing-Report-WEB.pdf [Accessed 8 July 2020].

Denham, E. (2019) Information Commissioner's Opinion: The use of live facial recognition technology by law enforcement in public places. Available at https://ico.org.uk/m edia/about-the-ico/documents/2616184/live-frt-law-enforcement-opinion-20191031.pdf [Accessed on 20 May 2020].

Diekmann, A.(2009) *Empirische Sozialforschung: Grundlagen Methoden Anwendungen*. Reinbek beim Hamburg:Rowohlt.

Duhigg, C. (2012) How companies learn your secrets. Available at https://www.nytim es.com/2012/02/19/magazine/shopping-habits.html?pagewanted=1&_r=1&hp [Accessed 28 May 2020].

Durham Constabulary. (2020) Checkpoint. Available at https://www.durham.police.uk/ Information-and-advice/Pages/Checkpoint.aspx [Accessed 23 May 2020].

Epstein, R. and Robertson, R.E. (2015) Search engine manipulation effect (SEME). *Proceedings of the National Academy of Sciences*, 112 (33): E4512–E4521; Available at https://www.pnas.org/content/112/33/E4512DOI:10.1073/pnas.1419828112 [Accessed 12 June 2020].

Evans, M. (2008) Cultural paradigms and change: a model of analysis. In C. Harfield, A. MacVean, J. Grieve and D. Phillips (eds). *The Handbook of Intelligent Policing*. Oxford: Oxford University Press.

Ferguson, A.G. (2017) *The Rise of Big Data Policing: Surveillance, Race and the Future of Law Enforcement*. New York: New York Press.

Few, S. (2004) Tapping the power of visual perception. Available at https://www.percep tualedge.com/articles/ie/visual_perception.pdf [Accessed 17 May 2020].

Fox, A.M., Sedelmaier, C.M. and White, M.D. (2019) The role of technology in the strategies for policing innovation program: challenges, solutions and lessons learned. Available at https://www.researchgate.net/publication/337981275_THE_ROLE_OF_ TECHNOLOGY_IN_THE_STRATEGIES_FOR_POLICING_INNOVATION_ PROGRAM_Challenges_Solutions_and_Lessons_Learned [Accessed 23 May 2020].

Fussey, P. and Murray, D. (2019) *Independent Report on the London Metropolitan Police Service's Trial of Live Facial Recognition Technology Facial Recognition Technology.* Project Report. University of Essex Human Rights Centre. Available at http://repository.essex.ac.uk/24946/ [Accessed 14 April 2020].

Grace, J. (2019) 'Algorithmic impropriety' in UK policing contexts: A developing narrative? Available at SSRN: https://papers.ssrn.com/sol3/papers.cfm?abstract_id= 3487424 [Accessed 7 February 2020].

Grubesic, T. and Murray, A. (2001) Detecting hot-spots using cluster analysis and GIS. Paper presented at the 5th annual international crime mapping research conference, Dallas: Texas. Available at https://pdfs.semanticscholar.org/c3db/1455ca 4f771195525cf128efcdc866145045.pdf [Accessed 10 February 2020].

Guilfoyle, S. (2015) Binary comparisons and police performance measurement: good or bad? *Policing: A Journal of Policy and Practice*, 9 (2): 195–209.

Hibberd, M. (2015) Observations from no-man's land. *Police Professional*, 15 July 2015.

HMIC. (2013) Stop and search powers: Are the police using them effectively and fairly? Available at https://www.justiceinspectorates.gov.uk/hmicfrs/publications/stop -and-search-powers-20130709/ [Accessed 13 May 2020].

HMICFRS. (2019) *Force Management Statement: Template and Guidance for Forces.* Available at https://www.justiceinspectorates.gov.uk/hmicfrs/wp-content/uploads/for ce-management-statements-2-guidance-and-template.pdf [Accessed on 10 June 2020].

HMICRFS. (2018) *Force Management Statements.* Available at https://www.justiceinsp ectorates.gov.uk/hmicfrs/police-forces/integrated-peel-assessments/force-managem ent-statements/ [accessed on 26 August 2020].

Home Office. (2020) *Home Office Annual Data Requirement (ADR) Data.* Available at https://www.gov.uk/government/publications/home-office-crime-and-policing-resea rch-and-annual-data-requirement-adr-data-privacy-information-notices/home-office-a nnual-data-requirement-adr-data-privacy-information-notice [Accessed 28 May 2020].

Howgego, J. (2019) A UK police force is dropping tricky cases on advice of an algorithm. *New Scientist*, 8 January 2019. Available at https://www.newscientist.com/a rticle/2189986-a-uk-police-force-is-dropping-tricky-cases-on-advice-of-an-algorithm/ [Accessed on 19 February 2020].

ICO. (2000) *CCTV: Code of Practice.* London: Information Commissioner's Office. Available at http://www.ico.gov.uk/upload/documents/library/data_protection/deta iled_specialist_guides/ CCTV_code_of_practice.pdf [Accessed on 24 February 2020].

Jackson, J. and Bradford, B. (2010) What is trust and confidence in the police? *Policing: A Journal of Policy and Practice*, 4 (3): 241–248.

Kearns, I. and Muir, R. (2019) Data driven policing and public value. Available at https:// www.police-foundation.org.uk/2017/wp-content/uploads/2010/10/data_driven_policing_ final.pdf [Accessed on 20 May 2020].

Koper, C.S., Lum, C. and Willis, J. (2014) Realizing the potential of technology in policing: A multisite study of the social, organizational, and behavioural aspects of implementing policing technologies. Report for the National Institute of Justice, US Department of Justice: Center for Evidence Based Crime Policy, George Mason University and Police Executive Research Forum.

Kumar, R. and Nagpal, B. (2018) Analysis and prediction of crime patterns using Big Data. *International Journal of Information Technology*, 11 (4):799–805.

Laney, D. (2001) 3D Data Management: Controlling data volume, velocity, and variety. Available at https://blogs.gartner.com/doug-laney/files/2012/01/ad949-3D-Data-Management-Controlling-Data-Volume-Velocity-and-Variety.pdf [Accessed 3 April 2020]

Leeds Institute for Data Analytics. (2018) Application of natural language processing for identification of online hate on Twitter. Available at https://lida.leeds.ac.uk/research-projects/application-natural-language-processing-identification-online-hate-twitter/ [Accessed 23 May 2020].

London Police Ethics Panel. (2019) *Final report on Live Facial Recognition – May 2019*. Available at http://www.policingethicspanel.london/reports.html [Accessed 14 August 2020].

McAleer, S.R., Kogut, P. and Raes, L. (2018) The case for collaborative policy experimentation using advanced geospatial spatial data analytics and visualisation. *Internet Science*. Available at https://www.springerprofessional.de/en/the-case-for-collaborative-policy-experimentation-using-advanced/15554220 [Accessed 6 July 2020].

Marr, B. (2018) How much data do we create every day? The mind-blowing stats everyone should read. Available at https://www.forbes.com/sites/bernardmarr/2018/05/21/how-much-data-do-we-create-every-day-the-mind-blowing-stats-everyone-should-read/#f6acd8660ba9 [Acessed 26 April 2020].

May, T. (2001) *Social Research: Issues, Methods & Process* (3rd edn). Buckingham: Open University.

Mayer-Schönberger, V. and Cukier, K. (2013) *Big Data*. New York: Houghton Mifflin.

Meijer, A. and Wessels, M. (2019) Predictive policing: review of benefits and drawbacks. *International Journal of Public Administration*, 42 (12): 1031–1039.

Miró-Llinares, F. (2020) Predictive policing: Utopia or dystopia? On attitudes towards the use of big data algorithms for law enforcement. Available at https://osf.io/preprints/socarxiv/a7juk/ [Accessed 12 February 2020].

NPCC. (2016) *Policing Vision 2025*. Available at https://www.npcc.police.uk/documents/Policing%20Vision.pdf [Accessed 5 May 2020].

Oswald, M., Grace, J., Urwin, S. and Barnes, G.C. (2018) Algorithmic risk assessment policing models: lessons from the Durham HART model and 'Experimental' proportionality. *Information & Communications Technology Law*, 27 (2): 223–250.

Paul, K. (2018) Google's algorithms are keeping us in a political bubble, study finds. Available at https://www.marketwatch.com/story/googles-algorithms-are-keeping-us-in-a-political-bubble-study-finds-2018-12-04 [Accessed 22 March 2020].

Pease, K., Ignatans, D. and Batty, L. (2018) Whatever happened to repeat victimisation? *Crime Prevention and Community Safety*, 20 (4): 256–267.

Pease, K. and Roach, J. (2017) How to morph experience into evidence. In J. Knutsson and L. Tompson (eds). *Advances in Evidence-Based Policing*. Abingdon: Routledge.

Perry, L.W., McInnis, B., Price, C.C., Smith, S.C. and Hollywood, J.S. (2013) *Predictive Policing: The Role of Crime Forecasting in Law Enforcement Operations*. Santa Monica: Rand.

Petit, H. (2018) The AI that is faster and more accurate than top human lawyers when spotting legal issues in contracts. Available at https://www.dailymail.co.uk/science

tech/article-5435479/The-AI-outperforms-human-lawyers.html [Accessed 22 May 2020].

Ratcliffe, J. (2019) Predictive policing. In D. Weisburd and A. Braga, (eds). *Police Innovation: Contrasting Perspectives* (2nd edn). Cambridge: Cambridge University Press.

Ratcliffe, J., Taylor, R., Askey, A., Thomas, K., Grasso, J., Bethel, K., Fisher, R. and Koehnlein, J. (2020) The Philadelphia predictive policing experiment. *Journal of Experimental Criminology.* Available at https://doi.org/10.1007/s11292-019-09400-2 [Accessed on 10 February 2020].

Ridgeway, G. (2018) Policing in the era of big data. *Annual Review of Criminology,* 1 (1): 401–419. Available at https://www.annualreviews.org/doi/abs/10.1146/annurev-criminol-062217-114209 [Accessed 22 March 2020].

Rowe, M. (2007) Rendering visible the invisible: Police discretion, professionalism and decision-making. *Policing and Society,* 17 (3): 279–294.

Santos, R.B. (2014) The effectiveness of crime analysis for crime reduction: Cure or diagnosis? *Journal of Contemporary Criminal Justice,* 30 (2): 147–168.

Seddon, J. (2008) *Systems Thinking in the Public Sector.* Axminster: Triarchy Press.

Stanko, B. (2008) Strategic intelligence: Methodologies for understanding what police services already 'know' to reduce harm. In C. Harfield, A. MacVean, J.G.D. Grieve and D. Phillips (eds). *The Handbook of Intelligent Policing: Consilience, Crime Control, and Community Safety.* Oxford: Oxford University Press.

Tyler, T.R. (2004) Enhancing police legitimacy. *The Annals of the Academy of Political and Social Sciences,* 593: 84–99.

Tyler, T.R. (2006) *Why People Obey the Law.* Princeton: Princeton University Press.

University of Wisconsin. (2017) *A Modern History of Data Science.* Available at https://datasciencedegree.wisconsin.edu/blog/history-of-data-science/ [Accessed 23 May 2020].

Von Gunten, L., Hümbelin, O. and Fritschi, T. (2014) *Administrative Data: Benefits and Challenges for Social Security Research.* Illustrated by Research Projects at the Berne University of Applied Science, Social Work Division. Available at https://ecpr.eu/Filestore/PaperProposal/c37024ae-ed80-4fc8-b8b2-0c22a14a648f.pdf [Accessed on 29 April 2020].

Walker, J. and Drawve, G. (2018) *Foundations of Crime Analysis: Data, Analyses and Mapping.* London: Routledge.

Washington Post. (2016) A new report shows the limits of police body cameras. Available at https://www.washingtonpost.com/gdpr-consent/?next_url=https%3a%2f%2fwww.washingtonpost.com%2fnews%2fthe-watch%2fwp%2f2016%2f02%2f05%2fa-new-report-shows-the-limits-of-police-body-cameras%2f [Accessed 3 May 2020].

Waterhouse, J. (2019) Criminals escaping justice due to IT system. Available at https://www.bbc.co.uk/news/uk-46964659 [Accessed 27 January 2020].

Wheeler, A. (2020) Admin data should be used more often in policing research. Blog post 13 May 2020. Available at https://andrewpwheeler.com/2020/05/13/admin-data-should-be-used-more-often-in-policing-research/ [Accessed on 17 May 2020].

Završnik, A. (2019) Algorithmic justice: Algorithms and big data in criminal justice settings. *European Journal of Criminology.* Available at https://journals.sagepub.com/doi/10.1177/1477370819876762 [Accessed on 26 March 2020].

Chapter 9

Improving intelligence analysis – meeting future challenges

Introduction

On the 3rd July 2020 news broadcasters across Europe disclosed a successful intelligence led operation, named Operation Venetic, which culminated in the arrest of 746 organised crime offenders and the seizure of £54m cash, 77 firearms and over two tonnes of illicit drugs. It was the epitome of a successful intelligence led operation. Police officers from across the continent had shared knowledge and technology to infiltrate EncroChat, an encrypted secure mobile phone instant messaging service provided to around 60,000 users worldwide (about 10,000 in the UK). As a spokesperson explained, 'The infiltration of this command and control communication platform for the UK's criminal marketplace is like having an inside person in every top organised crime group in the country' (NCA, 2020). The operation clearly showed how high-quality intelligence, when properly analysed and actioned, can transform the criminal environment.

Improving intelligence analysis is the core theme of this book and this concluding chapter seeks to review whether the current knowledge and practice is sufficient to meet future challenges. The police and wider law enforcement agencies have been associated with an intelligence-led approach since the 1970s, building upon examples found in the military and commercial sector. Predicting when, where and how offenders will strike is beneficial not only to law enforcement agencies but also to the commercial 'policing' sector (i.e. insurance and security companies) and the third sector (i.e. victim/community support groups). All of these organisations face similar challenges in that they seek to continually improve their services for their users whilst managing tighter financial budgets. The previous chapters have shown that an intelligence-led approach can deliver both of these aims and that is why significant sums of money have been invested. However, not all of this expenditure has delivered value for money and, over a number of decades, an intelligence-ed approach has been associated with criticism, scandal and intelligence failures across the world.

Of course, it is easy for commentators to dispense criticism, especially when they stand on the side-lines and suffer no consequences. In this, Sir Ronnie Flanagan (a previous Chief HMIC and distinguished orator) favoured a Theodore Roosevelt quotation to inspire police audiences:

> It is not the critic who counts, not the man who points out how the strong man stumbles or where the doer of deeds could have done better. The credit belongs to the man who is actually in the arena, whose face is marred by dust and sweat and blood, who strives valiantly, who errs and comes up short again and again, because there is no effort without error or shortcoming, but who knows the great enthusiasms, the great devotions, who spends himself for a worthy cause; who, at the best, knows, in the end, the triumph of high achievement, and who, at the worst, if he fails, at least he fails while daring greatly, so that his place shall never be with those cold and timid souls who knew neither victory nor defeat.
>
> (cited by Kowalczyk-Harper, 2016)

Police employees appreciate these sentiments because they understand the difficulties of decision making in complex operational environments and have little respect for those who rely on hindsight. Nonetheless, in any field of operation, poor decisions will be apparent, and it is the role of academics to establish the patterns that underpin them. Indeed, the requirement for police analysts to improve working practices and deliver improved operational and organisational outcomes has never been greater. As Flanagan (2008:4) said, 'policing is far too important to be left to the police alone', and this final chapter accepts his invitation. The preceding chapters have provided an overview of how the intelligence framework works, current techniques, good practice and the challenges for the future. The purpose of this chapter is to summarise these issues and suggest where improvements can be made. This will be done in three sections.

- Section 1: Will discuss the future direction of policing to better understand how intelligence analysis may need to evolve if it is to be fit for purpose. In this it will specifically explore the role of interconnectivity and partnership.
- Section 2: Will focus on the strategic elements that facilitate effective intelligence analysis. It will specifically focus on the role of leaders who provide strategic direction and develop the infrastructure (people, systems and resources) to deliver it.
- Section 3: Will focus on the role of the police analyst, suggesting how their knowledge and skills should develop, to improve analysis in an information rich world. It questions whether desk based analysis has the potential to become more innovative in the future.

Section 1: Future challenges for intelligence analysis

Future challenges for the intelligence community?

This book has listed numerous examples of intelligence failure. Although extra resources are often injected into the intelligence infrastructure to counteract these failures, because the systems and cultural practices remain constant, similar experiences can re-occur. An example of this was the investment in fusion centres, initially created from the failure to collate and pass intelligence owned by disparate agencies. Whilst having some success these structures have been regularly criticised, with Wardlaw (2015) arguing that fusion centres have suffered from the absence of a standardised model, mission creep, and under-developed or missing external agency partnerships. It appears even new bolt-on structures suffer old problems, as they increase bureaucracy and increase the number of system boundaries (silos) for practitioners to navigate.

Prior to suggesting change, an awareness of the past is helpful. A valuable example of this was during the 1970s when the Association of Chief Police Officers (ACPO) in England and Wales formed a sub-committee to improve the use of intelligence. This group commissioned the Baumber Report (ACPO, 1975), the Pearce Report (ACPO, 1978) and the Ratcliffe Report (ACPO, 1986), which all provided recommendations as to how an intelligence led approach could be improved. A key idea was that any subject of interest would only have one intelligence record, which would be accessible to all law enforcement personnel. Whilst an excellent idea, the proposal that different police forces would augment one core record as the subject crossed jurisdictional boundaries, was completely impractical. This was because the remainder of the 20th century saw an explosion in mobility, making it impossible for the 43 police forces in England and Wales to co-ordinate this level of activity. Due to diverse IT systems and infrastructures, individual forces had instigated bespoke intelligence systems and individual ways of working. This made it much more difficult to share information across borders and agencies.

An understanding of the immediate future is also important when suggesting change, especially as technology, data and demand are expected to accelerate. In China, artificial intelligence has revolutionised city living, especially through the use of robots and electronic surveillance to monitor behaviour compliance. This approach will be extended with the design and construction of smart cities across the Middle East. Closer to home, Price Waterhouse Cooper (2018) have estimated that, due to automation, a third of British jobs could be lost within 15 years. Schwab (2015) argues we exist in the early stages of a 4th industrial revolution, which will exploit and unite digital and physical innovation, to generate an even greater interconnected and interdependent world. To succeed in this environment will rely on even closer co-operation between government, private business and civil society. Deloitte (2018) argue this change will present a new epoch for policing as the service faces the demands of a growing and ageing society, a globalised economy, ongoing urbanisation, technological acceleration, data abundance, and political extremism. They summarise the challenge for the police, as having to:

1 Serve a fully digital world, with police related incidents forming a digital footprint.
2 Operate on disproportionately smaller budgets when compared with other public sector agencies (health, care and pensions), and other private sector agencies involved in community safety.
3 Face rapid unprecedented change, which will demand an unprecedented speed of response.
4 Harness cyber-physical systems.
5 Manage an unknowable volume of knowledge to establish 'what works'.
6 Operate with near total transparency.

In this data rich environment, Birkinshaw (2014) makes four specific points. First, he argues that the abundance of data has meant some level of evidence is available for most hypotheses being tested, which can complicate decision making. Secondly, organisations can become intellectually lazy as there is a tendency to default to data-mining approaches rather than use deeper understanding and experience. This has often been the case with police analyst products (Chainey, 2012). Third, he argues practitioners find it difficult to focus on single activities as they move between numerous information sources which vie for their attention – an issue that has implications for managing staff and external relationships. Finally, these factors can lead to decision inertia, as it is easier to request more information and postpone decisions. Whilst this inaction may be explained through the complexity of the decision, or the need to perform due diligence, it can generate either 'paralysis by analysis' or conversely make individuals default to a previous response without much consideration. Although decision making should be based on relevant data wherever possible, staff should be aware that some decisions can only be based on judgement and experience (Pease & Roach, 2017).

What specific ramifications will these changes have for the police? Commentators suggest the future will bring a more interdependent, technological and information rich society (Deloitte, 2018; Schwab, 2015), which has the potential to amplify current weaknesses within the intelligence community. Whilst investments in technology will be needed to improve the capability and compatibility of police systems, the most significant requirements will be associated with people and processes. The wide availability of information together with increasing interdependencies makes secrecy a less effective strategy. The police, often identified as pursuing an isolationist approach and reticent to engage fully in inter-agency working to exploit data sharing, will need to evolve. Although a full reversal is not anticipated (as complete transparency also has its risks in a law enforcement arena), smarter methods of working will be needed, particularly in understanding non-traditional police data, i.e. big data.

Further, the recruitment and development of staff (both managers and operators) will also need to evolve within the intelligence environment. Technical skills will become more essential as the need to process big data and use rigorous research techniques to enable critical analysis comes to the fore. Increasing levels of information vying for attention means that staff must focus on the correct issues, rather than being diverted by many other interesting, but irrelevant, elements. In summary, this environmental scanning shows that the future is likely to be transformative, and police intelligence systems will be at the forefront. This will require much more fundamental change than the piecemeal changes experienced previously. The remainder of the chapter will discuss these issues in more detail.

Section 2: Leadership - the importance of strategic insight to underpin effective intelligence analysis

Introduction

The evidence of high-profile intelligence failures is regularly documented across the world, from terrorist atrocities to misbehaving intelligence staff. Why then, are some organisations effective in the collection, analysis, dissemination, and the use of intelligence while others aren't? This phenomenon is particularly perplexing in those agencies who have implemented the National Intelligence Model (NIM), as this was supported by 816 pages of guidance, explaining exactly how an effective and efficient intelligence system should work. However, guidance is determinant on implementation and the notion of implementation failure is constantly raised throughout this book. It is particularly prevalent within the intelligence process, which is saturated with organisational and operational challenges. In this, the performance of staff deployed in leadership roles is particularly important as their actions trickle down to impact upon the working environment and the staff behaviour within it. As Molière (1622–1673) famously said, 'It is not only what we do, but also what we do not do, for which we are accountable' (Forbes.com, 2020). This second section will therefore concentrate on the elements of leadership which have a positive or adverse impact on the ability to improve intelligence analysis.

Strategic vision and the input–output–outcome challenge

A number of management consultants advocate that the first step in obtaining clarity in strategy is to 'start with the end in mind' (Covey, 1989). This means that leaders establish what they want to achieve and work backwards from this point. Unfortunately, this is not quite as simple as it sounds as, whilst the institution of policing has existed for many years, its actual purpose is constantly questioned, and subsequent objectives have been modified across time and location (Kirby, 2013). This means the responsibilities of the police are open to discretion. Whilst an earlier chapter outlined Goldstein's list of police responsibilities, Moore and Braga (2003) have also provided their list of seven priority areas, which include:

- Reducing serious crime.
- Holding offenders to account.
- Maintaining safety and order.
- Reassuring the public.
- Providing quality services.
- Using force and authority fairly and effectively.
- Using financial resources fairly, efficiently, and effectively.

Whether you agree with the list or not, it is important to recognise these issues aren't mutually exclusive. The Black Lives Matter movement in 2020 shows that, even if a police department enjoys an outstanding record in holding offenders to account, if officers abuse their authority and use undue force they won't be perceived as a legitimate agency in the eyes of their citizens. Moore and Braga (2003) argue that the police should be measured across all these factors, utilising a performance management system similar to a balanced score card system used by private industry. This is particularly relevant to the intelligence community who should be aware of the ramifications and potential adverse consequences that can emerge from different tactics. To understand the purpose of their organisation, leaders should be able to answer simple questions such as: What is our core business? How do we define success? What do we value in this business? Do we have the right skills, training and technology to conduct our business? Are we prepared to meet future challenges? Only when leaders know the answers can they provide clarity to the intelligence practitioner, who in turn understands their particular role, how success is defined, and how they create value in the intelligence process. However, this process can be constantly in flux.

Policing is a dynamic process and police forces are increasingly influenced by external factors. That creates the possibility that a police agency may change significantly in the way it delivers its services. A recent example is the 2020 Black Lives Matter movement, which generated fundamental questions surrounding how a police agency should operate and even whether this historic institution should actually be abolished. Whilst history suggests the police (as an institution) are unlikely to be disbanded, future compromise and change is possible. This can include demands for changes to personnel (mainly at senior leadership level), or the adherence to certain policing models (mainly requiring the implementation of community centric approaches). An example is Camden (USA), which in 2012 disbanded its police department. This enabled it to remove its police-union contract that had proved costly. It set up again, this time with more money to recruit officers – however this time it insisted on community-oriented policing and made its officers more accountable. Results in Camden, notably reductions in homicide and complaints against the police, have been positive (Politico, 2020).

Another radical proposal has been to suggest law enforcement agencies should adhere more to a harm reduction approach (rather than enforcement) and work more closely with health and social care agencies (College of Police, 2018). Growing research demonstrates that health issues play a key role within incidence of crime, harm and anti-social behaviour (Wood, 2020; Weisburd and White, 2019; Bartkowiak-Théron and Asquith, 2017; Schuller, 2013). There is little doubt that police demand is increasing most in social welfare issues, from those suffering homelessness or mental health crisis. Case studies in Chapter 5 provide examples of where smarter partnership working makes it possible to establish the underlying causes of a problem and instigate better interventions. Intelligence is no longer just a police concept, as harvesting multi-agency data can provide a holistic picture of individuals and communities, and can improve community safety more effectively. Whilst currently there are good examples of partnership working with some limited sharing of resources, this is often on the margins of policing (Keay & Kirby, 2018b; Bartkowiak-Théron & Asquith, 2017), and it is possible the future may bring aligned priorities and shared budgets.

Putting these strategic issues to one side, ultimately, whatever strategic vision is set, a policing model is needed to deliver the available resources in a fair, efficient and effective way (Moore & Braga, 2003). Chapter 3 shows there are numerous such models, each of which uses intelligence in different ways and emphasises different tactics and outcomes. However, the importance of amalgamating these models is increasingly being recognised. Problem solving approaches which are cognisant of community views and supported by intelligence and evidence led approaches are all well documented. As such discrete models, such as the NIM, which explicitly emphasise one element over another are insufficiently sophisticated to deliver either police or community needs. Basic NIM processes have failed to keep pace with policing demands. There have been attempts to tackle this. In the USA the research by Santos (2014) and Santos and Taylor (2014) on 'stratified policing' has shown some promising results in embedding analysis and the analyst role (Smith, et al., 2018; Santos, 2018). Stratified policing is an organisational framework that promotes the use of evidence-based practices, problem-solving and crime analysis at numerous operational and strategic levels (Santos & Santos, 2015). Whilst having some parallels to the NIM, it currently appears to have avoided some of the bureaucratic drawbacks of the model (Ratcliffe, 2016). Stratified policing aims to integrate evidence-based practices across all police rank structures, based on the premise that the police should address crime reduction strategies at different levels, from first responders through to chief officers. The ultimate aim is to transform police culture and institutionalise evidence-based strategies (Santos, 2018). However, it should be recognised that no model guarantees success, as any method can be poorly implemented. That is why strategic leaders should select their operating model carefully and implement it with vigilance.

A further issue is the point made by Goldstein (1979), that the police often place more emphasis on the 'means' than the 'ends'. It should be remembered that intelligence is the means, and the outcome of the intelligence is the ends. To assist in this discussion, all staff should understand the terms input, output and outcome. These labels, used in Management Science since the start of the century, map the process of how resources (i.e. people and money) are transformed into specific activity or outputs (i.e. arrests, intelligence products, etc.), which ultimately lead to a measurable outcome, such as a reduction in the amount of crime or the number of Organised Crime Groups who are disrupted from being able to commit crime (OECD, 2002). In military and commercial examples, the desired outcomes are unambiguous due to the implications of failure. If the opponents aren't neutralised (military) or profits increased (commercial), then lives can be lost or the commercial enterprise may go out of business. However, police related outcomes are much more nuanced, due to the considerable debate surrounding police priorities and the level of discretion available to operational officers. As such this strategic knowledge, in terms of what the organisation ultimately wants to achieve, is sometimes missed. Practitioners may become embroiled in tactics that are unduly influenced by organisational culture rather than evidence-based research. Examples include the constant changes to structure (i.e. specialist crime teams, new team names) or operating systems (different police models, types of covert police equipment and intelligence reporting formats). As well as consuming considerable energy, it can make the intelligence community appear isolationist (James et al., 2017), as it leads to elitist language when delivering specific actions (outputs) in overly bureaucratic formats. Whilst more procedures are followed, and boxes ticked, less emphasis is placed on the impact of the investment and whether the outcome could have been achieved in a more effective or inexpensive way. For those practitioners who feel this criticism is overly harsh, two questions can be posed. First, how many outcome/impact reports evaluating the success of outputs are conducted. Second, how often are comparisons made to examine the cost effectiveness of different approaches to achieve the desired outcome (i.e. do informants, mobile or static surveillance lead to better outcomes – and, if so, in what context). In summarising this section, if senior leaders do not have a complete grasp of the intelligence process and the outcomes they wish to achieve, there is little possibility of intelligence being optimised. Successful leaders will understand how intelligence should be used to optimise cost effectiveness. For example will a) spending months on prosecuting a suspect (enforcement), b) interrupting the activity of organised crime group members (disruption), or c) improving the security of a port susceptible to drug trafficking (prevention), generate the best outcome for the least cost? Whilst these input–output–outcome questions have a high priority in the private sector, this is less robust in the public sector. Unfortunately, the academic evidence illustrates that (generally speaking) police officers still favour intuitive approaches, rather than the knowledge of what works (Palmer et al., 2019).

Of course leaders do not face these challenges in a sterile environment. Their internal working environment involves constant change, involving legislation, procedures and a constant churn of staff, who have varying levels of knowledge and experience. Further, this new epoch is epitomised by an interconnected and interdependent world, which places new demands on them in terms of communicating with partner agencies and taking account of interdependencies. This challenge is further compounded by the exponential rise of available information requiring more difficult choices when deploying their finite resources. The ability to process the magnitude of information is problematic. A study estimated that 54 million commercial data workers across the world wasted 44% of their day on unsuccessful data activities (Alteryx, 2019). This time is lost through workers juggling different technology systems and manipulating their data into a useable format. One would expect police organisations, especially in the intelligence sector, to have similar challenges.

In summary, the challenges for those leaders who direct intelligence resources in the future will be significant, requiring greater knowledge (to navigate multiple data sources and follow an evidence-based approach), and the development of new skills (to operate in an interconnected world). Meanwhile individual practitioners will also have to adapt if intelligence analysis is to be improved and it is to this area that the chapter now turns.

Section 3: Implications for analysts

Introduction

So far, this book has shown that the intelligence arena is going through unprecedented change due to evolving technologies and an abundance of data. How then will the role of the analyst look in the future? This section discusses the evolution of the role by examining recent history and the current status of analysts. It then explores the future to examine what knowledge and skills will be required going forward.

The current status of the analyst role

The start of the new millennium was a period when the National Intelligence Model was at its height. This was a period when UK police forces were investing in their intelligence function and the analyst role sat at the centre of operations. However, in the following years a number of factors coincided to weaken this position. First, the introduction of the NIM was not universally accompanied by managers who had a comprehensive understanding of the approach. This meant some analysts were mismanaged, leading to sub-optimal intelligence products. This subsequently led to reduced operational benefits and further reduction in the operational use of analysts (Evans, 2008). Unfortunately, this reduction in prestige was further exacerbated through an international recession, and austerity measures that disproportionately affected police analysts (Keay & Kirby, 2018a). Ironically, this meant that at a time when more investment in police intelligence and analysis could have been used to better direct existing resources, the opposite occurred. All these factors mean that, across the UK and the USA, analysis is still not routinely adopted into all areas of police work (Santos & Taylor, 2014).

Nonetheless the evidence continues to show that analysts can play an important role in performance improvement. Indeed, there are many success stories where analysts have been pivotal to positive outcomes in reactive and proactive operations. Analysts have also collaborated with external academics to provide insight into operational and organisational outcomes. Chapter 3 has shown all contemporary proactive policing approaches endorse the importance of the analyst. Problem-oriented policing, which was recently shown by a systematic review to lead to an average 34% reduction in crime (Hinkle et al., 2020), shows a lack of analytic support is consistently associated with its implementation failure (Sidebottom et al., 2020). Similarly, implementation of evidence-based policing also highlights the value of analysts (Sherman & Murray, 2015), as 'knowledge' is core to understanding 'what works'. In the knowledge process, evaluation is key as it can lead to improvements in policy and practice, both in terms of directing what action should be taken, as well as what approaches should be curtailed. Unfortunately, evaluations are rarely conducted, and even when available they can be poorly conducted. For example, whilst most police pilot programmes are reported as a success, only a limited number are maintained. This is probably because these projects are only anecdotally endorsed as effective and undergo very little formal or worthwhile evaluation. It has been suggested that some programmes are enthusiastically discussed prior to an evaluation to support the senior officer's promotion prospects (Pease & Roach, 2017). Further, the argument of 'killing the cubs' (Pease & Roach, 2017) relates to when new leaders disregard the initiatives of their predecessors. When that initial enthusiasm of a new programme passes there is a more honest acknowledgment that the impact of the approach is limited, and practitioners move on to seek new solutions. Evaluations, be they through randomized control trials (RCTs) or quasi-experiments, require as much time, effort and investment as other forms of analysis and are critical in developing knowledge. Analysts are more likely to have the skills to support and conduct evaluations, which ultimately saves resources being wasted.

The future role of analysts and the skills required

The omnipotence of data as well as the fiscal pressure on police budgets underline the importance of the analyst role. Whilst once the analysis of criminal intelligence and organised crime were synonymous with police analysts, their role has become more diverse as data access has increased. With over 70 definitions of intelligence, it is fair to conclude that there are multiple tiers and perspectives associated with intelligence. As such analysts have been introduced into the following areas of policing, which include:

- Criminal intelligence.
- Organisational intelligence.
- Partnership intelligence.
- Intelligence emanating from Big data.

This natural evolution has grown through the varying perspectives and needs of stakeholders including police leaders. Most recently the emergence of 'big data' and digital data sources have become the latest dimension of intelligence (Ferguson, 2017). With information now ubiquitous, the scope for examining human behaviour is substantial, ranging from internet shopping, to political interests (Ferguson, 2017). Existing criminological theory can be augmented with big data to understand patterns of behaviour and improve intelligence development. This provides an ideal opportunity for the analyst to provide joined-up thinking, especially when aligned with data science and crime science approaches. The potential to aggregate this new data within existing practices will provide greater prospects of detecting and reducing crimes, whilst also improving organisational and operational efficiency and effectiveness. It is thought these issues may affect the analyst role in three ways.

First, there has been a natural diversification of analyst roles and this is expected to continue. Whilst the pressure on police budgets continues, the analyst role is important to make sure resources are targeted in the most cost-effective way. This can only be done if there is an emphasis on understanding data patterns and evaluating whether interventions are effective. As such it is difficult to think of any element of police work that would not benefit from an analytical function.

Second, the ubiquitous nature of data will drive new opportunities. Big data will be used to predict future offending and incident patterns. However, the process will be more complex in terms of collection, analysis, dissemination and presentation of information. Previous chapters have illustrated that large data sets pertinent to policing may be sourced from diverse agencies in a variety of forms. These may not be straightforward to collect and the analysis of data which may materialise in different forms (i.e. video, twitter) will be difficult to manage, analyse, and understand.

The third aspect is perhaps the most radical. The access to more diverse and ubiquitous data sets have the potential to generate online innovation, especially in relation to criminal investigation, offender management, and 'what works'. The examples provided through investigative journalism have illustrated the imaginative ways that insight can emerge through open source information. This has not yet been exploited by police analysts. Investigation and intelligence gathering are primarily viewed as the domain of police detectives who go about their business by knocking on doors, speaking to confidential informants, and engaging in surveillance. These are high cost activities in terms of resources, with an increased risk of wasted effort and reputational damage. The use of digital detectives remains to be exploited and there is currently limited imagination in the use of open source material to either profile suspect behaviour or identify patterns of behaviour surrounding high risk victims and events. As has been seen, human behaviour is often recorded through a myriad of electronic traces which continue to increase in frequency and sophistication. This approach is particularly interesting for the concept of disrupting offenders. Roach and Pease (2016) have shown offenders can 'self-select' themselves for police attention as they commit minor offences as well as more serious ones. In essence, offenders seldom specialise, and even serious offenders come to the attention of the authorities for smaller breaches of the law. So, for example, organised crime offenders have been seen to keep illegal pets, breach planning laws, or engage in fly tipping. This presents incredible scope to target offenders using focused deterrence approaches from the reduced cost and increased safety of the desk. Such an approach is also open to other public sector agencies, notably probation, social services and health which can assess client compliance from a distance. Obviously, such a process will need to be scrutinised from an ethical standpoint.

Future skills needed by analysts

It is difficult to specify what skills will be needed by analysts in the future, as it is leaders who set the strategy, and this often remains ambiguous and diverse. However, the discussion so far highlights some obvious trends. First, the default standard for analysis should be at a higher level than is generally seen at the moment. Weisburd and Neyroud (2011) have argued that police agencies need to develop a research capability that is both objective and rigorous – an approach they refer to as police science. This is echoed by other commentators who support a practical application of science being embedded in police activity (Cordner, 2019; Evans, 2008; Laycock, 2005). The term 'science' removes ambiguity and promotes objectivity, which are concepts that intelligence analysis has generally been missing. To better understand this, analysts need to be equipped with advanced research and analytical skills similar to those used in academia. Whilst the traditional analyst skill set is useful for basic police analytic tasks, it is clear that a wider, growing, and more challenging world of data requires an appropriate level of analysis. As shown throughout this book, scientific research is often undertaken in collaboration with academic institutions or other partnerships. This is positive for both police staff and academics as they both benefit from cross fertilisation. However, if analysts are to be at the core of knowledge-based approaches such as evidence-based and problem-oriented policing (Keay & Kirby, 2018a), more rigorous research methods are routinely required. This will lead to a greater strategic understanding and the production of more beneficial analytical products.

Further, there is an obvious need for enhanced data management skills. Herdale (2020) suggests 'it is clear that the current infrastructure for the police as well as the wider criminal justice system is not currently able to cope with existing, never mind anticipate data trends'; further explaining that the Royal Society has identified a significant and growing demand across the economy for data skills. As discussed in Chapter 8, the advances around big data mean that the construction and use of data is increasingly important. To assist this, some police forces are slowly starting to invest in data scientists or data analysts (the name varies), who are responsible for developing databases and extracting data. Additionally, there may be other skill requirements to conduct research or obtain data for the testing of hypotheses, such as data recoding. Being hypothesis-led and identifying what is needed, as opposed to what data is available, would yield a far greater return (Chainey, 2012; Townsley et al., 2011).

To maintain resilience and proactivity in this constantly changing world requires strong recruitment and the ability to maintain a progressive training programme. This goes beyond the basic analyst courses as discussed in Chapter 4 and requires specialised training programmes. This is not just for fresh challenges, e.g. new crimes – such as AI enabled crimes (Hayward & Maas, 2020), but to achieve professional programme standards and personal continuous professional development (CPD). Evans (2008) notes that, to effect change, analysts should keep up to date with the latest research and have the skills to meet new challenges in a practical setting. This means the analyst should be equipped to apply their training, experience and knowledge to new crimes and a changing environment. Currently the emphasis is for staff to learn at the point of need, which means skill acquisition is limited to what is required at a particular point in time. This can dilute the depth of the skill and generate a reactive rather than a proactive mentality. Further, even when possessing the relevant skills, they must be afforded the time to develop and use them. Miller (2020) notes that there has been much discussion on analysts being diverted onto 'firefighting' tasks. Indeed, Ratcliffe (2004) points out that good research takes time which analysts are seldom afforded. This requires managers to step in and provide clear guidance on analyst input and to shield them from meaningless, descriptive tasks that clog up the system (Cope 2004; Miller, 2020).

A future structure for analysts

Organisational structures for analysts differ between police forces and countries and there is little research on which is the most effective structure. In practice, analysts, who are engaged in different 'disciplines' of intelligence, rarely cross paths; they are often siloed and aligned with the priorities of the agency they act for. The dilemma has always been whether to keep analysts under central control or devolve them to operational units, to remain close to the problems they are asked to analyse. The UK experience is that analysts traditionally sit within intelligence units; however, as numbers have grown and roles diversified, they can be found across different departments (e.g. corporate analysis including performance data, integrity units). This has created fragmentation, with many analysts receiving different types and levels of training or CPD. This reduces the organisational ability to develop the knowledge, skills and techniques to improve intelligence analysis.

One option, favoured by many in the intelligence community, would be to progress a dedicated hub that caters for a variety of research and analytical needs. This would align all analysts with either a single dedicated management structure to provide a range of analytical services for the force, or provide some central accountability for direction and development. The diagram below (see figure 9.1) proposes a stronger alignment between analyst groups. Some forces may be closer to this structure than others. This is because some organisations keep IT functions separate, whereas others show increased collaboration between departments, particularly in setting up new databases and IT systems. This hub can comfortably integrate the partnership, crime and performance roles, as well as allowing for closer working and strategic management of diverse analyst groups.

Specifically, the alignment of data science with other elements of analysis would be a unique step forward for many police forces. This brings the end user of data together with those that are designing and developing data bases and software architecture, i.e. data modelling and data extraction. This continues to be problematic. For example, during the N8 CPD analyst course (see Chapter 4), participants constantly discussed data issues, ranging from data quality, missing data and what was actually present in existing systems. Police analysis has tended to be data-led as opposed to being hypotheses-led, a possible side-effect of NIM demands for data and regular 'analysis' products that could lead to descriptive rather than insightful products. The support provided by a hub would provide improved resilience amongst the analyst community (Miller, 2020) and maintain standards whilst encouraging innovation. The downside (for some) of specialist and dedicated senior management is that the analyst lacks local accountability for their product.

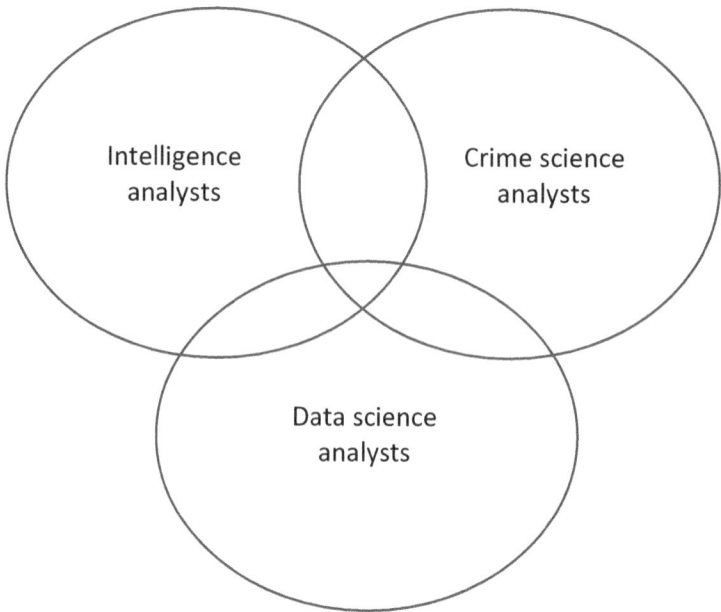

Figure 9.1 Research and analysis hub – a potential model for police analyst structure

Conclusion

In recent years it has been increasingly acknowledged that intelligence plays a major role in improving police interventions, which lead to improved public outcomes. Notwithstanding the great strides forward, many improvements can still be made, and this final chapter has shown a number of factors to be particularly germane.

Initially it should be recognised that decisions should be future proof. Society is changing in terms of demographics, which is generating more demand on the police. Unfortunately police budgets are not growing at the same pace as society, therefore smarter and more targeted interventions, through improved analysis and intelligence, are needed. In this process strategic leadership is key for a number of reasons. First, there needs to be greater awareness as to the benefits of an intelligence-led approach as well as its limitations. Many incidents at first labelled as 'intelligence failure' have emanated from unrealistic expectations. Knowing a crime is possible does not mean actionable intelligence is available (i.e. where and when exactly it will occur and by whom) to prevent or disrupt it. The police use of intelligence is constrained by a highly regulated legislative and procedural framework to maintain both standards and reputation, therefore it is the duty of strategic leaders to be clear about what the approach can achieve and to educate stakeholders on the limitations as well as the opportunities.

Secondly, it should be remembered that intelligence is but a facilitator (the means) to deliver better outcomes (the ends) and should not be viewed as an end in itself. If the overarching strategy or objectives (to which the intelligence relates) is/are flawed then positive benefits cannot be delivered. In any intelligence process it is critically important to have in place a feedback loop connected to an evaluation system. Insufficient understanding of why a particular intervention has (or has not) made an impact generates a significant weakness in knowing how best to allocate resources. Such ambiguity will only continue to reinforce a practice of delivering similar outputs without fully appreciating their consequences.

The third critical point for leadership is to establish a vision. The NIM created a new reality in intelligence analysis which was embedded across many parts of the world. However, much of the emphasis was on structure and process. Whilst there have been developments (the stratified policing model is one), a question arises as to whether a new, more ambitious vision needs to be set. This would place the emphasis on a more outcome focussed model which uses good practice to deliver the most cost-effective outcomes. In such an approach, decisions would need to be made about the structures that are required nationally and those that are required locally. Within any model, an understanding of big data, and how to use it, is required. This would extend from the most effective exploitation of national systems such as the Police National Database, to exploring the potential of large non police databases. Exploitation of these databases requires a new paradigm and a willingness to extend desk-based approaches.

A further critical theme that emerges from this book is that the delivery of effective and efficient intelligence analysis requires knowledgeable and skilled people, supported by a capable infrastructure. This needs to extend past the intelligence community in terms of understanding and valuing intelligence analysis. Analysts who are at the heart of this process require particular support and, to be truly proactive, their skills must be relevant for the times. Two issues have surfaced: the move towards larger and more diverse datasets as well as the need for analysts to be stronger in their research skills to provide critical analysis rather than deliver default, descriptive products. Systems are also of critical importance if the movement of information is to become seamless and able to transcend borders and silos. The infrastructure to manage diverse and large data sets and visually present intelligence on a real time basis presents technological and cultural challenges. Ultimately, all these factors are interdependent, requiring a system where effective managers, practitioners and infrastructure come together in a mutually supportive environment.

This book has illustrated that a wide array of knowledge and techniques currently exists to allow practitioners to deliver high quality analysis. Many of these techniques can be developed further. One example is social network analysis (SNA), which has been slow to develop despite available research to show its value (Burcher & Whelan, 2018). Whilst analysts are well versed in producing network or association charts, these can be developed further by examining the network before *and* after policing activity (rather than just focusing on the network prior to the intervention). This can provide further insight as to how the relationships have changed post intervention, and what police opportunities these newly formed patterns provide for further intervention (Duijn et al., 2015).

To finish, we turn to an argument made by the Director of the Chicago crime hub, a prestigious organisation committed to reducing crime (*Chicago News*, 2019). During a recent presentation he highlighted that society wasn't doing a particularly good job of reducing violent crime. He said this was in stark contrast to developments in health (which had nearly eradicated polio), and design (which had transformed car safety). This type of argument is well rehearsed. Many commentators have compared the police with disciplines ranging from engineering to health. These comparisons have much to praise them, as they highlight the lack of a scientific basis associated with policing which ultimately slows its development. However, they fail on one often neglected point, which is that the police face a thinking adversary who constantly adapts their approach. Unlike a car design that can be tested in laboratory conditions, when colliding with an unmovable object, policing occurs in an extremely dynamic environment. This is amplified due to the volatility of the actors in the process (i.e. offenders, victims, and witnesses). The overall police response is also influenced by the police call taker, the responder and the supervisor, who can all think and act in slightly different ways. The importance of these changing dynamics is supported by the significant research conducted on 'what works'. It shows that whilst there are evidence-based approaches to tackle crime and incidents, context is extremely important, as not all good practice works everywhere. It is the critical role of the analyst to understand this environment as best they can, to establish the patterns of consistency and unpredictability. Only with this insight can the most appropriate response be recommended. In such a dynamic environment intelligence analysis will always remain central if available resources are to be used wisely.

References

ACPO. (1975) *Report of the ACPO Subcommittee on Criminal Intelligence (Baumber Report)*. London: Association of Chief Police Officers.
ACPO. (1978) *Report of the ACPO Working Party on a Structure of Criminal Intelligence Officers (Pearce Report)*. London: Association of Chief Police Officers.
ACPO. (1986) *Report of the ACPO Subcommittee on Operational Intelligence (Ratcliffe Report)*. London: Association of Chief Police Officers.
Alteryx. (2019) *The state of data science and analytics*. Available at https://pages.alteryx.com/idc-infobrief-state-data-science-analytics.html?_ga=2.131134925.33338981.1591113137-418304826.1591113137 [Accessed 14 January 2020].

Bartkowiak-Théron, I. and Asquith, N. (2017) Conceptual divides and practice synergies in law enforcement and public health: some lessons from policing vulnerability in Australia. *Policing and Society: An International Journal of Research and Policy*, 27 (3): 276–288.

Birkinshaw, J. (2014) Beyond the information age. Available at https://www.wired.com/insights/2014/06/beyond-information-age/ [Accessed 14 February 2020].

Burcher, M and Whelan, C. (2018) Social network analysis as a tool for criminal intelligence: understanding its potential from the perspectives of intelligence analysts. *Trends in Organised Crime*, 21: 278–294.

Chainey, S. (2012) Improving the explanatory content of analysis products using hypothesis testing. *Policing: A Journal of Policy and Practice*, 6 (2): 108–121.

Chicago News. (2019) What's next for the University of Chicago Crime Lab? Available at https://news.uchicago.edu/story/whats-next-university-chicago-crime-lab. [Accessed 30 August 2020].

College of Police. (2018) Public Health. Available at https://www.college.police.uk/What-we-do/Support/uniformed-policing-faculty/Pages/Public-health.aspx [Accessed 10 February 2020].

Cope, N. (2004) Intelligence led policing or policing led intelligence: integrating volume crime analysis into policing. *British Journal of Criminology*, 44 (2): 188–203.

Cordner, G. (2019) A practical approach to evidence-based policing. In R.J. Mitchell and L. Huey (eds). *Evidence Based Policing: An Introduction*. Bristol: Bristol University Press.

Covey, S.R. (1989) *The 7 Habits of Highly Effective People*. New York: Free Press.

Deloitte. (2018) Policing 4.0: Deciding the future of policing in the UK. Available at https://www2.deloitte.com/content/dam/Deloitte/ie/Documents/PublicSector/deloitte-uk-future-of-policing.pdf [Accessed 18 May 2020].

Duijn, P., Kashirin, V. and Sloot, P. (2015) The relative ineffectiveness of criminal network disruption. *Scientific Reports* 4, Article number: 4238. Available at https://www.nature.com/articles/srep04238 [Accessed 17 June 2020].

Evans, M. (2008) Cultural paradigms and change: a model of analysis. In C. Harfield, A. MacVean, J. Grieve and D. Phillips (eds). *The Handbook of Intelligent Policing*. Oxford: Oxford University Press.

Ferguson, A.G. (2017) *The Rise of Big Data Policing: Surveillance, Race and the Future of Law Enforcement*. New York: New York Press.

Flanagan, Sir R. (2008) *Review of Policing: The Final Report*. London: HMSO.

Forbes.com. (2020) *Quotes*. Available at https://www.forbes.com/quotes/6902/[Accessed 12 June 2020].

Goldstein, H. (1979) Improving policing: A problem-oriented approach. *Crime & Delinquency*, 25(2): 236–258.

Hayward, K.J. and Maas, M.M. (2020) Artificial intelligence and crime: A primer for criminologists. Available at https://journals.sagepub.com/doi/abs/10.1177/1741659020917434 [Accessed 1 July 2020].

Herdale, G. (2020) Data analysis skills in policing (Blog). *TechUK.Org*. Available at https://www.techuk.org/insights/opinions/item/17765-data-analysis-skills-in-policing [Accessed on 10 June 2020].

Hinkle, J.C., Weisburd, D.W., Telep, C.W. and Petersen, K. (2020) Problem-oriented policing for reducing crime and disorder: An updated systematic review and meta-analysis. *Campbell Systematic Reviews*, 16 (2). Available at https://onlinelibrary.wiley.com/doi/full/10.1002/cl2.1089 [Accessed 16 August 2020].

James, A., Phythian, M., Wadie, F. and Richards, J. (2017) The road not taken: understanding barriers to the development of police intelligence practice. *The International Journal of Intelligence, Security, and Public Affairs*, 19 (2): 77–91.

Keay, S. and Kirby, S. (2018a) The evolution of the police analyst and the influence of evidence based-policing. *Policing: A Journal of Policy and Practice*, 12 (3): 265–276.

Keay, S. and Kirby, S. (2018b) Defining vulnerability: from the conceptual to the operational. *Policing: A Journal of Policy and Practice*, 12 (4): 428–438.

Kirby, S. (2013) *Effective Policing?: Implementation in Theory and Practice*. Basingstoke: Palgrave MacMillan.

Laycock, G. (2005) Defining Crime Science. In M.J. Smith and N. Tilley (eds). *New Approaches to Preventing and Detecting Crime*, Crime Science Series, pp.3–24. Collumpton: Willan.

Kowalczyk-Harper, H. (2016) No title given. Available at https://medium.com/@MsHannahTweets/to-quote-theodore-roosevelt-it-is-not-the-critic-who-counts-not-the-man-who-points-out-how-the-cead5273cfa6. [Accessed 15 September 2020].

Miller, O. (2020) Analysts and policing. *WeCops Blog*. Available at http://www.wecops.org/blogs/2183 [Accessed 23 June 2020].

Moore, M.H. and Braga, A. (2003) The 'bottom line' of policing: What citizens should value (and measure!) in police performance. Washington DC: Police Executive Research Forum, 30. Accessed at http://www.policeforum.org/assets/docs/Free_Online_Documents/Police_Evaluation/the%20bottom%20line%20of%20policing%202003.pdf [Accessed 27 May 2020].

NCA. (2020) NCA and police smash thousands of criminal conspiracies after infiltration of encrypted communication platform in UK's biggest ever law enforcement operation. Available at https://www.nationalcrimeagency.gov.uk/news/operation-venetic [Accessed 12 July 2020].

OECD. (2002) *Glossary of Key Terms in Evaluations and Results Based Management*. Original report, re-printed 2010.

Palmer, I., Kirby, S. and Phythian, R. (2019) Assessing the appetite for Evidence Based Policing: A UK based study. *International Journal of Police Science & Management*, 21 (2), 91–100.

Pease, K. and Roach, J. (2017) How to morph experience into evidence. In J. Knutsson and L. Tompson (eds). *Advances in Evidence-Based Policing*. Abingdon: Routledge.

Politico. (2020) The city that really did abolish the police. Available at https://www.politico.com/news/magazine/2020/06/12/camden-policing-reforms-313750. [Accessed 30 September 2020].

Price Waterhouse Cooper. (2018) Will robots really steal our jobs: An international analysis of the potential long-term impact of automation. Available at https://www.pwc.co.uk/economic-services/assets/international-impact-of-automation-feb-2018.pdf [Accessed 19 July 2020].

Ratcliffe, J. (2004) Intelligence Research. In J. Ratcliffe (ed.). *Strategic Thinking in Criminal Intelligence*. Sydney: Federation Press.

Ratcliffe, J. (2016) *Intelligence-led Policing*. Abingdon: Routledge.

Roach, J. and Pease. K. (2016) *Self-Selection Policing*. London: Palgrave.

Santos, R.B. (2014) The effectiveness of crime analysis for crime reduction: cure or diagnosis? *Journal of Contemporary Criminal Justice*, 30 (2): 147–168.

Santos, R.B. (2018) Police organizational change after implementing crime analysis and evidence-based strategies through stratified policing. *Policing: A Journal of Policy and Practice*, 12 (3): 288–302.

Santos, R.G. and Santos, R.B. (2015) Evidence-based policing, 'what works' and stratified policing, 'how to make it work'. *Translational Criminology*, 8: 20–22.

Santos, R.B. and Taylor, B. (2014) Integration of crime analysis into police work. *Policing* 37 (3): 501–520.

Schuller, N. (2013) Is crime a question of health? *Safer Communities*, 12 (2): 86–96.

Schwab, K. (2015) The fourth industrial revolution: What it means and how to respond. Available at https://www.researchgate.net/deref/https%3A%2F%2Fwww.foreignaffairs.com%2Farticles%2F2015-12-12%2Ffourth-industrial-revolution [Accessed 23 April 2020].

Sherman, L. and Murray, A. (2015) Evidence-based policing: from academics to professionals. *International Criminal Justice Review*, 25 (1): 7–10.

Sidebottom, A., Bullock, K., Ashby, M., Kirby, S., Armitage, R., Laycock, G. and Tilley, N. (2020) *Successful Police Problem-Solving: A Practice Guide*. Jill Dando Institute of Security and Crime Science, University College London. Practice guide. Available at https://discovery.ucl.ac.uk/id/eprint/10093612/ [Accessed 3 May 2020].

Smith, J., Santos, R.B. and Santos, R.G. (2018) Evidence-based policing and the stratified integration of crime analysis in police agencies: national survey results. *Policing: A Journal of Policy and Practice*, 12 (3): 303–315.

Townsley, M., Mann, M. and Garrett, K. (2011) The missing link of crime analysis: a systematic approach to testing competing hypotheses. *Policing*, 5 (2): 158–171.

Wardlaw, G. (2015) Is the intelligence community changing appropriately to meet the challenges of the new security environment? Available at http://press-files.anu.edu.au/downloads/press/p319221/pdf/ch082.pdf [Accessed 19 May 2020].

Weisburd, D. and Neyroud, P. (2011) Police Science: Toward a new paradigm. *Journal of Current Issues in Crime, Issues, and Law Enforcement*, 7 (2): 227–246.

Weisburd, D. and White, C. (2019) Hot spots of crime are not just hot spots of crime: examining health outcomes at street segments. *Journal of Contemporary Criminal Justice*, 35 (2): 142–160.

Wood, J. (2020) Private policing and public health: a neglected relationship. *Journal of Contemporary Criminal Justice*, 36 (1): 19–38.

Index